# mentally ill mothers
# and their children

# mentally
# ill mothers
# and their
# children

Henry Grunebaum
Justin L. Weiss
Bertram J. Cohler
Carol R. Hartman
David H. Gallant

The University of Chicago Press
Chicago and London

*Henry Grunebaum*, M.D., is project director and associate clinical professor in the Department of Psychiatry, Harvard Medical School, and senior psychiatrist at the Massachusetts Mental Health Center and the Cambridge Hospital.
*Justin L. Weiss*, Ph.D., is project codirector and assistant clinical professor of psychology at Harvard Medical School and chief psychologist at the Massachusetts Mental Health Center.
*Bertram J. Cohler*, Ph.D., is assistant professor in the Committee on Human Development, the Department of Education, and the College, University of Chicago.
*Carol R. Hartman*, R.N., D.Nsc., is associate professor in the School of Nursing, Boston College.
*David H. Gallant*, Ph.D., is research associate in psychiatry at the Harvard Medical School and chief psychologist at the Newton Guidance Clinic.

The University of Chicago Press, Chicago 60637
The University of Chicago Press, Ltd., London
© 1975 by The University of Chicago
All rights reserved. Published 1975
Printed in the United States of America
International Standard Book Number: 0–226–31021–3
Library of Congress Catalog Card Number: 74–5740

To our mothers and
the mothers of our children

# Contents

# Foreword

Henry Grunebaum and his colleagues have made a truly significant contribution to our understanding of disturbed mothering and its treatment. They have also illuminated important principles of normal development. By describing their work as it has evolved over more than a decade, the authors of this volume provide an instructive example of how clinical psychiatric research can be introduced and renewed within the context of an active, general therapeutic program.

The scope of this book goes beyond a tidy, easily categorized package. Repeatedly the reader comes upon unexpected excursions. The authors alert him that he will not find "an account of a carefully designed, coordinated, and controlled research program." Yet within these pages are included fascinating reports of several closely analyzed, small, but statistically buttressed investigations. Elsewhere in the volume there are vivid accounts of clinical experiences, as well as useful recommendations for the management of an interdisciplinary treatment program.

A rare feature of the long-term venture on which this book is based is interdisciplinary collaboration, in which the contributions of persons from different disciplines are clearly distinctive yet obviously command mutual respect. Another aspect of this work which has been maintained since its beginnings in 1960 is attention to the issue of informed consent. In 1974, the question of consent has been thrust upon clinicians and researchers by political activists. What is refreshing in the work of Grunebaum and his colleagues is their genuine, unforced seeking out of mutual consent of all the parties involved, with the explicit recognition that such consent facilitates both therapeutic and research processes.

It is impossible with books such as this to summarize to one's satisfaction the wealth of diverse points which are presented. Rather than make such an attempt, I shall quote, almost at random, some of the findings, hypotheses, and points of view which I found especially thought-provoking and cogent.

*Grunebaum and Weiss:* "As long as the focus of physicians is on the individual to the exclusion of the larger social units, joint admission will seem somewhat alien and in conflict with therapeutic objectives." "Bringing a baby onto a hospital ward involves realistic negotiations between the relevant parties to the agreement: the staff of the ward (especially the doctor and the nurses), the patient, her husband, and her family. If all of these parties have arrived at a decision through an understanding of the expectations, conflicts, and opportunities involved for each in a joint admission, then only rarely will there be serious and unresolvable difficulties once it is undertaken." "The single most useful indicator of when a mother is ready to take care of a child is when she feels ready." "A simple diagnostic classification is not particularly useful."

*Hartman:* "A woman's conflicts about motherhood may be viewed as paradigmatic of all of her maturational and interpersonal conflicts. If psychiatric treatment assists her in resolving the conflicts inherent in her withdrawal from mothering, she can then move closer to functioning more freely and with greater satisfaction in other areas of her life." "Despite the chronic nature of a mother's psychopathology and family difficulties, the traumatic effect of repudiating motherhood is the crucial element leading to the admission to the hospital." "It is possible to have a degree of success with women who do not relate in a close manner with their babies, and...it is also possible to fail with a mother who involves herself with her baby."

*Gallant:* "The children of psychotic mothers...had greater intratest scatter: they passed and failed items over a larger range of age norms than did the normal controls." "In both groups, children of psychotic mothers and children of nonpsychotic mothers, the children with [perinatal] complications had greater scatter than did children without [perinatal] complications." "Perinatal complications have greater potential for developmental deviation in children of psychotic mothers than in children of normal controls." "The joint admission program exerted a favorable influence upon the children's development. However, its effect was not uniform; it was greatest upon cognitive development, and it exerted least impact upon the development of interpersonal relationships. There was no indication that the program was harmful to the children in any way." "Non-joint admission children did more poorly in some aspects of cognitive development, and joint admission children consistently did better, than children of normal controls. A hypothesis advanced to account for these results was that a mental hospital ward may provide a superior, enriching, growth-enhancing environment for the cognitive development of the children."

Cohler: "[Psychiatrically] hospitalized mothers also tended to believe that mothers do not feel uncomfortable in learning to meet their infant's needs, while nonhospitalized mothers admitted to greater concern regarding this childcare issue." "[The psychiatrically] hospitalized mothers do not believe it is possible to establish a social relationship with a baby." "Hospitalized mothers did view the child as a separate being, but one who is passive and who is unable to communicate or achieve reciprocity with his mother." "Mothers hospitalized earlier after childbirth tended to have a greater number of sons than mothers hospitalized later." "Boys tend to cry more and are more fretful as infants, are awake for a larger part of the day, are more active, more prone to illness, and more variable in their overall development." "Caring for boys may be especially difficult for a woman who already feels ambivalent about becoming a mother."

Grunebaum et al.: "The relationship between the patient and her husband proved to be a critical determinant of the degree to which a patient was able to profit from hospitalization and to use the joint admission program constructively."

The reader will wish to examine the text in detail to assess the extent to which the authors have been able to document these and related viewpoints and findings. Among those who have worked extensively in research on treatment with psychotic patients, there is a curious tendency, perhaps engendered by the prolix contradictions of the psychoses, to assume either of two opposite postures: standing off from systematic conceptualization, asserting that these problems are too complex and ineffable, or proclaiming dogmatically and pretentiously that the truth has now been found or lies just around the corner if one follows a recommended path. Grunebaum and his colleagues take neither of these positions but have persisted modestly and courageously to observe and formulate and then to test their formulations. I was pleased to note that the authors themselves raise questions about the limitations of small samples and the merits of alternative interpretations of their findings. I believe that their conclusions, even those which are frankly preliminary but based upon both hard-won research data and clinical experience, warrant thoughtful consideration and serious efforts at replication and extension.

Having taken part in a program that has extended over a number of years, the authors expectably would now handle some matters differently than they did at the beginning. One example of this is noted by Grunebaum and Weiss, who observe that in the early 1960s the customary approach to the marriage of a hospitalized woman was to have the husband seen by a psychiatric social worker separately from his wife. The authors state that they would now place more emphasis on the conjoint treatment of the husband and wife in addition to the wife's individual psychotherapy. I would propose a further extension of a conjoint therapeutic approach, which would include the use of family and network therapy. The observations in this book provide conceptual support for broadened therapeutic explorations with mothers who are undergoing "puerperal breakdown": the authors conclude that not only the husband, but the extended family, particularly the parents of the new mother, as well as neighbors and friends, are critical in the new mother's ability to adapt to the developmental crisis of motherhood.

Similarly, the authors have conceptualized the mother-baby dyad as a unit undergoing development; family theorists would now prefer to move one step further and examine the crises and phases of development of the family as an open system which would include other family members, as well as mother and baby, all reciprocally having crucial impacts upon one another, growing together, and splitting, as an expression of a shared developmental process. The empirical findings of the book support a systems concept of this kind. However, despite some preliminary efforts, no one has yet carried the conceptualization of family development forward with the degree of detail that has often been presented for the development of the individual personality and here for the mother-child dyad.

This book both breaks new ground and, at the same time, invites further explorations to which the authors themselves no doubt will contribute. Both in the past and from reading this volume I have learned much from this stimulating group of clinicians and researchers, and I am delighted to introduce this overview of their work to new readers.

Lyman C. Wynne

# Preface

When the mother of one or more young children is admitted to a mental hospital—particularly if it is her first such admission—a series of emotionally meaningful events ordinarily ensues.

1. There is a *separation*, typically sudden, between the mother and child or children. Young children invariably have difficulty in comprehending the circumstances and reasons for the sudden absence of important people, but this particular kind of separation is rarely understood at all because it cannot be explained. Studies of early childhood development have established that, other things being equal, separation of mother and infant or toddler is likely to affect the child adversely. The point need not be elaborated here—it is dealt with extensively in the text which follows.

2. The provision of *surrogate care* for the children is usually less than adequate. It is typically arranged in a hurry, often with an ambivalent commitment on the part of all concerned, for no one is certain how long the care will be needed. Not infrequently it involves a sudden change of environment for the children and even, on occasion, separation of siblings. Among other consequences, invalidation of the woman as a competent mother by virtue of her disturbed behavior and hospitalization usually leads to a change in the established equilibrium within the family. Her husband, mother, and other relatives may well feel justified in their belief that the patient, by virtue of her

impaired judgment, decreased energy, and/or self-confessed murderous thoughts, is unfit to be close to the children. This conviction, supported by the common view of psychotic behavior as unpredictable and "incurable," is extremely hard to modify.

3. Like other patients, mothers of young children often experience temporary *relief* from unmanageable burdens upon entering a mental hospital, since they typically break down in the context of their inability to meet the extensive demands of caring for a young child. A factor which adds to the burdened feeling is that the child or children who require so much of the mother may be centrally involved in her most disturbing thoughts, fantasies, or fears. On admission to the hospital, psychotic mothers are often glad to be the recipients of attention, care, and concern from others for a change.

4. However, once this initial stage has run its course, many hospitalized mothers begin to feel guilt or shame about what they perceive as an abandonment of their children, with lowered self-esteem and feelings of failure. They may also resent the "surrender" of their maternal responsibilities to others. What often results is a state of intense *ambivalence*; the mother is uncertain about her own readiness and competence to return to caring for her children but is resentful of the surrogate, who in most cases is her own mother and is therefore already the repository of powerful ambivalent feelings.

In *Psychotic Mothers and Their Children* we describe some of the ways in which an interdisciplinary group of clinicians and investigators attempted to respond to this particular set of circumstances of mothers and children. The various sections of the book present a series of interrelated efforts to understand — and to help — psychotic mothers who participated in a program of "joint admission" at the Massachusetts Mental Health Center in Boston. We have used the term joint admission to designate any instance in which an infant or young child lived with and was cared for by his mother on a psychiatric ward for some period of time during the mother's hospitalization.

## OBJECTIVES

The objectives of the book, like its contents, are somewhat

diverse. We have had the following purposes in mind: (1) to describe phenomenologically the administrative, diagnostic, and interpersonal considerations involved in planning a joint admission; (2) to provide a theoretical and clinical review of the nature of postpartum emotional disorders and an epigenetic conceptual scheme for investigating the psychology of maternal personality and attitudes; (3) to report and discuss a pilot investigation of the development of joint admission children; (4) to delineate a framework for mothering-oriented therapeutic nursing care throughout the hospital course and after discharge; and (5) to present a detailed analysis of the relations between therapeutic nursing processes and outcome.

## OVERVIEW

The reader will *not* find between the covers of this book an account of a carefully designed, coordinated, and controlled research program. The history of the joint admission project was such that people from different disciplines with different perspectives and methodological approaches began their work at different times; their "admission" to the project was not "joint." One direct result of this evolutionary growth was that the several studies reported were not conducted with the same patient population; there is some overlap of cases, but scarcely enough to permit the degree of integration which would be desirable.

A brief summary of the chronological development of the project will assist the reader to put the various sections of the book into perspective. The joint admission project began in November 1960 when Dr. Henry Grunebaum, then the senior psychiatrist on one of the wards of the Massachusetts Mental Health Center, suggested that a young mother on his ward might find it useful to consider caring for her child there. Dr. Grunebaum saw beyond the possible clinical utility of this innovation and recognized an opportunity to study the expectations and responses of the patient, the ward staff, and the other patients. He therefore enlisted the collaboration of Dr. Justin L. Weiss, head of the Clinical Psychology Service, and Dr. Linda Hirsch Schoeman, then a psychology intern. Interview data collected by Dr. Schoeman and case history material provided by the patient's therapist, Dr. James Barrett, were interpreted and integrated by Drs. Grunebaum and Weiss to form the nucleus of part 1.

The apparent success of the first joint admission led to others, with Dr. Grunebaum providing consultation and guidance to the clinical staffs of wards in addition to his own. After twelve cases had been studied, projective psychological tests administered to the mothers were analyzed for a study (Weiss, Grunebaum, and Schell, 1964) relating psychological characteristics to clinical judgments of the utility of joint admission.

In 1963 Dr. Carol Hartman, at that time a doctoral candidate in psychiatric nursing at Boston University, joined the project staff. The choice of a nurse to take a central role in our investigation of the clinical processes of joint admission was dictated by our first experiences with mothers and babies on the ward. It had become clear that the nursing staff, by virtue of their "round-the-clock" responsibilities for the patients, were in the best position to observe and influence the mother-child relationship. The attitudes, feelings, and skills of the nurses and attendants with regard to mothering in the hospital were therefore the most appropriate focus of our assistance, along with the direct help we could provide to the mother. In part 2 Dr. Hartman has presented her own formulation of psychological decompensation in early motherhood as a maturational crisis. Following this general orientation, she describes a sequential framework within which the work of the nurse-therapist with the hospitalized mother may be examined, and then illustrates the use of this framework with a detailed study of the interactional processes in eleven joint admission cases. Finally, she presents both conceptual and case material relating to continuing care after discharge from the hospital.

Dr. David H. Gallant joined our group in 1965 after some years with the group of investigators at the Boston Lying-In Hospital (now Boston Hospital for Women) who participated in the National Collaborative Study of Cerebral Palsy. Dr. Gallant's experience there had been with systematic, repeated behavioral and psychometric measures of infants and young children, and he approached the matter of evaluating the youngsters of our psychotic mothers, both those in the joint admission program and those who were not, with a similar orientation. In part 3

Dr. Gallant reviews much of the available literature concerning the offspring of psychotic mothers; unfortunately, for our purposes, this literature has much more to say about adult offspring than about early childhood development. He then reports the findings and conclusions from a small-sample pilot study of joint admission children and discusses some of the factors which may contribute to the differences in the development of children of normal and psychotic mothers.

Although Dr. Cohler joined us as early as 1962, it seemed most logical to leave for the last major section of the book his extensive theoretical and empirical work on maternal character, psychopathology, and child-rearing attitudes. Some of what is reported here constituted part of his doctoral dissertation in clinical psychology in the Department of Social Relations, Harvard University. Additional analysis of the data was carried out during a postdoctoral fellowship in the Laboratory of Social Psychiatry in the Department of Psychiatry, Harvard Medical School. In part 4, Dr. Cohler presents a discussion of the various theoretical perspectives on character, after which he relates character formation to specific conflicts which mothers may experience in child rearing. Then, following a review of the literature on the assessment of maternal character, he describes the development of the Interpersonal Apperception Technique, a method for coding picture-thematic material. Finally, he relates maternal character to measures of psychopathology and child-rearing attitudes—the latter assessed by the Maternal Attitude Scale which was also developed by .Cohler on the project and described elsewhere—and integrates his theory and findings.

In part 5 we have sought to distill from these various clinical, theoretical, and empirical approaches to understanding and helping disturbed mothers and their children some general observations concerning the nature of psychological decompensation in early motherhood and the characteristics of women who are vulnerable to it and who respond well to mothering-oriented therapeutic nursing care. We have tried to integrate what has been learned from our multifaceted approach to the disturbed mother and her child and to draw some implications for both theory and therapy.

It is our hope that the book will be of particular interest to several groups of readers in the mental health field. Psychiatrists and others with either administrative or therapeutic responsibilities for patients who happen to be the mothers of young children may be moved by this material to consider whether their own wards and institutions are or might become open to a joint admission program. Along with psychiatric nurses, visiting nurses, and others who are engaged in trying to assist troubled mothers, they may find in this book ideas which are of value both conceptually and pragmatically. Those with theoretical and research interests in psychopathology and its relation to personality may wish to examine particularly the sections on postpartum disturbances and on maternal attitudes and character in hospitalized and normal mothers. The systematic study of the relations between process and measures of outcome has relevance for those interested in psychotherapy research. Beyond these specialized groups, we hope that this book will reach and stimulate readers who are concerned with institutional change or involved with the problems of psychologically disadvantaged childhood.

## ACKNOWLEDGMENTS

While the various sections of the book have been written by the members of the research staff who had primary responsibility for developing and carrying out their respective studies, the nature of our collaboration was such that each of us made ongoing contributions to the work of the others. Our consistent use of the first person plural throughout the book is an appropriate reflection of this pleasant state of affairs.

We are most grateful to many colleagues and pleased to acknowledge their help here. Dr. Jack R. Ewalt, Bullard Professor of Psychiatry, Harvard Medical School, and Superintendent of the Massachusetts Mental Health Center, lent his immediate administrative support to the first joint admission and followed through with the cardinal necessities of life for any research enterprise—space, time, and institutional sanction. Dr. Milton Greenblatt, then Assistant Superintendent and Director of Psychiatric Research at MMHC and later Commissioner of Mental Health of the Commonwealth of Massachusetts, provided both encouragement and consultation in the initial stages of the project. For their cooperation and support we are indebted to many members of the clinical staff at MMHC—the psychiatric residents, nurses, attendants, and social workers who shared problems with us and who helped to make their patients available to us.

Dr. Gerald Stechler of the Departments of Psychiatry and Psychology, Boston University, was a helpful consultant on several occasions and was of particular importance in the early stages of the project as we sought to clarify our experiences and thoughts and to draft a proposal for grant support. Dr. Louis Sander, also of the Department of Psychiatry, Boston University, not only welcomed our adaptation of his developmental framework for issues in mother-child interaction but helped us to improve the accuracy of its translation into a scale of maternal attitudes. Drs. Caroline Chandler and Howard Davis of the National Institute of Mental Health gave us their enthusiastic support and constructive comment at several steps along the way.

Several project staff members whose names are not reflected in the authorship of the chapters of this book deserve much more than this brief mention for their important contributions in specialized areas. Dr. S. Norman Sherry conducted pediatric examinations on most of the children seen between 1963 and 1967 and was tremendously helpful to the mothers in the course of these examinations. Mrs. Jean Fasman, our research social worker, added new perspectives through her visits to the homes where joint admission children were being cared for before and after their hospital stay. Dr. Peter Van Der Walde and his staff were instrumental in introducing a joint admission program to the Medfield State Hospital, a venture which was studied by Dr. Donald Meeks. Mrs. Judith S. Grunebaum, M.S.W., conducted interviews with the mothers in Dr. Cohler's sample. Miss Ruth E. Schell, Ed.M., Staff Psychologist at MMHC was a devoted associate who not only conducted the psychological testing on the early sample of cases but also performed a multitude of coordinative functions. The special pictures used with the Interpersonal Apperception Technique were created by Goett and Phyllis Ward. Dr. Lois Levin assisted in the development of the coding manual and the scoring of the IAT. Mrs. Dorothy Randall, M.A., serving as our first child psychologist from 1963 to 1965, provided us with many valuable clinical observations of the children of our earliest mothers.

We acknowledge our debt to three effective research assistants in the beginning phases of our work: Miss Ann Maslow and Mrs. Linda C. Brunn assisted with the observation and testing of the children, and Mrs. Linda Copen helped with the development of the Maternal Attitude Scale and various additional research and clerical responsibilities. Devoted and efficient secretaries are a vital part of any undertaking such as this, and we have been pleased to have had the help of the following women in this capacity: Mrs. Margaret Little, Mrs. Debra Bennett, Mrs. Rosalie Brown, Mrs. Christine Forester, Miss Angela Nickerson, Mrs. Barbara Grenell, and Mrs. Claire Gilpatric. The typing of the final manuscript was largely the responsibility of Miss Alice Carr and Miss Kathy Brooks.

In the editing of these pages for publication we have had the assistance of Mrs. Patricia Eden and Mrs. Joyce Olsen. The manuscript was further polished by the application of Mrs. Grace Margolien's talents and brought to completion by the fine editorial touch of Mrs. Judith Sensibar.

Our final acknowledgment, and perhaps our greatest debt of all, is to the mothers and children who are the subject of this book. It was their trust and their willingness to help as they were being helped which made much of our work a pleasure. While it is true that some of the most intensive aspects of the project were conducted with a relatively small number of women, it should also be remembered that some phases of it (for example, the pretesting of various versions of the Maternal Attitude Scale) required as many as five hundred women. To all these unnamed heroines we express our gratitude.

Financial support for this project was provided principally by NIMH Grant Number 7-R11 MH 02435 from September 1963 through August 1967, and the book was written with partial support of NIMH Grant Number 2-R01 MH 13946. The Milton Fund of Harvard University provided initial support in planning the study, and the Laboratory of Social Relations of Harvard University provided financial support for the reliability studies of the Interpersonal Apperception Technique. The computations reported in the present volume were aided by grant number 6P-2723, National Science Foundation, to the Computation Laboratory, Harvard University.

# part 1

## planning
## for joint admission

*Henry Grunebaum*
*Justin L. Weiss*

To the Right Honorable his very good Lord Therle of Salisbury.

Right Honorable and my very good Lorde. It is supposed by those of councill with this Gentlewoman in a controversy betwene her and her brother before youre Lordship that if youre Honor onderstode the casse the pore Gentlewoman is in concerning her weakenes of mynde it might move you the more to pytty her and to deale the more favorably with her if the rigor of Law shold bee agaynst her. In this respect under youre Honors correction I am bolde upon theyre ernest sollicitation of me to certefye youre Honor that she is as melancholick a creature as may bee without totall Loss of her wittes the which to preaserve in sum sorte (for to restore to perfect integrity I durst never ondertake) hath bene not my smalest care these two or thre yeares. Now if her belovedst chyld shold bee geven from her i am in great dowbt my Lord she wold with greef fall clene besydes her selff never to bee recovered by any arte. Thus mych I have upon others importunitye bene bold to advertis youre Honor off. The Lord of Lordes direct youre Lordship in this and all things ells to his glory and increase of youre honor

youre Honors to bee commanded
peter Turner Doctor of physick
[1606]

From R. Hunter and I. Macalpine, *Three Hundred Years of Psychiatry, 1535–1860* (Oxford University Press, 1963).

# Introduction to Part 1

A young woman was in the hospital being treated for a psychotic reaction. Her sixteen-month-old son was being cared for at home by his father, with help from a baby-sitter, but this initial expedient was wearing thin. The maternal grandmother, who is the most frequent surrogate mother in such cases, was far from an ideal choice for various reasons. In this context, necessity became the mother of invention, and it was proposed to the patient that she might feel ready to undertake a return to mothering while still in the hospital.

In chapter 1 this first venture at the Massachusetts Mental Health Center is viewed in two perspectives: (1) the development of the treatment from the time the idea was raised, and (2) the expectancies and reactions of the hospital staff to this somewhat dramatic innovation. Chapter 2 attempts to generalize and to integrate the administrative and clinical experiences of the authors after a relatively large number of such cases had been treated in the same institution. The chapter deals with practical considerations in the implementation of a program of joint admission and provides guidelines for selection and treatment planning in individual cases. The concerns of all parties to the arrangement are taken up in turn: the hospital administration, the ward staff, the patient, her husband, and her mother.

Several types of marriages are discussed in terms of their psychodynamic contributions to the breakdown of the wife and their modes of dealing with the illness, hospitalization, and recovery. Since the patient and her family must of necessity come to terms first with the relinquishing and then with the resumption of her maternal responsibilities, joint admission is compared in the last part of chapter 2 with the traditional arrangements for surrogate mothering during a psychiatric hospitalization.

# 1

# The Baby on the Ward

Bobby was sixteen months old when he came to live on one of the wards of the Massachusetts Mental Health Center so that his mother, under treatment for an acute psychotic reaction, could take care of him. This event was the catalyst which led to all the clinical, empirical, and theoretical studies which are reported in this book. The reader will soon recognize that this work evolved cumulatively; cases, colleagues, concepts and methods accumulated at an uneven rate as we went on over a total period of six years, and we grew as we learned and learned as we grew. The book therefore reports not a single, coherent, predesigned research project but a series of loosely complementary studies involving overlapping but not identical populations.

Thus we have thought it appropriate to begin the book at the point where our work began. We called Bobby's entrance into the hospital a "joint admission." While in some cases, especially at hospitals other than our own, mothers and their children have indeed been admitted jointly, we have used the term to describe any situation in which a mother assumes the live-in care of her child on the ward at some time during her hospitalization.

This chapter is reprinted, with minor revisions, from "The Baby on the Ward: A Mother-Child Admission to an Adult Psychiatric Hospital," by H. U. Grunebaum, J. L. Weiss, L. L. Hirsch, and J. E. Barrett, Jr., *Psychiatry: Journal for the Study of Interpersonal Processes* 26 (1963): 39–53. © 1963 by The William Alanson White Psychiatric Foundation, Inc.

This chapter will present and discuss the first joint admission to our hospital, with particular emphasis upon the intrahospital negotiations which facilitated the introduction of this new program. The expectations and later reactions of staff members and patients will be described at length in order to illustrate the factors which must be taken into account in planning and carrying out a successful joint admission, one that can conceivably serve as a therapeutic tool, an aid to investigation, and a stimulus to institutional social change.

The importance of the early mother-child relationship to personality development has been well documented by clinical and research data in pediatrics, child psychiatry, and human and animal studies in psychology. The adverse effects upon the child of prolonged separation from his mother have been especially well demonstrated in the observations of Freud and Burlingham (1942), Spitz and Wolff (1946), and Bakwin (1942). However, traditional practice in mental hospitals and psychiatric wards has required that mothers admitted for care be separated from their infants and children.

The practice of separating psychotic mothers from their children appears to rest upon at least four assumptions involving the consequences of interaction among the mother, the child, and the hospital milieu: (1) The mother's acute psychotic reaction stems, in part, from her inability to deal with her hostility toward the child, who is perceived as a source of demands and threats. Thus her treatment and recovery, especially in postpartum reactions, is contingent upon removing her from contact with the child. (2) The mother's behavior, arising to some extent from disturbed feelings and fantasies and reflecting impaired judgment, represents a potential psychological and physical danger to the child. (3) The disturbed behavior of other patients represents a potential psychological and physical danger to the child. (4) The presence of a young child on an adult mental hospital ward would be extremely disruptive to the therapeutic management of the ward and therefore harmful to patients.

Recently reported experiences in British hospitals raise serious questions concerning these assumptions. Douglas (1956) observed that mothers with postpartum psychotic reactions were unlikely to relapse if they were given an opportunity to care for their babies in the hospital. This report of six patients treated successfully on the "neurosis ward" of the West Middlesex Hospital illustrates dramatically the effectiveness of permitting the mother to assume increasing responsibility for the child in a context of psychotherapeutic and institutional support. The work of Main (1958) at Cassel Hospital suggests similarly that it is beneficial for mothers with postpartum neurotic depressions to have their infants or toddlers in the hospital with them. The Cassel Hospital program, begun in 1948 at the request of a mother who had no one else to care for her child, has since 1955 "made it a condition of admission that mothers should bring their babies and young children with them" to this hundred-bed private psychiatric hospital. More recently, several such admissions to McLean Hospital, Belmont, Massachusetts, involving more severly disturbed mothers, have come to our attention (James Haycock, personal communication).

We regard the patient in the mental hospital as needing help in accomplishing certain tasks of living rather than as suffering from an illness which requires treatment in social isolation. Broadening the scope of the hospital to include an opportunity for mothers to assume increasing responsibility for the care of their babies is a way of helping them accomplish a task for which their past experiences did not sufficiently prepare them. Often the relationship of such patients with their own mothers is poor, and society offers fewer mother substitutes than it once did. With the baby in the hospital, observations can be made of the patient's difficulties and successes, and these can become part of staff and psychotherapeutic interaction. Therefore, while the problems raised by joint admission are many, we believe that joint admission has advantages which make it a potentially significant development in psychiatry.

In order to understand fully the development and execution of the plan for the joint admission, it will be helpful to know something both of the hospital milieu and of the emotional problems confronting the patient and her family.

## NATURE OF THE HOSPITAL

The Massachusetts Mental Health Center, under its earlier name of Boston Psychopathic Hospital, was among the first state mental institutions to concern itself primarily with the study and treatment of behavioral disturbances rather than with the provision of custodial care. It is an unusual state hospital in a number of important ways, among which are its small size (approximately two hundred adult inpatients), its role as a psychiatric teaching hospital in the Harvard Medical School, a strong research orientation, a very high staff-to-patient ratio, a relatively low proportion of so-called chronic patients, emphasis upon psychotherapy as the treatment of choice, and an advanced milieu treatment program which attempts to reduce the huge gap between the individual's role as a mental patient and his other significant social roles. At the same time, many of its attributes also distinguish it from the private hospital. Its patient population, which reflects the full range of the socio-economic scale, consists largely of acutely psychotic persons, plus some with neurotic, borderline, and character problems. In addition to those who come through the usual medical and psychiatric channels, a number of patients have been referred by the courts. It should also be noted that treatment at all levels is carried out primarily by people in various stages of training.

There are four adult services of approximately fifty patients each. The wards, all unlocked, are characterized by a fairly high level of activity and social interaction by male and female patients together. The staff of each service consists of a consultant, a chief psychiatric resident, six first-year residents, a clinical psychologist, nurses, attendants, social workers, and occupational therapists. While the *administrative responsibility for the ward and the day-to-day decisions fall to the chief resident*, under the general supervision of the hospital's clinical director, the consultant also serves somewhat general advisory and supervisory functions.

## THE MOTHER

Into this context came Mrs. P, a plump, twenty-two-year-old woman whose major difficulty was related to the change which occurred in her life when she gave birth to a son the day before her college graduation in June 1959. Mrs. P made it clear that becoming a mother was a bitter disappointment to her because of her desire to continue her education in anthropology at the graduate level. Her mother had been critical of her own husband's backwardness, and had often expressed strong intellectual and social ambitions for her oldest child, the patient. The younger siblings were expected to help with the chores, while the patient was to do her homework and be successful in school—which she was. She grew up a rather shy child without real friends, since other children did not meet her mother's standards for her. She was taught nothing about sexual matters and thus was afraid of her "degrading" feelings.

She met her husband in college, and they were married with the understanding that both would continue their studies. Her unplanned pregnancy in the fall of 1958 meant to the couple that only the husband would be able to pursue his academic work in graduate school. During the pregnancy the patient became increasingly withdrawn and unable to express her feelings toward her husband. She began to neglect her household work; her husband took over many of these duties, but with ambivalence and criticism. During this time the patient initiated a long series of intimate sessions in which she and her husband "analyzed" each other.

Bobby arrived following a full-term, normal pregnancy and a breech delivery after a long labor. Mrs. P was assisted in the neonatorum by her next younger sister, who had earlier carried the burden of household chores while the patient studied. The patient had wished to breast-feed but was unable to do so because Bobby spit up. Her husband felt her milk might be "bad," but she insisted that Bobby was sick and had to be taken to the hospital, where he was operated on for pyloric stenosis. Following the operation he did well, and became an alert, charming, and active child. But Mrs. P felt increasingly inadequate as a wife and especially as a mother, and experienced a generalized decline in vitality and a loss of interest in her surroundings. She was particularly troubled by her son's growing independence and later related a critical incident which pointed up her feelings about his separateness. She had attempted to prevent his seeing his bowel movement flushed down the toilet, believing that he would be upset, only to recognize that he was merely curious and that the anxiety was her own.

Her acute decompensation, characterized by feelings of depersonalization, ideas of reference, and severe anxiety, took place early in the summer of 1960, a week after she, her husband, and their year-old son had arrived to spend the season with her in-laws in another part of the country. She was hospitalized there for six weeks, during which there was a partial symptomatic recovery. When the family returned home at the end of the summer, she was seen at the Massachusetts Mental Health Center by a senior staff psychiatrist to whom she had been referred for follow-up care. On her initial visit he found her to be seriously depressed, withdrawn, and confused. She said, "My mind is weak, it's full of sand." She was admitted to the hospital on 6 September 1960.

## PAVING THE WAY

When the intake diagnostic studies had been completed and a treatment plan was being formulated, the question arose as to who would take care of the baby. At the time of admission a neighbor was with him during the day. At night the father took care of Bobby, and, though he found this quite gratifying, it was interfering with his academic work. Mrs. P thought that the child should be sent to her mother. At this point the consultant (Dr. Grunebaum), who was familiar with two brief attempts at McLean Hospital to have hospitalized mothers care for their babies, wondered whether the P family might benefit from such an arrangement. Mrs. P believed that she was incapable of loving Bobby, and the consultant reasoned that her work on this problem might be facilitated if she had the opportunity to utilize models provided by the staff and to discuss in therapy her day-to-day interactions on the ward with Bobby. In addition, her previous hospitalization had not led to a lasting recovery.

   The possibility of admitting the child to the hospital was first discussed by the consultant with the two psychiatrists most directly concerned with Mrs. P—the chief resident on the service and the resident working with her in treatment. The therapist's reaction was decidedly negative. He doubted that Bobby's presence would be beneficial to the treatment, and preferred to have Mrs. P gradually increase her time at home and discuss in her therapeutic sessions her feelings about the baby and what was going on at home. He also thought that being in the hospital with his mother would harm the baby, chiefly because Mrs. P was unable to accept Bobby and tended to try to "live by the book" in bringing him up. It was his belief that a more suitable environment would be available at home with a baby-sitter supplementing the father, whom he described as a "fairly loving sort of guy." The therapist had been working with Mrs. P for a month and was understandably not receptive to a radical, new procedure which might interfere with his treatment efforts. After reading the Cassel Hospital report, however, he accepted the idea. He now felt that the baby's presence might be a boon to psychotherapy, and he could find in the article no evidence to support his fear that there would be adverse effects upon the baby.

The chief resident also was reluctant, though perhaps not so much as the therapist. He felt that there was good reason to keep the P family intact if possible, and he was especially aware of Mrs. P's concern that her baby be well cared for, preferably by her own mother. But he anticipated that bringing Bobby into the hospital would raise many difficult administrative problems for him, and would create a "side show" on the ward. He was concerned that Mrs. P would become a "special" patient, which would increase the distance between her and other patients. He thought the staff might resent the extra work involved, which would in turn increase Mrs. P's feelings of loneliness and worthlessness. He also expressed apprehension about the response to Bobby by several female patients on the ward who were quite hostile to their own children. However, he recognized that certain features of his ward might serve as effective safeguards against these dangers. In the first place, it was possible to assign Mrs. P to a single room so that she might have some degree of privacy with Bobby. The high staff-to-patient ratio made available adequate supervision on the ward to protect Mrs. P against the negative feelings which might arise on account of her special status. Furthermore, Mrs. P was rather solitary and uninvolved in ward activities, so that she would not, he felt, become a focus of ward problems.

Next, a green light was required from the upper administrative level of the hospital. The proposal met with varying degrees of enthusiasm as it was successively referred to higher authority, but the ultimate endorsement was readily obtained.

The general strategy evolved was that Mrs. P would be

strongly encouraged to take full responsibility for Bobby's care on the ward, but that the head nurse would serve as a kind of model—not in doing things for Mrs. P, but in supporting her ability to do them for herself and in facilitating things where necessary. The head nurse at first had grave doubts about taking a baby onto the ward. Being unmarried, she could not easily see herself as a model for motherhood and was, in fact, afraid that she would not know what to do. As a nurse she was quite strongly oriented toward patient care, and she expressed negative feelings about "using patients for research." She thought that a great deal of additional work would be required of herself and the attendants, and that the ward was not physically equipped with such necessities as crib, playpen, special facilities for food preparation, and so forth. However, she did have sufficiently positive feelings about it so that when some assistance was provided for the arrangement of these details, she accepted the idea.

Next came a series of administrative decisions regarding the total treatment plan for the family. It was now almost two months since Mrs. P's admission, and the therapist had been working with her both in individual treatment and as the psychiatrist with direct administrative responsibility for her on the ward—functions which are sometimes split between two staff members. The consultant and the therapist agreed at this point that the former should assume administrative responsibility for Mrs. P, with the latter continuing as therapist. The reasons for the split were clear. The administrator was to be manifestly involved with the "baby project" and in regular contact with Mrs. P in order to help her work through and manage the various problems of current adaptation, including her relations with staff and patients. His previous pediatric training would be useful if the baby should need medical attention. The therapist would primarily concern himself with Mrs. P's feelings about herself, and he did not wish to take a stand for or against the baby project. The patient's husband, who had been indicating a desire to enter psychotherapy in his own right, also began seeing another member of the staff on a regular basis.

Up to this point, the question of bringing Bobby into the hospital had not been broached to Mrs. P, since we felt it was necessary to carry out the preparations described above in order to insure that things would go smoothly in the event she agreed to the plan.

In Mrs. P's second interview with the consultant, she spoke about the fact that she felt worthless and just didn't care. He wondered aloud whether she would like to care for her baby here in the hospital. Her immediate emotional response was one of agreement—she grinned broadly and said that she would. She spent the next two interviews discussing all the rational difficulties involved in following through on her emotional commitment. She said that she "could take care *of* the baby but would not care *for* him"; that she herself was a baby and needed to go home to her own mother; and that if Bobby came in she would be a special patient, the only one with a baby, and might feel as if she was living in a goldfish bowl. The consultant agreed that it would be difficult to learn to love her child, and that she would be somewhat special on the ward, but reminded her of her initial smile when she thought of caring for Bobby herself, and assured her that she would have help from the staff in achieving her goals.

The following week there was a conference at which Mr. and Mrs. P, their social worker, the chief resident, the patient's therapist, and the consultant were present. Mrs. P was asked whether she wanted to bring the baby into the hospital. When she began by saying that this plan was hopeless and futile, she was reminded of her initial grin. She wondered whether Bobby would not suffer by losing his father, but was reassured that being in a hospital does not mean that a boy loses his father. The time for decision had come. There was a long and uncomfortable pause. Previously Mr. P would have been inclined to tell his wife what to do, and, indeed, she now looked to him for the answer, but he had been exploring this problem in his own treatment and was able to remain silent and let her know that this was her decision to make. Finally Mrs. P said she would like to have the baby come in as soon as possible. It was agreed that they would spend Monday through Friday in the hospital and weekends at home. Mr. P would also be in regular contact with the social worker. The hospital personnel most intimately concerned with the care and treatment of the family would meet weekly in order to share information and discuss problems as they arose.

Immediately after the family conference, the chief resident assembled all the patients on his ward and told them that a baby would be admitted the next week. He emphasized the hospital's philosophy of individual care and treatment, and expressed the staff view that Mrs. P's optimal treatment situation should include her continuing to care for her baby. He stressed also that the doctors and nurses would assist and support her, and that certain facilities on the ward (a private room) would serve to keep the baby's presence from being "everyone's concern all the time." The response of the patient group appeared to focus on several principal questions: What will be the long-range effects on the child? Who will protect him from harm on the ward? Will he get an inordinate amount of attention? Will there be more than this one baby? These questions were dealt with by the chief resident and the group quite directly, and patients were also encouraged to take up their feelings with their individual therapists. In general, the patients in the group expressed considerable positive support for the idea, as well as concern.

Now that Mrs. P had decided to have her child come to the hospital, the staff had made appropriate plans, and the patients had been informed, Bobby was admitted. He was just sixteen months old.

## THE TREATMENT

*Individual Psychotherapy.* Mrs. P was seen by her therapist four times a week for two months before Bobby's admission and for two months following his admission, and three times a week for another four months as an outpatient following her discharge. She initially discussed her feelings of intense worthlessness as a person, with much alternation between sobbing and control. Her reluctance to follow the dictates of her punitive conscience gradually became clear. She spoke of knowing what she must do but hating to do it, with particular reference to the drudgery of caring for a child, which she tried to do "by the rules." She saw her husband as all-good and all-competent, and herself as all-bad and incompetent. She felt that the way to health was simply to use "willpower," to "make" herself do as her husband directed. She attempted to draw the therapist into attacking her with criticism, but slowly, with his refusal to do so and his pointing out her need to be attacked, she began to ask for guidance. She felt helpless and weak and wished to be shown, but she was beginning to perceive her anger at being helped in this way. It was at this point in treatment that the question of Bobby's coming into the hospital was raised. Characteristically, she wanted her therapist, her administrator, and her husband to decide, but with support she was able to make her own decision.

Almost immediately after Bobby's arrival she began to experience and to accept her anger toward her husband. She came to see these feelings as related to her envy of his masculinity and power, which had been enhanced by her placing him in a position which she perceived as omnipotent. In the second session after Bobby came in, while the therapist was examining with her some specific details of the child's care, she suddenly abandoned the position of poise and control, of denied feelings and intellectualized incompetence. She dramatically shouted, "I hate it! I hate it!" in relation to Bobby. Once she had achieved this breakthrough, Mrs. P continued to express and investigate her anger about being a woman. With support from her therapist and increasing gratification from her interaction with Bobby, she began to assimilate the idea that she could be both a competent and a feeling mother.

Upon her discharge from the hospital four months after admission, Mrs. P continued her progress in psychotherapy and at home. She remained in treatment another four months, terminating when Mr. P completed his graduate work and the family moved to the section of the country where his parents lived. In a letter eleven months after discharge, Mrs. P described with satisfaction the ways in which she continued to learn and appreciate the role of a woman. At the same time, she was beginning to channel her intellectual aspirations by enrolling in a language course. Two years after discharge, Mrs. P had given birth to a daughter and continued her satisfactory adjustment.

In reviewing their work together, Mrs. P and the therapist felt that she had made significant movement in the following areas: (1) reduction of the intense rivalry with her husband, especially in relation to Bobby's care and to her disappointment about her career ambitions; (2) some resolution of the question of who was in control in the marriage, particularly with respect to the anger-provoking matter of her being overweight; (3) increased freedom to express appropriate anger at Bobby as well as to love him, since she came to see that anger was not always destructive; (4) her growing feeling, first fostered by her caring for Bobby in the hospital, that the one thing she could do better than her husband was to be a mother and care for Bobby. (In connection with the last point, her having insisted that Bobby was sick and needed to go to a hospital when he had had pyloric stenosis was a particularly important memory.) She came to see that she did not need to be "her mother's girl" but could be "her own woman, her husband's wife, and Bobby's mother," in the words of her therapist. She felt that the transition from child and patient to woman, wife, and mother was clearly facilitated by the experience of caring for her child in the hospital.

*Other Therapeutic Relationships.* In addition to her psychotherapy, Mrs. P had important relationships in the hospital with other members of the staff. She consulted her administrator more than once a week at first about the many practical problems of caring for her baby on the ward, and also for pediatric advice. Upon her discharge, this supportive relationship was continued in half-hour weekly sessions. Throughout, one of the main issues discussed was her concern that the administrator could not like her but could only respect her for her ability to care for her baby.

With the head nurse Mrs. P was quite distant and formal until she was able to see and share the pleasure which they both had with Bobby. She was surprised that the nurse could find Bobby "so kissable." Mrs. P was particularly close to the occupational therapist on her ward. This relationship began with their reading together the occupational therapist's copy of "Dr. Spock." During their hours, Bobby would sometimes come along and run back and forth between them. At first his mother ignored him, but the occupational therapist picked him up and played with him. Gradually however, Mrs. P played more and more with him until they were finally having a wonderful time together. She would hesitantly ask the occupational therapist,

"Do you think he is handsome? Sometimes I think so." At the time of discharge, Mrs. P asked the occupational therapist to come to her house for tea. Thus the relationship ended with Mrs. P's being able to give something of herself in return.

Few manifest changes were noted in Bobby during his two months of hospital living, and those which could be observed seemed to be in response to the closer relationship Mrs. P began to develop with him. His mother commented that he appeared to miss the hospital during his first weekends at home. In general, Bobby entered and departed as a happy, active, and friendly child.

*Mr. P's Progress in Therapy.* Mr. and Mrs. P appeared to be intensely competitive in their marriage, she with respect to his career, and he with respect to her housekeeping. Since she was the less secure, he gradually adopted a sadistic, and she a masochistic, role in their frequent quarrels. His self-esteem fed on defeating her; yet he experienced her failures as his own, for he could not differentiate clearly between himself and his wife. With the birth of their son and her decreasing self-confidence as a mother, his competitiveness increased, and he neglected his work to prove he could do hers better than she could. His wife's hospitalization, which left him in total charge of their baby, thus contained an element of gratification.

In therapy Mr. P was able to work toward achieving an identity separate from his wife. He saw this process of differentiation, however, as a painful necessity rather than something rewarding in itself, especially after the baby joined his wife in the hospital. The turning point came with Mr. P's realization that the nurses knew how to help his wife in a way that would increase her confidence and independence rather than destroy them. He now began to see security and gratification in permitting a differentiation of their roles. On the return of his family to the home, he worked with increasing success to learn how a couple could act to complement and supplement one another rather than to compete destructively.

## IMPACT UPON THE HOSPITAL

The reactions of patients and staff were assessed by means of interviews and ward observations over the period of the baby's stay. Psychiatric residents from all inpatient services were asked to complete questionnaires, and the residents on Mrs. P's ward were interviewed individually, as was a representative sample of patients, day and night nurses, and attendants on the ward.

*Residents' Reactions.* The residents were initially dubious about the plan. They feared that the baby's presence would upset other patients ("Is it *fair* to other patients?") and would result in Mrs. P's being treated as special. They thought that the baby might be hurt and wondered what the long-term effect of such an experience would be on him. Most agreed, however, that the positive value of keeping a mother and child together was sufficient reason to give the plan a try. One female resident, for example, remarked, "I don't feel it's particularly beneficial for the child to be brought up in a mental hospital, although there are certainly advantages to eliminating some of the separation problems when mothers become ill."

   Of all the groups studied, the residents placed most emphasis on the research aspects of the plan. Some felt that it was being done "merely for research purposes" and without enough consideration for therapeutic issues. Others lauded the hospital's continual spirit of innovation and flexibility. Compare the remark of one resident, "This is an example of a research idea rather than a therapeutic gesture," with that of another: "The flexibility . . . [of structuring] the hospital situation to meet the needs of the patient and her son seems a laudable innovation in principle. . . . Other patients . . . might want a similar arrangement, and I do not feel that this would create unworkable problems but might further facilitate psychotherapy."

   Gradually the residents seemed to become more accepting of the idea, as demonstrated by the fact that, up to the time of this writing, nineteen other mothers have been admitted with their babies. Some residents did state that their patients resented Bobby's presence and that these feelings had to be taken up in psychotherapy. None, however, felt that this issue had been responsible for otherwise avoidable complications in therapeutic progress.

*Ward Staff Reactions.* In anticipating that the baby's presence would be disruptive, the ward staff members were concerned not so much with therapeutic efficacy as with having more on their hands than they could reasonably manage. Since they felt directly responsible for the conduct of the ward, the nurses were personally involved in the possibility that it would be upset. They felt they would have to keep a constant eye on Bobby, and also on the patients, both for fear of the patient's harming him ("I was thinking of the baby being hurt") and because of the uncontrollable feelings which his presence might arouse in patients ("He might be affected by raging, screaming behavior"). They expressed concern that "court cases" would abuse him sexually, and in general felt that the hospital was no place for a baby. They also wondered if patients would feel jealous of the attention which might be given to Mrs. P and Bobby.

The nursing supervisor supplied additional data on the intensity of these initial reactions. She told us that many nurses had hoped the plan would not be carried out or would fail, in order to justify their resentment toward the "gung-ho research psychiatrists." They were worried that they would have to watch the baby, feed him, clean him, and so forth. They further indicated that if they had wanted to care for babies, they would have worked in a children's hospital.

The nursing supervisor emphasized that, once the plan was instituted, one of the nurses' biggest difficulties was understanding their role in relation to the baby. Nurses often tend to be possessive of their patients. Having accepted the responsibility for the baby's care, they were not happy about sharing it with the mother. A number of the unmarried nurses expressed (perhaps without full awareness) their resentment toward Mrs. P, who despite her psychosis was married and had a child, while they, although "normal," were single and childless. One of the most upsetting requests made of the nurses was that they provide Mrs. P with a model for feminine identification, helping her with the baby only when she needed help. Many of the nurses said quite directly that they felt inadequate to this task because they were not mothers; some seemed to feel that they were "not good for the baby." Although in fact they were often helpful to Mrs. P, most nurses rarely played with or cuddled Bobby.

After about a month, the staff was clearly more comfortable

with the idea of having a baby on the ward, although there was still an occasional problem. An attendant said, "We have madmen here and they have never hurt the child." Perhaps because most of the attendants were male and therefore experienced less personal conflict in the situation, they seemed to adjust more readily than the nurses. But the nurses also became more accepting as they understood more clearly the psychiatrists' expectations of them, and as they observed that nothing dreadful was occurring on the ward. In fact, many of the personnel were surprised and some, perhaps, disappointed that the patients were not more upset. The only patients whom the staff mentioned as having been especially angry about Bobby's presence were a few mothers whose problems centrally involved their relationships with their own children. In general, however, the ward staff enjoyed having Bobby around, regretted his departure, missed him, and felt that the plan had been quite successful therapeutically without having had any noticeably upsetting effects on the patients or upon themselves. One attendant summed up his experience as follows, "My opinion when the baby first came in was that everyone was anxious, and after a while it was just part of life, like the sun coming up in the morning."

*Patients' Reactions.* Fifteen of the forty-five patients on the ward were interviewed. They ranged in age from sixteen to fifty—a male and a female adolescent, three men in their early twenties, one divorced middle-aged man, five unmarried young women, and four mothers in their thirties and forties.

Since there were important clinical reasons for bringing Bobby into the hospital soon after the decision had been made, it was not possible to conduct an interviewing program beforehand. Patients were interviewed between two and four weeks after the admission. It was reasoned that the respondents would have had sufficient time to assess for themselves the impact of the experiment but not so much that they would forget or seriously distort the memory of their earlier anticipations.

The interviews were semistructured and open-ended. The following general questions were asked: (1) When, how, and from whom did you first learn that Bobby was coming? (2) How did you feel about it then, and what thoughts did you have about how it would work out? (3) What is your understanding of why this is being done? (4) What are your thoughts and feelings about it now, from the point of view of yourself, Bobby, Mrs. P, and other patients? (5) In what ways have you been involved with the baby? Did you play with him? (6) How would you feel if there were other babies on the ward? (7) How would you feel if Bobby left?

Two main themes were expressed by patients in their anticipatory reactions: (1) They or others might harm the child either physically or psychologically. (2) The baby would deprive them of a good deal of attention and protection from ward personnel. On the other hand, the patients, like the staff members, were able to see some of the positive values in having the baby brought to the hospital. One woman emphasized that it was important for the baby to be with his mother. Quite a few patients felt that the child wasn't really old enough to suffer any emotional trauma as a result of being in a mental hospital, and that the advantages of being with his mother were greater than were the disadvantages of being in the hospital.

Ward observations were made during the week prior to the baby's arrival (after the chief of service had announced the plan) and for several weeks following. We had expected that Bobby's arrival might have an appreciable effect on the ward, that activity might center about him, and that possibly some patients might have to be restrained from hurting him. However, his presence was quickly accepted as a matter of fact, and none of the patients hurt him or threatened to do so. Many played or chatted with him when they passed him in the corridor, especially early during his stay, but essentially all went about their daily routine much as before. As Mrs. P became more able to involve herself with Bobby, she separated herself and her child somewhat from the rest of the ward, thus contributing to the diminishing amount of fuss made over him. A male attendant reported, "I offered to fix his supper, and she told me politely but firmly that she was doing it herself. It was the first indication I had that she was running the show."

It is important to note that the patients on the ward constitute a sufficiently organized social unit to impose group standards of behavior and to enforce sanctions on offenders. Hurting the baby would not be acceptable to the individual patient nor to the ward group. A schizophrenic young woman said, "I try to act right in front of him and have been getting more mature since he's been here." A depressed middle-age woman observed, "There is enough feeling of protection, not only from doctors but also from other patients.... Just as in the street when you see a child in front of a car, you snatch him up, so there is little danger in the ward."

While ward behavior on the whole did not appear significantly changed, individual patients expressed strong feelings about Bobby to the interviewer. Their attitudes about him appeared to be consistent with their own dynamics and often involved projection of internal feelings onto the baby. A schizophrenic girl of twenty-four, who longed for her family in the Midwest, said, "He makes me sad, as I'd like to be with my parents." An adolescent girl who was often caught rummaging through others' possessions feared that "he might go into others' rooms and they might not like it." A young male graduate student who was having difficulties involving himself in independent research said, "The baby provides an opportunity for the bird-watchers (researchers) to move on the ward."

Not unexpectedly, the women tended to have strong feelings about having one of their number caring for her child on the ward, and typically they were rather critical of Mrs. P. One mother said, "If he were mine he wouldn't be standing on chairs.... I don't think she's as responsible as she might be.... Some of us don't think hospital food is good. In my room I always have fruit. She doesn't invest the time or effort to get fruit." Another remarked, "She is pushing him too hard, that's no good. I tried to tell her in a nice way but she won't listen. It seems to me that she is too dreamy.... I should talk, but my children never got hurt because of my carelessness."

These mothers were also moved by the experience of seeing another woman successfully caring for her child. One said, "Sometimes a mother will be glad to be separated from her child, but she will be here as long as she feels that way, because she will be guilty about not going home." Another said, "He makes me grieve for my own child." These women generally did not play much with Bobby, stating that they did not believe that they should interfere with another mother's child. We had the impression that this was often a reaction formation. For example, one commented, "I try to control my maternal feelings so as to let her do it—as I would like to think he was mine." Another stated, "I am jealous of her and so I stay away."

Other female patients were led to consider various aspects of their adjustments as women. One schizophrenic young woman said, "I know I was not capable of caring for a child in my marriage, now that I see how much care is needed." A borderline patient remarked, "He brings out the maternal instinct in me." An adolescent commented, "I love babies. Since I'm young I'd like to get ready for when I get married. You learn how babies respond, how to like a baby by playing with him."

Certain common categories of response could be distinguished: (1) Feelings that the patients and the baby might be mutually harmful. (2) Feelings of envy of the attention the baby received. (3) Withdrawal from emotional involvement with the baby. Some patients responded in terms of only one of these themes, others showed more than one. In general, it was noted that the more negative a patient felt about the baby, the more he tended to avoid him.

At least five of the fifteen interviewed patients expressed strong feelings that they might hurt the baby. Most of them also stated that the ward of a mental hospital was an inappropriate place for a child. Often they commented that the baby himself was unpredictable, especially in regard to aggressive behavior. A schizophrenic young man, who spoke in therapy of his fear of his own aggressive impulses, avoided the baby, saying, "You can't depend on his action. If he feels angry he may just kick someone." A middle-aged borderline psychotic woman was concerned lest she hurt him as she had her own son. Mrs. P herself commented, "It was obvious that patients who were otherwise unpredictable were extra nice with Bobby."

Three patients reported strong envy of the attention paid the baby and avoided playing with him. A schizophrenic young woman, who was very jealous of the slightest attention shown anyone but herself, expressed her resentment directly: "He will take time away from the patients who need help. It's an adult unit, not a children's unit." Another patient said, "He gets the guidance that I need."

The tendency to withdraw from any emotional involvement

with him was particularly characteristic of four. These patients were conspicuous for their lack of participation in ward activities in general. When asked how she would feel if Bobby were to leave, one woman replied, "I'm not attached to him. I might perhaps say that I wonder how he is, but I don't think I'd have any particular feelings." A middle-aged depressed man who was quite lonely and isolated said only, "I don't mind having him around, but I mind my own business." He objected to any changes in the status quo and was against having more babies on the ward lest "other patients take advantage of it ... and turn this place into a nursery." A very ill young woman with chronic schizophrenia referred to the baby as "it" throughout the interview and said such things as, "If it were to cry or something, I just wouldn't want to be responsible for it."

Although these feelings of aggression and jealousy, of self-questioning and withdrawal, were aroused by having a baby on the ward, a great many adaptive and affectionate responses were also noted. Few patients failed to comment that Bobby cheered up the ward, that he made it seem more like a home, and that he was a cute and delightful baby. The baby's mother said, "I was surprised at the positive reaction of the other patients. I thought that people would object. Most everyone was very encouraging." An attendant said about one of the sicker patients on the ward, "She is hostile and withdrawn and seclusive, but she has the time of her life with the kid, playing with him and baby-sitting."

Many patients reported that Bobby aroused in them feelings which were used for purposes of self-understanding. A young male schizophrenic observed, "He enables other patients, me in particular, to see new things, to become aware of feelings. Each new presentaiton that you have, you become aware of other things." A middle-aged woman said, "I was in my room with him. I force myself to be with him sometimes, when I think I can control myself. When my tolerance point is low, I stay away because I don't want to hurt him." A young girl confided, "Sometimes I do act like him just to amuse him.... I used to act pretty silly myself." Similar comments were made by most patients, except for the group that consistently avoided Bobby. Some remarked that he was fortunate to be a child. A severely ill young schizophrenic woman said, "He is so cute and innocent—

I'd like to be a kid again." Another young woman felt, "If he is adjusting so well, I should be." Perhaps most illuminating is the remark of a desperately lonely paranoid young woman who said, "Just to look at his little face, he's so cute, it helps."

## DISCUSSION

Of the intense feelings aroused in staff and patients by the proposed admission of a baby to an adult psychiatric ward, the predominant manifest fear was that harm would come to the child. Less overtly, the staff was concerned about having to take greater responsibility, and the patients feared that less care would be available to them. These feelings were strongest in those who were to have the most day-to-day contact with Mrs. P and less intense in people who could view the issue "intellectually" from a distance. Patients with strong negative affect about the baby were inclined to avoid him and thus to protect him from themselves. This solution was less available to personnel who were directly involved with the child, by virtue of their positions of responsibility on the ward.

Helping the staff and patients with their initial feelings usually involved three phases: a rational explanation of the proposed change, with an attempt to define roles and expectations; a free and open discussion of the consequent feelings and associated fantasies; and a commitment to be available for the working through of any problems which might arise. One may expect that similar feelings will emerge whenever the admission of a baby is being considered for the first time. While each institution has its own dynamic social structure and the methods of communication among personnel and patients will therefore vary, we would like to call attention to the tremendous amount of support the ward staff must be given.

Certain characteristics of the institution helped to make this innovation both possible and successful. Among these were: (1) *The tradition of change*, an important element of the humanitarian revolution in psychiatry. The resistances encountered thus appeared to stem more from the specific idea of admitting the child than from a strong investment in preserving the status quo. Clear-cut administrative support from the superintendent of the hospital was invaluable. (2) *The tradition of research.* There is a strong group commitment to investigative goals, although the intensity of this commitment varies considerably according to roles and individual values. Intrinsic to this innovation was the explicit provision for a study of its impact. Thus the feelings of conflict, fear, and inconvenience experienced by the staff and patients were tempered by the knowledge that those who initiated the new procedure attached importance to these feelings and sought to understand them. (3) *Institutionalized forms of emotional support and communication.* Regular meetings and conferences of patient groups and ward staff at different levels also facilitate for those involved the feeling that their opinions are valued and their need for information is recognized. (4) *The active participation of patients in their own treatment.* The prevailing orientation at MMHC emphasizes the responsibility of the patient to make his own decisions whenever possible. More generally, it stresses the psychological assets of the patient as prime factors in the recovery process. Fundamental in the success of this case was the fact that the mother made her own decision to bring the child into the hospital. (5) *The norms for conduct on the wards.* Certain aspects of the hospital milieu, such as the unlocked doors and the mixing of male and female patients, tend to foster socially appropriate behavior. These norms are fairly well maintained, and while patients may occasionally hurt themselves, serious attacks upon others are rare. The adult patients tend to feel a certain protectiveness toward the adolescents on the ward, and the mores which underlie this .feeling are no doubt strengthened when an infant or young child becomes part of the group. (6) *The interest of the staff in the social context in which mental illness develops.* Concern with the families of patients is also traditional at MMHC. Furthermore, recently increased emphasis in psychiatry upon the psychopathology of family units has had a strong impact upon diagnostic and therapeutic thinking in the hospital.

The four assumptions underlying the traditional separation of the hospitalized mother and her child may now be reexamined.

1. *The mother needs to be separated from her child to promote her recovery.* In the case of Mrs. P, it was clear that the mother was better able to work in therapy on her hostile feelings about her child when he was physically present. As Main (1958)

has pointed out, when the hospital isolates the mother from the child, her fear and resentment of him are reinforced, and her self-image of destructiveness, inadequacy, and worthlessness is confirmed. In addition, it seemed to be useful to the father to be separated from his child and to learn how others could support his wife's efforts in a way he had not done. While we cannot generalize from one case, we must at least call into question the assumption that all psychotic mothers need to be separated from their children.

2. *The mother's illness may be harmful to her child.* There was no evidence to support this belief in the case of Mrs. P. We were impressed that the mother was able to identify with the nurses and other personnel and achieve greater acceptance of her role as a mother and woman. Most hospitalized psychotic mothers return to caring for their children after discharge. How well they do so depends in part on what they have gained from their hospitalization. Sobel (1961), reporting on the children of eight sets of schizophrenic parents, has observed that such children appear to be adversely influenced when the discharged mother resumes responsibility for the child, as compared with continued foster home placement. Pao (1960) discusses the difficulties encountered by five severely ill schizophrenic women on resuming care of their children following periods of hospitalization of months to several years. He emphasizes the feelings of separation anxiety aroused in the mother by the loss of her dependent relationship with the hospital at the time of discharge. These feelings are similar to those experienced by a child, who may react with behavioral regression to the loss of the mother surrogate, having been earlier sensitized to feelings of loss when the mother entered the hospital. He points out that failure to deal in psychotherapy with the mother's dependent wishes and separation anxiety may lead to her inability to help her child, to rehospitalization, or to both.

Our experience supports the findings of Douglas (1956) in suggesting that discharged mothers may be better prepared to care for their children if the problems of mothering have been experienced during the hospitalization and made a focus of treatment. For it is not only mental health professionals who are concerned about the effects of a mentally ill mother on her child. The mothers themselves are likely to be deeply troubled about their possible influence on the future growth and development of their children. Their presenting problems often revolve around the care of the child; fears of abusing, neglecting, or harming him are common, as well as excessive worry about him and inability to care for him. During the evaluation and over the course of treatment, these fears are often understood to be rooted in earlier troubled relationships and to have surfaced under the stress of difficulties within the marriage. Nonetheless, the concern for one's children and about one's effect on them is a reality for all parents which must be taken seriously by those who work with mentally ill mothers.

Joint admission should offer mothers the opportunity to express their fears and worries and to reality-test the distortions and exaggerations in the context of actually caring for their children in a supportive and therapeutic setting. When the mother assumes responsibility for her child in the hospital, her own feelings of dependency upon the institution may be modulated by the increased self-regard which comes from providing nurturance and care for another. It is thus reasonable to assume that joint admission can ameliorate the difficulties reported by both Sobel and Pao. If one considers in addition the weight of evidence from many studies against the prolonged separation of small children from their mothers, then the possible harm the mother's illness may cause the child—though every attempt should be made to evaluate it explicitly—should not ipso facto dissuade one from using joint admission.

We would emphasize that there may be mothers who are at times too disturbed to care for their children, and that in the case presented the mother was supported by the nurses and occupational therapist and was engaged in intensive psycho-therapy, for which she had considerable resources.

3. *The patients on the ward will actively harm the child or will adversely influence him.* We found that when patients felt hostile toward the child, they tended to avoid him. In addition, it was apparent that patients supported each other in acting maturely in his presence. On a few occasions, patients who were attempting to be playful appeared to frighten the child, but this was nothing more than might occur in ordinary circumstances with strangers outside the hospital. We saw no evidence of harm, but we did observe the pleasure Bobby derived from his

contacts with many of the patients. However, the possible long-term effects of this hospital experience upon children must be assessed more adequately than we have so far been able to do.

4. *The management problems presented by a small child on an adult psychiatric ward are prohibitive.* The success of even one case invalidates this assumption, yet there are real difficulties involved in helping a mother to care for her child in the hospital. Others must consider their own institutional organizations in terms of the potential interpersonal resources for beginning this kind of plan, considering the major feelings and consequent problems which a joint admission is likely to engender.

It has not yet been possible to assess with precision the broader effects of a child's presence upon our adult wards. However, we have observed certain changes and "side effects." The regulations which had hitherto prohibited visits by children under sixteen were soon forgotten and later officially changed as children routinely came to see their parents on the wards. This occurred with so little consequence that it was almost unnoticed, and now people wonder why this rule ever existed. We have the impression that the hospital is more cheerful and homelike, and many who come on the wards for the first time are quite amazed at what they see. It appears to us that the baby's presence mobilized, not only in his mother but in other patients, adaptive resources and mature social behaviors that were less available before his arrival.

Furthermore, after twenty such cases and more than two years of exposure to playpens on the ward, there is unquestionably a greater interest on the part of our staff in the families of patients and in how we may be useful to them. (See Grunebaum and Weiss, 1971, for a report on the first twelve of these cases.)

In summary, the facilitation of the mother's treatment, and the lack of any evidence of harm to the child, suggest that joint admission merits serious consideration as another possible therapeutic bridge between being a mental patient and returning to one's place in society. Instead of requiring the patient and her child to separate, the hospitalization supports the mother's need to learn how to live with the child, and reinforces her potential for experiencing pleasure in the relationship. Further, we believe that joint admission of mother and child offers a unique opportunity to study their interaction during the mother's acute disturbance and through her recovery, with the possibility of clarifying much of what has hitherto been surmised through reconstructive evidence.

# 2

# Clinical and Administrative Guidelines for Planning Joint Admission

The concept of a joint admission rests on certain specific assumptions about the nature of psychosis and the functions of hospitalization and treatment. While recognizing the possible genetic elements or predispositions in some cases of psychosis, the somatic origins or implications of some symptoms, and the efficacy of therapies directed toward changes in bodily state, our concept of joint admission assumes that patients who come to a mental hospital are to be understood and responded to as persons with problems in living rather than as persons who have a disease and require isolation. A second assumption is that while the personality of the patient may show certain deviations from normal, as has indeed been discussed at length in this book, the therapeutic approach to joint admission requires an appropriate balance in emphasis between the patient's intra-psychic conflicts and defenses and her interpersonal roles and relationships.

If we view the patient who requires hospitalization as needing help in accomplishing certain tasks of living, then broadening the scope of the hospital program to include an opportunity for the mother to assume increasing responsibility for the care of her baby is a way of helping her with a task for which her past experiences did not sufficiently prepare her. Joint admission renders the patient's mothering behavior and feelings directly observable and therefore directly accessible both to her and to the staff for purposes of therapeutic support, understanding, identification, and growth.

Taking the point of view that a central task of hospitalization is to help the mother assume increasing responsibility for her own life has certain consequences for the use of joint admission. It does not mean that one writes in the order book, "Admit baby." It means that bringing a baby onto a hospital ward involves realistic negotiations between the relevant parties to the agreement: the staff of the ward (especially the doctor and the nurses), the patient, her husband, and her family. If all of these parties have arrived at a decision through an understanding of the expectations, conflicts, and opportunities involved for each in a joint admission, then only rarely will there be serious or unresolvable difficulties once it is undertaken. In order to examine more closely these negotiations and the conditions under which they take place, it will be useful to discuss the issues which arise with each of the parties: the hospital staff, the patient, the husband, and the family.

The focus of the present chapter is administrative, in a broad sense, since it deals with matters of case selection and initial negotiations and with the social context of the patient and the hospital as these relate to the likelihood of success in joint admission. It leaves for part 2 the detailed presentation of therapeutic process and outcome and the central role of the nurse.

## THE HOSPITAL

*General Characteristics.* Hospitals which have successfully undertaken joint admissions differ greatly. The Massachusetts Mental Health Center (MMHC) in Boston, at which our own program was conducted, is a small (200-bed) research-oriented university teaching hospital. The Cassel Hospital in England and the McLean Hospital in Belmont, Massachusetts, other pioneers in joint admission, are both small, private institutions, which treat not only psychotic patients but also neurotic individuals disturbed enough to require hospitalization. These three institutions are devoted solely to the care of mental patients, and all three place a strong emphasis on individual psychotherapy based upon a dynamic theory of psychopathology. They are well staffed, both qualitatively and quantitatively, but have the disadvantage—from the standpoint of joint admission—that the staff is unlikely to feel comfortable in taking the responsibility for infants or small children when the mother is unable to do so. Thus, if a mother must interrupt her care of her baby, the child will usually have to go home or be placed in foster care.

Quite different is the experience of institutions such as the West Middlesex Hospital in England, a general hospital, where Douglas (1956) carried out some of the earliest joint admissions. Here the ready availability of nurses made possible the care of the child in the hospital even though the mother was not prepared, either initially or during a subsequent crisis, to assume responsibility for him. The nurses undertook to meet the physical needs of the child; the mother was encouraged to do as much for the child as she felt able, and was encouraged to discuss her feelings about this with a psychotherapist. Thus the mother came to know the baby at her own pace and had the daily reassurance that, despite all her own strange, mixed feelings toward her infant, he still survived with the detached physical attention given by the nurses. As her fear of her own negative feelings to the child lessened, she gained increasing confidence in caring for him.

Douglas's experience was corroborated by that of Daniels at the University of Chicago (as reported by Daniels at the 1965 meeting of the American Orthopsychiatric Association). Because the pediatric and maternity service staffs are available to provide "backup" in a general hospital, the mother is able to assume responsibility as she becomes ready. On the other hand, some workers have noted that many pediatricians and obstetricians tend to be overly concerned about the hazards to a baby cared for by a mentally ill mother.

The large public mental hospital, in the United States and most other countries, is the primary facility for the care and treatment of patients with psychosis. Because there had been no published reports of joint admission to large mental hospitals, we were interested in learning whether babies could be admitted with their mothers to the wards of such institutions. We were fortunate in kindling the interest of Dr. Peter Van Der

Walde, who was in charge of the admission unit of the Medfield State Hospital in Medfield, Massachusetts. This is a rather typical large state mental hospital in a rural area, and its treatment program depends heavily on drug and milieu therapy; individual psychotherapy is rarely available. Dr. Van Der Walde undertook, with our consultation, to initiate joint admissions at Medfield, and Dr. Donald Meeks, then a social work student at MMHC, interviewed many of the patients and staff of the ward before and after the first joint admissions to learn something of their reactions (Van Der Walde, et al., 1968).

The first joint admission at Medfield was the case of a twenty-year-old mother suffering from a postpartum schizophrenic episode. (Her child at this time was three months old.) The joint admission was initiated as a transition between hospitalization and her return home. The transition proved to be extremely important because she had no previous mothering experience and was extremely apprehensive about being quickly thrust back into the community to care for her child unaided. The joint procedure gave her an opportunity to deal with her fears about her role as a mother within the protective confines of the hospital. Judging by the comments of the mother during and after the joint admission and in the extended period of follow-up that has occurred since, the experience seems to have been successful. At the time of this first admission, the anxiety of the nurses increased tremendously. Their repeated statements that the mother was still too sick and that she would therefore neglect her baby were a reflection of their anxiety about their own responsibilities for the well-being of both baby and mother. Yet within a very short time the nurses felt very secure.

The nurses gave the patient advice and aid as it was needed, but they never assumed her duties. They adjusted very well to their role as milieu therapists, and their role behavior was without overinvolvement or overwhelming anxiety.

It was clear, after nine joint admissions, that the procedure was quite feasible on the wards of this large state mental hospital, and that the patients did well. Since the unavailability of public transportation to this institution makes partial hospitalization difficult, joint admission was often used to prepare the patients for discharge to the community. Instead of sending the patient home to her family for increasing periods of time, a part of the family was brought to the hospital. Van Der Walde and his colleagues found that other patients on the ward responded positively to the presence of a baby.

Specific staff expectations about patients will differ, depending on the type of hospital; Van Der Walde and Meeks found that the nursing staff at a state hospital, as Medfield is, is psychologically geared to cope with overt psychotic reactions and does so effectively. However, nurses consistently show difficulty in dealing with the acting-out behavior of a neurotic or character-disorder patient. This proved to be the case with the fourth joint admission, a patient with a neurotic depressive reaction. During her stay, this patient began overtly to reject her husband and children, and in many ways attempted to force her responsibilities onto the other patients and nurses. The nursing staff reacted with hostility toward the patient and her physician, and therefore allowed her behavior to continue without intervention. It was obvious that the nurses equated lack of psychotic symptoms with lack of pathology. It was therefore difficult for them to conceive that the patient's rejecting behavior could be symptomatic. This issue was taken up directly with the nurses, and thereafter they were able to handle the problem much more effectively. However, one can very likely anticipate a similar problem with future nonpsychotic admissions. This experience underlines the importance of integration and communication among the staff if a new program is to work effectively in a hospital.

Formal follow-up interviews with ward personnel after the first joint admission showed their general reaction to be one of pride and accomplishment in a project well launched. Specific reactions expressed by two or more nurses interviewed in the follow-up study included: "I felt that the baby's presence was a positive morale factor for the patients"; "I was surprised that there was so little anxiety on the part of ward personnel once the baby was here"; "The patients who had to give up their babies [born out of wedlock] responded to the baby"; "It was a tremendous experience for me"; "The mother took good care of the baby and there was little additional drain on the staff." They saw the project as effective and adding to the treatment potentialities of the hospital. On the whole, the nurses' morale and involvement in the program became stronger with each admission.

We have noted that when one of the wards in a hospital undertakes a joint admission and the outcome is positive, the staffs on other wards are likely to be eager to have a baby "of their own." The competitive wishes, while understandable, should be tempered with particular care and patience, otherwise poor case selection or premature joint admission without mutual agreement will almost surely follow. Each new unit must recognize that there are no short cuts to doing its own preparatory work, and that its unique administrative, social and staff characteristics must be taken into account.

*Administrative Issues.* We come next to certain matters of administrative importance in initiating a joint admissions program. As a general rule, innovations which originate with and have the strong personal involvement of the individual responsible for that unit have the best chance for success. Even so, there are bound to be resistances to change, and in our experience neither the resistances nor the strategies for dealing with them are entirely unique to joint admission. These have been presented in some detail in chapter 1. Most joint admission projects have been initiated by the psychiatrist in charge of a ward, and, in some, the head nurse of the ward has played an instrumental role.

Top-level administrators are understandably often anxious about matters of legal liability, and, in common with others at all levels, they have concern about possible danger to the child. However, we are unaware of a single instance anywhere of legal action arising out of a claim that a child has been harmed, or for that matter, of an instance in which a child has been physically hurt.

It is clear that the decision to participate in a joint admission must be made voluntarily by both parents of the child. However, parental consent does not usually constitute a waiver of responsibility from a legal point of view if a child is harmed. An interesting legal precedent may be found in a recent ruling of the Supreme Court of the Commonwealth of Massachusetts which stated that a minor and his parents may consent for him to be the donor to his identical twin in a kidney transplant. The court reasoned that to have refused would doom the ill youngster and would lead to psychological harm to his surviving brother (Alan Dershowitz, personal communication). Thus the legal issue in joint admission is likely to be whether the procedure is undertaken with the child's ultimate emotional and physical well-being as a goal. Insofar as the mother's caring for the child may permit mother and child to be reunited more quickly, and insofar as efforts are made to foster a healthier mother-child relationship, it should be evident that the child's best interest will often be served by a joint admission. Therefore, a hospital is unlikely to be held liable if reasonable precautions are taken.

*Facilities and Arrangements for the Child.* What facilities are necessary in order to admit a baby to a psychiatric ward? Clearly there are real advantages in having a single room for the mother and child; if additional space is available for them to sleep separately, so much the better. Main (1958) has described living together in an "atmosphere of domestic comfort" and even homey disorder "which would not be alien to it" as workable and desirable. Some simple kitchen facilities such as refrigerator and stove are necessary for the preparation of formula and baby foods, but older children have eaten regular hospital food. A washing machine and dryer are also useful. At MMHC no special provisions have been made for play equipment; the mothers have found ways to keep their children occupied. Since we have had no joint admissions of school age children, no educational facilities have been required. All other equipment needed, such as crib, play pen, and carriage, is usually brought in by the father. An extra crib was found to be useful so that a mother could go home weekends without taking the crib back and forth.

Since patients are expected to participate in the treatment program, the joint admission mother must have a baby-sitter during her therapy appointments and other required activities. Each mother has managed to find appropriate sitters from among the other patients on the ward, and we have required only that the head nurse approve the choice. We also arranged for a pediatrician to be available for the children when necessary.

*Pediatric Observations.* Dr. S. Norman Sherry provided consultation to our hospitalized mothers and regular pediatric examinations of their children. He was impressed with the many similarities between these patients and the mothers he sees in his pediatric office and clinic practice. However, he observed also the stress, at times overwhelming, which some of the patients experienced in handling the multitude of demands inherent in raising a child. In addition, the mother-child relationship is vulnerable to the upheavals that may be taking place in the mother's relationships with other adults. Consequently, pediatric guidance which attempts to clarify expected change in the baby's behavior during the normal course of development is of limited value to the mother unless the doctor can broaden his focus of investigation to include her thoughts and feelings about the behavior and activities of the baby.

Dr. Sherry reported that mothers who have required psychiatric hospitalization during the period of time in which they are raising small children typically doubt their ability to mother, feel inadequate and doomed to failure, and are unable to separate other problems from their child-rearing activities. Child-rearing is less pleasurable to these mothers because it is so fraught with anxiety and doubt. If the pediatrician can reassure the mother that he is aware of these factors, he will be in a better position to exert positive influence upon her relationship with her offspring.

After the mother is discharged from the hospital, though she may resemble mothers in the general population and may express very similar concerns about her child, the pediatrician must continue to take an understanding and flexible approach in which the mother's responses to the baby are a major focus. A minor issue such as washing the hair of a two-year-old daughter can be a big crisis for both mother and child. Consequently, the pediatrician's attention to the details of daily activities provides information about those matters which are of concern to the mother. Stress may be indicated by the mother's repeated comments about a particular behavior, by her avoidance of a topic normally discussed during the visit, or by comments about seemingly inconsequential behavior. The mother's problem is precisely that she does not know what to expect of herself or the baby.

## THE WARD STAFF

*Nursing and Attendant Staff.* The various professions who work on the mental hospital ward approach a joint admission from different vantage points determined by their training and their role traditions. The attitude of the ward personnel is crucial, and their tasks, especially those of the nursing staff, will be discussed in greater depth in the following chapters. The professionals most directly involved with the day-to-day responsibility for the well-being of mother and child are usually psychiatric nurses.

The care and treatment of the mother falls into a work area nurses traditionally define as their own; however, having a baby on the ward may be viewed as alien to the professional identity and experience of the nurse who has chosen to work with adults rather than children. It is of interest to note that before Fowler and Brandon (1965) opened their unit for mothers and children, "the two sisters in charge of the villa were sent to the local maternity unit for a course of instruction in general infant management." The task is made yet more difficult if the nurse is encouraged or expected to help the patient in the mothering role. The unfamiliarity of this role does not make the nurse immune to strong negative reactions to some of the mothering behavior she may observe on the part of psychotic women. To use a cliché, the nurse may feel that "I don't know much about being a mother, but I know what I don't like."

It therefore follows that if the ward staff is involved from the beginning in plans for a joint admission, conflicts and negative feelings of this kind can be anticipated and discussed, and a firm basis is established for sharing new problems as they arise.

The problems of differential staff reactions are well illustrated by the Medfield State Hospital's third joint admission, a very disturbed schizophrenic girl and her child. The day staff experienced a transient anxiety, but the therapeutic atmosphere quickly returned. However, the night supervisor and personnel exerted considerable pressure to undermine the procedure directly and subtly. Their behavior is attributable to two factors: anger at the greater attention accorded the day shift, and inadequate structure for dealing with the program. They felt powerless and understaffed. The feeling, manifesting itself in apprehensiveness and overcautiousness in dealing with patients, was transmitted to the mother as anxiety, and she became increasingly anxious.

The various reactions clearly point to the fact that the success of such a program as joint admission depends on free communication among staff and on support of the nurses by ward physicians. Steps were quickly taken to correct the lack of communication in the present instance by having the physicians talk directly with night personnel and by communicating through the day shift. When the anxiety was worked through, the situation improved. Yet the anxieties of the late shifts never completely disappeared, and active expressions of it were much more easily provoked than on the day shift. This was especially true of the night supervisor, whose employment of delaying tactics, through the administrative staff of the nursing service, crystallized the need for the full cooperation of all levels of the nursing service.

Frequent consultation is mandatory, especially for those who are inexperienced in joint admissions. The attitudes and feelings of the nurses and attendants and also the timing and quality of their interventions are significant factors in determining how well the mother will be supported in her effort to care for her child. The staff tends either to take over functions which the patient is able to manage for herself, or to leave her entirely to her own devices. Sometimes staff reaction to a patient's impending discharge can be a problem. The discharge of the patient just discussed is a case in point. The day shift had had the greatest investment in, and the least anxiety about, this patient. Suddenly, just prior to discharge, they became almost unanimously critical of the patient as a mother, criticizing her ability to care for her child or herself. The personnel began openly pushing the patient into increasing dependence upon them, resulting again in a gradual deterioration of the patient. In a meeting of nurses and doctors, it was found that the nurses were experiencing a separation anxiety. They had formed such a deep and strong investment in this patient that they found it difficult to terminate her. They expressed fear of a relapse which would reflect badly on them and undermine their faith in the program. When such anxiety was brought into the open, the nurses were better able to handle the situation. The patient again rapidly improved to her highest level of performance and was eventually discharged.

As will be discussed in ensuing chapters, certain types of patients tend to evoke these extreme staff responses.

When we were involved in assisting the staff at Medfield State

Hospital to plan a joint admission program, one of the most helpful steps was to invite several key members of their nursing staff to visit the MMHC wards in the company of Dr. Carol Hartman, the research nurse of our project. The Medfield nurses, generally somewhat older than those at MMHC, married, and parents of adolescent or grown children, came away from their visit to our wards with enthusiasm and some feelings of healthy rivalry. One of them put it quite directly: "If they [the younger, unmarried nurses] can do it, we can do it better." The Medfield nurses began to feel that the joint admissions would offer them new opportunities, not just more work.

It is our impression that more mature nurses are less threatened by a psychotic married young mother than are younger nurses, who may feel keenly their unmarried state. We have also observed that the nurse who has raised her own children is often more comfortable assisting a younger woman with a baby or small child. On the other hand, an older and experienced nurse may be tempted to assume an inappropriate degree of care for the child, and her age may also facilitate the exaggerated transference of the patient's ambivalence toward her mother. Pearce has stated that he prefers as nurses married women whose children are no longer babies (1965 meeting of the American Orthopsychiatric Association). We believe it possible that age and marital status of the nurse are likely to determine initial, rather than long-term, differences in the handling of joint admissions.

Not infrequently the mother, ambivalent about seeking or receiving help from other women, may turn to a male ward attendant, who is then faced with many of the same issues that concern the nursing staff. The male attendant may not know how to mother, but he can be most supportive of the patient in ways she can accept. Attendants have, in general, not been so closely or intensively involved in the care and concerns about a mother and her child, and they have found their avuncular role comfortable.

*The Ward Psychiatrist.* In advance of the first joint admission, psychiatric residents at the MMHC were concerned about two adverse possibilities: the effect of the baby's presence on the other patients who might feel deprived of attention, and the effect of the mentally ill mother and other patients on the child. On the other hand, because there was considerable positive value attached to innovative clinical research, most psychiatrists at the MMHC were in favor of the undertaking. Reports from Medfield State Hospital were rather similar, but there the psychiatrists seemed to put greater emphasis on the fear of being blamed if something should go wrong.

Several generalizations about the participation of psychiatrists have emerged from our experience. First, we have noted repeatedly that regardless of the treatment orientation a psychiatrist prefers, if he is interested in the interpersonal milieu of the ward and believes in its therapeutic importance, then he is likely to undertake joint admissions when the opportunity arises. This observation comes not only from the MMHC but from the British joint admission reports. On the one hand, Cassel Hospital utilizes psychotherapy "informed by psychoanalysis" and had recently added group psychotherapy at the time of Main's report. On the other hand, the reports of Baker, Morison, Game, and Thorpe (1961) and of Douglas (1956) focus on the use of electroconvulsive therapy and drugs together with ward nursing care. All these workers highlight the interpersonal context of treatment and are enthusiastic about the use of joint admission.

The greatest resistances to joint admission stem from the view that the presence of a baby will interfere with the mother's recovery; this often masks the doctor's feeling that his relationship with the patient will be disturbed. Residents are well aware that patients interact with many other staff people the "other twenty-three hours of the day," and that their relationships with their families are not abruptly cast aside upon admission to the hospital. Nonetheless, the doctor who admits a baby to the care of its mother on the ward becomes a *witness* to emotionally charged interaction rather than just hearing about it in his office, where the only charged interaction is between the patient and himself. This fact, we think, explains why, in certain training settings, residents may experience joint admission as complicating and a diversion from their main business, psychotherapy. The resistances to "rooming-in" are probably similar in nature. Perhaps as families come to be viewed as a significant ecological unit both for the genesis of maladjustment and for its treatment, these feelings will be lessened. As long as the focus of physicians is on the individual to the exclusion of the larger social units, joint admission will seem somewhat alien and in conflict with therapeutic objectives.

Whereas the psychiatrist who openly opposes joint admission makes his position clear, the doctor who brings in the patient's baby as a last straw in a difficult clinical situation (poor communication between him and his patient, his failure to perceive and interpret gross denial of distress, etc.) poses a more subtle problem. The action is usually motivated by the feeling on the part of both doctor and patient that a change—almost *any* change—might do some good. Joint admissions born out of therapeutic desperation are almost certainly headed for trouble; a genuine working alliance is the best guarantee against this misuse of joint admission.

## THE MOTHER

The central participant in the negotiations to initiate a joint admission program is the mother. What criteria are useful in assessing whether or not a mother should undertake the program?

*Diagnosis.* There are no specific psychiatric diagnostic entities which either suggest or contraindicate joint admission, in our opinion. This view is consistent with the criteria used by Mitchell and Turton (1966) in admitting patients to a twenty-five-bed ward for short-stay periods. "All women with children below school age were offered the facility of bringing their children into the hospital, irrespective of diagnosis, whether psychotic or psychoneurotic. Hostility to the children, either latent or manifest and whether expressed verbally or physically, was not a contraindication, nor was the severity of the mother's condition." Mitchell and his colleagues were able to admit the children of nine schizophrenic women, of two with psychotic depression, and of one diagnosed as schizoaffective. Also admitted were the children of psychoneurotics and several immature and addicted mothers. Similarly, Glaser (1962) notes that selection of patients should not depend strictly on diagnostic category. "Mothers who are undoubtedly schizophrenic, even when suffering gross hallucinations and delusions, may care most devotedly for their children. On the other hand, mothers with neurotic illnesses may be quite incapable of fulfilling their maternal role in spite of the help offered." Our experience is similar to that of these workers—the usual diagnostic categories are of little relevance. What criteria, then, are useful?

We have found that, as might be expected, the most immediate priority in treating a newly admitted psychotic mother is not to ascertain whether she can care for her child. The first order of business must be to ensure the mother's protection from the dangers of disturbed affect, thought or behavior. (We have heard of an instance of suicide, when a mother felt that the staff was not really interested in her but only in how well she could perform as a mother.) The hospital staff must let the mother know that it is, above all else, interested in her well-being.

Mrs. R, a twenty-three-year-old nurse whose family had a history of mental illness, was admitted to the hospital in an acute schizophrenic turmoil three weeks after the birth of a daughter. Eight days after her admission, when she had calmed down only slightly, the patient precipitously decided she wanted to take care of her daughter. The staff too was overly eager to have her do this, but when the baby came on the ward, the patient rapidly became panic-stricken again. The infant responded to her mother's panic with shrill screams, although when other people held her she was easily calmed, comforted, and fed. The baby was sent home and the patient soon recompensated.

What the hospital personnel *can do* in the beginning is to help the family arrange for the baby to be well cared for. When a mother enters the hospital, the arrangements for care of her children are usually made by her family. This is often done on a temporary basis, with tentative and poorly defined plans, since the family has no clear idea of how long the mother will be away and how long she will be unable to care for her children. The hospital staff, which may be expected to have some estimate of the length and course of hospitalization, is in a good position to assist with the planning of surrogate child care prior to admission. Of particular importance is that the child or children be placed with someone who is willing and able to care for them, and that the ties to father, siblings, and, in the case of older children, peers and school, be as little disrupted as possible.

No mother will thank a hospital for asking her or allowing her (which may be *felt* to be the same thing) to take care of her child when she feels incapable of doing so. A crucial indication that joint admission may succeed is the mother's spontaneous positive interest and feeling when the subject is broached, and the single most useful indicator of when a mother is ready to take care of a child is when she feels ready. However, as we have noted, different wards will demand varying degrees of competence and responsibility from the sick mother, depending on the ability of the ward personnel to take care of the baby. If the mother expresses interest in caring for her child and it is suggested to her that she must take the initiative in making appropriate plans with the nursing staff, then the manner and promptness with which she undertakes this task are the best guide to her readiness to begin a joint admission. The patient's actions will speak louder than her words, and sound clinical judgment requires close attention to the mother's behavior during this critical period.

At Medfield State Hospital, for example, one disorganized postpartum mother at the time of the second joint admission began to request that she also be allowed to do this. The then current joint admission mother confronted her quite directly with the point that she was in "no shape to do this" and that she had better "shape up if you want your child." This confrontation was surprisingly well handled. In fact, as a preliminary step toward her own joint admission procedure, the disorganized mother apprenticed herself to the joint admission mother. The collaboration was of considerable benefit to her, for she had until then felt inadequate to take care of her child, her first, and little interest in helping her had been expressed.

While the usual diagnostic categories are not particularly useful, we have found it helpful to think about the prognosis for joint admission and its impact upon the patient's clinical course by dividing the psychotic mothers into three more or less distinct groups according to their histories and presenting problems.

*1. Acute, child-centered reactions.* Patients in this group have a history of reasonably successful prepsychotic adaptation, particularly at work and school. They appear to come from intact families with whom they retain close ties. Strong masculine striving and serious conflicts over femininity are prominent, and becoming a mother is thus particularly stressful. These women tend to become disturbed during pregnancy, although they may not become psychotic and in need of hospitalization until some months later, after the delivery. Of our three groups, this one comes closest to the usual definition of "postpartum psychosis," though our experience leads us to reject the term as a diagnostic classification because of its heterogeneity.

The child involved in these cases is often a first child; the patients almost always report that they would like to love the child and feel guilty because they cannot. Caring for the child in the hospital helps these mothers come to terms with their hostility toward the child, lessens the guilt aroused by having abdicated maternal responsibility, and affords them the opportunity to develop both positive feelings and a sense of competence in caring for the child in a supportive setting. The joint admission seems particularly useful in these cases since it focuses the patient—in her life on the ward, in her interaction with the staff, and to some degree in her psychotherapy—directly on the problems central to the decompensation. And these women, whose breakdowns involved conflicted feelings about the young child as a major dynamic issue, appear to have the best prognosis for rapid recovery.

A typical example of a case which falls in this group is that of Mrs. C, a twenty-six-year-old woman admitted to the hospital nine months after the birth of her second child. She was in a depressed and anxious state and was fearful that she might kill her children and husband. Mrs. C, whose nickname was Billy, had been a "tomboy," wanted to be a WAVE, and was afraid of men. Sexual relations with her husband were never satisfying, and her husband experienced premature ejaculation. She had had life-long sexual fantasies of relationships with her girl-friends. Her first child was a son, a source of great gratification and pride, but her second child, a daughter, made her very anxious. It was felt that the birth of a girl had led to anxiety about her own poor feminine identification and that caring for the child would be useful. She was very competent in caring for the child and was discharged after a few months. The follow-up, two years later, demonstrated a considerable improvement in her general adjustment. The father was more active in the care of the children, and the patient enjoyed sexual relations much more.

*2. Acute marriage-centered reactions.* In the second group, we have also noted fairly good prepsychotic adjustment, particularly before the marriage. Here the principal feature appears to be sado-masochistic needs, which may be manifested in both passive and rebellious interpersonal relationships. While a woman in this group initially complains of difficulties in caring for her baby, who is usually not her first, it soon becomes clear that the illness is primarily related to the struggle with her husband and her general dissatisfaction in the marriage. These patients appear, retrospectively, to have married in an effort to get away from home and the unresolved difficulties with their own mothers. While the marriages have been marked by strife, they do not become intolerable until there are several children on the scene. The children often seem to bear the brunt of the marital struggle. It is somewhat typical in this group of families that, as the husband becomes more successful at work, he finds that his profession takes him more and more away from home, a home he is glad to leave because of the many fights with his wife and because of his own needs to avoid closeness. Psychotherapists who work with couples of this kind have written of them as involving the "love-sick wife and the cold-sick husband." A mother in this group may welcome the opportunity to care for her child in the hospital as a support to her self-esteem as a good mother. On the other hand, the mother may just as often welcome the hospitalization as a respite from the demands of her home, and she may be quite unreceptive to a suggested joint admission. For this group as a whole, joint admission may be supportive but is not centrally involved in helping the patient with her problems. Therapeutic efforts in these cases must focus on the marriage for optimal results.

Mrs. S, a twenty-six-year-old nurse, married to a doctor, was admitted four and a half months after the birth of a son. Her psychotic reaction, which had begun six days after delivery, had not been diminished by a series of sixteen electroconvulsive treatments. She did well caring for her child on the ward and was discharged after three months. There are three significant things about her course. First, during several brief periods of upset behavior while she was on the day care program, it was necessary to send the baby home and keep her in the hospital. We felt that this emphasized our interest in her and not merely in her mothering. Second, she made clear how much having to care for her child made her face and cope with her problems. During the admission, she said, "If it was just me, I would have killed myself, but I had this responsibility." And two years later she said, "If I had not cared for the baby, I would not have had an opportunity to learn to love him." Third, and most relevant to our present discussion, the patient was involved in a particularly unrewarding and difficult marriage. She had been promiscuous and frigid as a single girl, and her frigidity had continued in her marriage. Some degree of resolution was, however, achieved; our follow-up information a year later indicated that she seemed satisfied with her husband as a source of money and social position, and she felt that he was pleased to have a very attractive hostess who made few demands on him for time and affection.

*3. Exacerbations of chronic problems.* Relatively poor pre-admission adjustment, with a history of chronic depression and/or psychotic periods, characterizes the third group. These patients come to the hospital when stress exacerbates these long-standing problems. Their own early development has, in many cases, been featured by deprivation and abusive treatment, and their strong needs to be taken care of leave them with little to give their children. Joint admission has not worked out well in these cases unless it was introduced fairly late in the hospital course; earlier than this, the needs of the child constitute an additional demand upon an already overburdened mother. Needless to say, these are among the most difficult patients to help with any psychotherapeutic approach. However, it is well to remember that discharging these chronically depressed and often marginally competent women to care for their children at home—unobserved, unhelped, but in a setting that does not arouse the guilt or anger of the hospital staff because they do not see what goes on—is no solution either. The most appropriate procedure would seem to be a joint admission late in the hospital course as an aid to the mother's transition from hospital to home, and the provision of adequate aftercare at home.

Mrs. E, brought unwilling to the hospital by her husband, carried her four-month-old infant and refused to be separated from her. The patient was the oldest of ten children born to a mother who was told never to have children and whose father was a demerol addict. At an early age, Mrs. E was responsible for the younger children whenever mother went to the hospital to have another. However, when the sixth sibling was born, a change in her personality was noted, and simultaneously her father told her mother that she was never to be disciplined because she was "perfect." Since that time, she seems to have been withdrawn, confused, and vague, and in the marriage has always been dependent upon her husband to deal with the outside world. He did the shopping, cared for the house, and arranged their social life. Her increasing disorganization after the birth of their second child began to interfere with his going to work, since he found it difficult to trust her with the children. Finally he sought help, bringing her against her will to the hospital, and she was admitted with her baby. The nurses soon found that her care of her child was too negligent and irresponsible to be tolerated. The patient's behavior with her child and her emotional communications to the staff engendered strong feelings of hopelessness, and the baby was sent home to stay.

These three groups became apparent in the course of our clinical experience, and we were interested to note that very similar groups were delineated by Pearce. On the basis of his experience at the University of Saskatchewan Hospital, Pearce distinguished three groups of hospitalized mothers as follows:

1. In this group of patients, usually neurotic but sometimes with bizarre symptoms, the birth of a child activates a conflict about mothering. This conflict is characterized by the following history in some of these patients. There has been a previous birth of a stillborn, deformed, or otherwise abnormal baby in a context of conscious death wishes or thoughts of abortion, resulting in powerful guilt feelings from the mother's belief that her wishes or thoughts were the cause of the outcome. The

breakdown may occur in this setting or after subsequent pregnancies which arouse extreme guilt about the mother's wishes. Pearce felt that joint admission was very helpful in these cases since it permitted the focusing of therapeutic efforts upon the mother's main problem—the guilt and fear related to her destructive potential.

2. His second group consists of patients with a personality disorder such that interpersonal relationships in general are deficient and the mother-child relationship in particular may be especially difficult. Joint admission can be useful here in helping the mother with her child. Treatment should include serious consideration of whether the mother's difficulties in relating will lead to repeated problems for herself and the child and how this should be taken into account in deciding whether or how soon to have more children.

3. The last group seems quite similar to our third group— women with serious chronic emotional disturbances. The birth is merely the latest stress factor in a vulnerable system, and therapeutic management should be vigorously directed toward reducing the stress and ameliorating the psychotic behavior. Joint admission should be delayed, and if hospitalization is prolonged, the joint admission is likely to be helpful.

Considerations other than diagnosis have also been important in the evaluation of admission policy to a mother-baby unit at Shenly Hospital in England, as reported by Glaser (1962). She notes that in the beginning, admission was offered to any mother whose illness required treatment in the hospital and in whose case separation appeared likely to be harmful to mother or child. This resulted in the admission of patients with, for example, long-standing neurotic or personality disorders or schizophrenic states which had no relation to pregnancy or the postpartum period. Later, the unit tended to admit only patients whose illness bore a more clear cut relation to the birth of a child. On the other hand, Bardon's unit has evolved in the direction of the wider use of joint admission in sicker and more chronic patients as a way of assessing the mother's adequacy in order to evaluate the need for separation from the child or the provision of added support after discharge (Bardon et al., 1968).

At Medfield we found that joint admission was often of diagnostic value, since neurotic mothers, in particular, were stressed by the admission of their children, and their acting-out behavior in response to this stress was then available for therapeutic work. Previously, these mothers would have been discharged after the initial observation period because they were not psychotic. Under such circumstances, their pathological behavior would never have been available for discussion. As it was, this behavior was more closely evaluated, and their need for treatment and the problems of their families became strikingly apparent. The joint admission allowed the hospital to offer meaningful service to a group of patients who otherwise would have returned to unfavorable and unchanged home situations.

On the other hand, at our own hospital, mothers who have been considered for joint admission tend to be among the "healthier" patients on the ward. We suspect that the staff is more likely to discharge a sicker patient to care for her child at home rather than to admit the child and become a witness to what may sometimes be quite pathological interactions. In addition, it appears that patients from the lowest socioeconomic groups may be underrepresented among our joint admissions because their child-rearing techniques are often divergent from those which are familiar and comfortable to the middle-class ward staff.

*Review of Eight Cases with Poor Outcomes.* One of the ways of approaching the problem of case selection for joint admission and optimal joint admission procedures is to consider cases which encountered serious difficulties. In our review we encountered eight such cases, each of which can be studied from two aspects: how the patient's personality has led to the difficulties; and how, within such context, caring for the baby can be made most useful. We may add that these cases seemed to occur most frequently early in our experience.

The first group of three cases appear to be those in which either the mother was admitted to the hospital with her child because she refused to be separated from him, or the baby joined his mother before she was ready to care for him. Common to these women is the fact that they did not have a therapeutic alliance with the hospital and with their physician at the time of the admission of the child. In all three instances the baby had to be sent home, if only overnight. One of the women was an acute schizophrenic who rapidly recompensated, brought her baby in after three days, and immediately decompensated again. The joint admission was simply too early, and the baby had to go home; the mother refused to try it again. The other two instances were chronic schizophrenic women who refused to be separated from their children, had severe and intractable marital problems, and feared that their husbands might leave them and take the children. Here the contract with the mother was one-sided, for the hospital staff had no choice about admitting the baby; as a therapeutic alliance was built, it became possible to send the baby home and focus attention on the mother's problems.

Another group who had difficulties in joint admission was characterized by severe problems in impulse control. These four mothers had taken overdoses, slashed their wrists, been promiscuous, beaten their children, and led disorganized lives. Some came from backgrounds of poverty and deprivation. While the official diagnosis was sometimes schizophrenia, the problem in caring for the child was always in the area of impulsive behavior. Only one of these mothers was able to continue the joint admission, and even in this case it was occasionally necessary to send the child home for a weekend. This woman differed from the others in the strength of her relationship with her psychiatrist and in their agreement to focus therapeutic work on her difficulties in controlling aggressive behavior toward her children.

The other three mothers did not have an alliance either with their psychiatrists or with the hospital, and their cases were further complicated by the degree to which the patients provoked, or became the scapegoat of, intrastaff conflict.

The final instance of serious difficulties in caring for a child was that of a very deprived woman with chronic depression who, while different from the other unsuccessful cases in that she did not act on her impulses, was nonetheless unable to give to her child and found caring for him intolerably burdensome. As far as she was concerned, the hospital was a place in which to be given to; she did not expect to have to give to a child.

*Summary of Selection Criteria.* First, it appears that a simple diagnostic classification is not particularly useful and that patients with a wide variety of diagnoses have profited from joint admission. Second, it seems that the more acute the onset of the psychosis and the more directly it is related to the child's birth and development, the more immediately useful the joint admission is to the mother. Third, joint admission and other therapeutic efforts directed specifically toward the mother-child relationship should be considered for reasons of evaluation of long-standing problems when the mother's personality and attitudes are felt to be adverse influences upon the child. Unfortunately, the medical model of mental illness does not give adequate attention to the level of maternal functioning after hospitalization, and the typical mental hospital staff is so burdened that long-range preventive or rehabilitative efforts are often disregarded or are dismissed as an impossible luxury.

## THE HUSBAND AND THE MARRIAGE

While the patient's relationship with and feelings about her mother are of great developmental and contemporary significance and are centrally involved in her psychodynamics, treating decompensation which arises in the context of bearing and rearing children requires an understanding of the difficulties in the marriage. Some degree of unresolved conflict between husband and wife is intrinsic to the breakdown, and as we have looked more closely at marriages, we have been impressed with the high frequency of these difficulties.

It has been helpful for us to think of three broad classes of marital situations, each having somewhat different implications for the planning of the joint admission and the course of work with the family. Problem marriages can usually be classified as (1) new, (2) unstable, or (3) stable but imbalanced.

*The New Marriage.* In the *new* marriage, either or both partners may still be seriously hampered from full participation because of difficulties in separating from parents or unresolved conflicts between different backgrounds and values. One frequently has the sense, in marriages of this type, that the partners have important work to do together which they have avoided or have had too short a time to accomplish, and that parenthood confronts them before they are emotionally ready. The arrival of a baby often triggers feelings of rejection, deprivation, displacement, and resentment in the husband at a time when the wife needs support more than ever before in the marriage. On the other hand, we have had cases in which the premature demands of parenthood conflict with highly valued needs or goals of the wife, such as career aspirations, which have not yet been integrated into the marriage; in these instances, it is *her* feelings of anger or deprivation which set in motion the downward course of the marriage.

The case of Mrs. P, who was presented in some detail in chapter 1 as our first joint admission mother, is an unusually clear example of the breakdown and treatment of a woman in a *new* marriage. It will be recalled that her son was born the day before her college graduation, and that the pregnancy had thwarted her desire to go on to graduate school.

In the following case an intense struggle between the patient and her family was central to the initial difficulties in a new marriage, and a joint admission was helpful in launching the couple on their own course together:

Mrs. M was admitted to the hospital at the age of seventeen, two weeks after the birth of her first child, a girl. She had been the most rebellious and determined child in a traditional Italo-American family—the apple of her father's eye. After dating for three years a boy to whom the family objected, she became pregnant so that marriage would be mandatory. Her father had often said he would kill any of his children who became pregnant out of wedlock. The wedding was finally arranged after much open strife within the family. Ten days after Mrs. M delivered, it was discovered that the patient's brother had been responsible for the pregnancy of her closest friend. It was in this setting that she became acutely depressed. The work accomplished during the hospitalization was to help the patient's parents begin to let their daughter lead an independent life and to provide very strong support for the husband and the marital relationship. Mrs. M recovered rapidly, taking care of her baby skillfully in the hospital. Eight years and three children later she was doing well as a mother, her husband was successful in business, and their independence as a family was unquestionably established.

When the marriage is a new one and there are also problems due to different cultural backgrounds, the birth of a child can precipitate a family crisis.

Mrs. C, aged twenty-one, was admitted to the hospital in an acute confusional and depressed state three weeks after the birth of a daughter. She had grown up in Italy during World War II in a situation of considerable physical and emotional deprivation, and reported that there were times that she had lived in a cave and gone without food. She married a young American soldier stationed in Italy and came to the United States following her marriage. She was mildly depressed at the birth of the baby, feeling alone and far from home among strangers. It was difficult for her to begin breast-feeding, and her husband told her she was a bad mother because the baby did not like her milk. Both husband and wife found the baby's crying intolerable and could find no way to relieve it.

Following admission, Mrs. C was given a course of nine shock treatments. The baby joined her on the twentieth hospital day and stayed until her discharge two months later. With considerable support from the nurses, she was able to take over the care of her child, and her husband was encouraged to become increasingly supportive rather than critical. It was helpful to Mrs. C that they were able to return to Italy immediately following her discharge; follow-up by letter indicated that she was maintaining the gains she had achieved in the hospital.

Emotional breakdown in new marriages is often a function of the immaturity of the couple. Their expectations of each other may be unrealistic, and the responsibilities of parenthood may be frightening. In these instances, a joint admission will often help the young mother to learn to care for her child in a supportive setting which takes some of the burden off her anxious husband.

Mrs. S, twenty-two years old, was admitted three weeks after the birth of a daughter. The patient's mother, an assertive woman with a successful business, had sent her own husband away for good when the patient was five. Mrs. S met and married her husband during college, but the unplanned birth of their first child occurred in a context of increasing marital difficulties, especially in the sexual area. Intercourse had been painful to the patient and therefore limited in frequency even before the period of abstinence prior to the delivery. Mrs. S's hospitalization was precipitated when her husband told her he had met a girl who could make him happier than she did. The patient did well in the hospital, gaining increasing satisfaction from caring for her baby. Given her own mother's attitudes, it was difficult for her to tolerate the presence, much less the affection, of a man and to accept motherhood as a good thing. Her husband, on the other hand, was made anxious by the closeness involved in marriage and was happiest when working on his sports car. The joint admission was merely the first step in a therapeutic process involving much work with both members of the couple—separately and together.

In general, we have been impressed that joint admission can be particularly useful in new marriages. It affords an opportunity for the couple to work together on a common task—helping the wife to assume care of her baby. It focuses therapeutic efforts on the question of what developmental issues must be worked out in order for the couple to move from being married to being parents. Often we have seen that the couple has not allowed itself sufficient time as a couple before becoming parents. But not all women with new marriages are dealing with the tasks of this period; indeed, a number of them appear to have developed rather rigid and imbalanced patterns of relating to their husbands. In such cases, where the situation is not in flux and the negotiation of developmental tasks meets stubborn resistance, the marriage may be "new" only in a temporal sense.

*The Unstable Marriage.* We employ the term *unstable* to refer to marriages which are in turmoil, often chronically, and may be in danger of dissolution. They may be, but are usually not, relatively young marriages. They are distinguished from new marriages by the clearly observable reverberations of incompatible character traits and modes of expressing love and anger. Narcissism, immaturity, insufficient capacity for delay of gratification, and tendencies toward impulsive action are typical hallmarks of at least one, and often both, of the partners. While we do not suggest an identity between such marriages and those called "schismatic" by Lidz, Cornelison, Fleck, and Terry (1957), who delineate them as one type of schizophrenogenic family, the two have much in common. We, however, are describing parents of young children while Lidz and his associates are dealing with the families of adolescent or young adult schizophrenics. They speak of a "state of severe chronic disequilibrium and discord ... mutual distrust ... recurrent threats of separation," and these phrases convey the flavor of the marital interaction in our unstable group.

Not infrequently in these marriages we find a husband whose defenses against his dependency are expressed in terms of a need periodically to "get free" of the commitment to the marriage in order to reassert his independence and masculinity. In such instances, sometimes an insecure and frightened wife expects the birth of a new baby to bind the husband into a shaky marriage—a commitment he has not made previously either to her or to his other children. What happens is just the reverse; the presence of the baby sooner or later leads to increased frustration of the husband's dependency needs, stronger feelings of being tied down, and a heightening of the preexisting tendencies toward withdrawal, usually in a context of resentment and escalating reciprocal accusations.

A wife's psychotic breakdown at this point is often a desperate reaction to the loss of support. Its meaning in an unstable marriage is complex and varied. From the husband's viewpoint such an eventuality may serve to confirm his accusations—he "knew she was crazy all along"—and to justify his further withdrawal. The following examples illustrate the supportive use of joint admission in an unstable marriage.

The psychotic reaction of Mrs. K, thirty-seven years old, occurred in the context of a ten-month separation from a marriage of fourteen years' duration. It was clear that the breakup of the marriage meant to Mrs. K that she had lost both husband and employment, since she had worked with him in a partnership. When divorce proceedings were initiated, the patient began to feel increasingly vague, depressed, and worried about her health and that of her child. She was especially upset at her husband's insistence on exercising his right to visit the baby while he had infectious hepatitis. On admission to the hospital, she was incoherent and showed inappropriate affect, posturing, and some feelings of persecution. She spoke of her sixteen-month-old daughter as being her only tie with people and requested that she be allowed to have the child join her. However, she was ambivalent about this, since she worried that it might be more of a burden than she could handle. It was felt that caring for her child would foster her ability to be realistic rather than to be overwhelmed by her fantasies; so three weeks after admission, little Jenny joined her mother on the ward. Immediately the patient became more organized and effective; three weeks later she was discharged, functioning well. She became better able to set limits with her husband, began a new career, and took good care of her daughter, who had been so important to her during the recovery from her illness.

The case of Mrs. W, aged thirty-two, provides another instance in which the birth of a child was merely the final straw in precipitating a psychosis in a woman with a marriage made unstable by mutual recriminations over the causes and care of two mildly deaf children. The marital relationship had become increasingly tempestuous over a number of years following the diagnosis of congenital deafness; the patient had frequent temper tantrums and was accusatory and pervasively critical of her husband. He responded by withdrawal, silent contempt, and deprecation of her mothering abilities. Mrs. W's hostility turned increasingly to depression. The hospitalization was precipitated by the birth of a third child and the fear that this child would also suffer from mild nerve deafness. She took good care of her child in a joint admission, being an experienced and competent mother. While this was a boost to her self-esteem, it appeared that the most valuable outgrowth of the hospitalization was the fact that she and her husband, with the help of a social worker, were able to resolve some of their marital problems and refocus the feelings which had been displaced onto the children.

The case of Mrs. A illustrates the repetition of an earlier breakdown under the strain of marital difficulties. Not long after recovery from an acute adolescent turmoil she married a young man who was frequently unemployed and who gambled a great deal. She was often depressed at the lack of financial and emotional support. When a crisis arose soon after the birth of her second child, a boy, she became acutely confused and more seriously depressed. She was admitted to the hospital where she cared for her son, and treatment included work with the husband. When he promised to try to grow up and take more responsibility, the patient improved rapidly, but she was readmitted subsequently with similar symptoms in the context of the next pregnancy and her husband's reversion to his previous gambling pattern.

These cases exemplify the difficulties in the unstable marriage where characterological problems lead to chronic disharmony and dissatisfaction. When the woman's feelings about her ability and worth as a mother are centrally involved, joint admission is specifically indicated. In other cases, when the marital problems appear to be more basic to the patient's difficulties than are her feelings about mothering, a joint admission may often be helpful to the mother-child relationship and offer her the opportunity to bolster her self-respect, but it will impinge little on the central problems of the marriage.

*The Imbalanced Marriage*. Fairly common in our sample are marriages which appear to be in a stable equilibrium but are imbalanced in terms of reciprocity of roles and mutuality of regard. For instance, we have seen hospitalization occurring after the birth of a child to couples in which the husband has been working at two jobs and has left the care of the house and children completely to his wife, essentially spending no time with her. Not infrequently, a woman with rigid intellectual defenses of an obsessional character, sometimes verging on paranoia, will decompensate when she is forced to stop working and stay home to care for the child that her husband has insisted she must have. Less commonly, we have seen couples in which the husband is ineffectual, alcoholic, and chronically out of work, while the wife manages by dint of her own efforts to keep the family together and functioning. Although it is more usual in such cases that the husband is regarded as the "sick" partner, sometimes the wife decompensates and is hospitalized.

Once again we may note the similarity between our marital typology and the family concepts of Lidz and his associates. The stable but imbalanced marriage has much in common with what the Lidz group calls "marital skew," defined by them in terms of the domination of family life by the psychopathology of one parent together with the submission of the other. Unlike Lidz's cases, our imbalanced families are not typically threatened by dissolution or open conflict; what is most striking is the maladaptive marital pattern, with stress precipitating a breakdown in the wife.

In the imbalanced marriage, the roles of the partners tend to be defined, fixed, and not subject to negotiation, but they are also skewed with one partner dominant. Usually the husband is the dominant one, at least at a behavioral level. However, sometimes one finds a wife who is nurturant and protective of a weak and passive man. In these cases the opportunity to care for the child in the hospital may be supportive of the wife's self-esteem and useful in fostering a better mother-child relationship. Sometimes the husband can come to have greater respect for his wife as he sees her gaining increasing competence in her role as mother. It is more usual, however, for these women to return to their homes with their marriages essentially unaltered. In this regard the marriages are much like those of the paranoid women described by Dupont, Grunebaum, and Ryder (1971): hospitalization had little effect on the rigidity and pathology of these families.

Husbands who have strong negative feelings about their wives' undertaking joint admission pose an especially difficult problem. In these cases we have usually found that the husband considers himself to be the sole judge of whether, how, and under what conditions his wife should have responsibility for the care of the child. Asymmetrical marriages of this kind, with one partner in the role of authority and the other the incompetent subordinate, are probably best understood in terms of how the two personalities meet each other's needs. Women within this kind of marriage have not generally done well during their hospitalization, since the imbalance is a powerful force in maintaining the patient's helplessness. We recall one case in which the husband's threat was explicit: "I want her to stay in the hospital until she's entirely well, because if she comes out and breaks down again, that will be the end."

An example of the supportive use of a joint admission in an imbalanced marriage is the case of Mrs. W:

Mrs. W, a twenty-eight-year-old woman, was admitted to the hospital with a paranoid psychosis four months after the birth of her third child. She came from a deprived background with an alcoholic father who had assaulted her sexually. She was married to a truck driver who threatened and controlled her, particularly through the grudging and conditional doling out of the household money. She was tremendously afraid of her husband and took a passive and obedient role in the marriage. Initially opposed to a joint admission, he was persuaded to allow her to care for the baby in the hospital, and he was quite impressed by the degree to which the staff supported her and saw her as a warm, affectionate, and understanding mother. She made a good symptomatic recovery but needed considerable help in learning to set limits with the baby in terms of not responding to her every whimper and cry. The marriage remained strong with the roles of the partners basically unchanged.

On the other hand, joint admission can be almost irrelevant to the clinical course of a patient in an imbalanced marriage.

Mrs. R, an attractive black woman, was admitted to the hospital with paranoid symptoms two months following the birth of her first child, to whom she soon gave excellent care on the ward. Both she and her husband had had previous marriages. He was working in the post office after a twenty-year career in the army as a noncommissioned officer. Before the birth of the child, she had worked as a secretary and had had some control over her own income and time, but now the husband demanded that she spend her entire time caring for their child, give up visiting her sick mother, stop seeing her friends, and allow him to do all the shopping. When she protested, he pointed out that she was being unreasonable since his way was more efficient and effective. Indeed, he was willing to assist her with any household tasks, even the most menial, always demonstrating that he could "do it better." It was clear that in many ways the wife welcomed her husband's domination, and her history demonstrates that she had always chosen to work as a secretary for autocratic men. Following her discharge from the hospital, he soon took the position that her therapist was trying to interfere with his making the decisions at home and forced her to terminate that relationship was well.

The only successful effort to breach the husband's position occurred in a single diagnostic interview during which an older male psychiatrist discussed with him the fact that what "worked" with men in the army did not work with women, on account of their inherent "peculiarity." It was pointed out that one had to handle them in somewhat inefficient and otherwise unreasonable ways, but that it worked better if one treated a wife in this manner. The husband subsequently referred to this interview as the high point of his contacts with the hospital. However, this approach could not be maintained by the wife's therapist, a young woman, since the husband could relax his demands only if permission were given by a male whom he perceived to be in a benevolent but strong position.

*Summary.* We have focused attention on the importance of the marital relationship in the emotional illnesses of mothers of young children, and we have offered a classification of marriages which has evolved from our clinical experience. Again and again we have been impressed with the central importance of marital disharmony in the breakdown of married individuals. Many patients who are viewed as suffering from what used to be called "postpartum psychosis" have in fact marital, rather than maternal, problems. The birth of the child unmasks and focuses on preexisting problems in the marriage.

If marital problems are considered so central to the mental illnesses of the young mothers about whom we have been writing, then what is the role of joint admission? We suspect that when marital roles are mutually supportive and subject to change as growth and new experiences require, then hospitalization for emotional illness is rare. Specifically, if a husband and wife can negotiate the transition from being married to being parents, outside help will not be needed. When, however, they cannot, a variety of possibilities exists. In these instances a joint admission can play different roles and accomplish different therapeutic benefits. These range from the supportive experience of caring for a child, a task which a mother may have handled well in the past, to learning for the first time how to gain satisfaction through becoming competent as a mother. In parallel with these experiences are the therapeutic effects on the marriage, which may range from working out specific, long-standing character problems to negotiating for the first time the reciprocal relationships of mother and father. If therapeutic efforts are directed toward the marital relationship, they will often be rewarded, as is suggested by Dupont, Grunebaum, and Ryder (1971), who found that in marriages where one partner had been hospitalized for a psychosis, individuals often reported that the marriage had been helped by the experience, especially when it was the focus of therapy.

It should be noted that during the years of the joint admissions described in this book, we usually arranged for the husband of a hospitalized woman to be seen by a psychiatric social worker, on a continuing basis where possible, but separately from his wife. Conferences involving husband and wife were usually held at the time a joint admission was to be made. From the perspective of the present, we would place more emphasis in certain cases on the conjoint treatment of husband and wife in addition to the wife's individual psychotherapy. The general guideline for such a recommendation is quite simple: it should be suggested in those cases where the marriage is a palpable source of emotional difficulty, provided that neither partner is totally unwilling to acknowledge his or her part in it.

## THE PATIENT'S MOTHER

Surrogate care is an issue not only for the mother, the child, and the hospital but also for the individual who may be undertaking this responsibility, which is often unexpected and unfamiliar. The specific nature of the relationship between the mother and that person may require special intervention, but any substitute mother will usually welcome whatever support and assistance the social service department of the hospital has to offer.

The most frequent individual called upon to offer surrogate care to the children of psychotic mothers is the maternal grandmother, and her relationship with her daughter is thus of central importance to the course of that care. Unfortunately it is common for psychotic mothers to have disturbed relationships with their own mothers. The clinical material of the following chapters will dramatically illustrate that the patient's perception of and feelings about herself as a mother are most intimately related to how she perceives, feels about, and reacts to her own mother and to other helping persons who embody similar characteristics of role or personality. Furthermore, much of what the patient—especially the patient who is a mother for the first time—knows about child care comes from her own family experience.

Sampson, Messinger, and Towne (1964), in their detailed study of seventeen schizophrenic mothers, have placed special emphasis upon the relationships of these patients to their mothers and families of origin, and have delineated two core groups among these women. The first group is labeled the "separation cases" because the central dynamic issue for them is the transition from the parental to the marital family. This transition is "experienced as a struggle about leaving the mother and the role of the daughter and establishing an identity as a separate adult." In each of these cases, the authors felt that "the struggle was lost again and again." In various ways, the marital family itself was transformed into something like the original parental family, and the continued role of the daughter and child was both sought and urged upon the wife.

A good example of a separation case is Mrs. F, who was admitted to the hospital at the age of twenty-eight suffering from a depressive reaction at the time her first child was fifteen months old. The patient's mother was a strong, aggressive, dominant, somewhat masculine woman who ordered and directed the patient's life, arranging such details for her as selecting and buying her clothes. Because of her parents' disapproval of her marriage, the patient turned to her husband and mother-in-law for the same direction. Her husband taught her about sex and about keeping a home; he even knew more about cooking than she did. Though he was warm and patient, he frequently took it upon himself to correct her in public. She similarly turned to her mother-in-law for guidance and instruction, particularly in the care of the baby. Mrs. F had maintained a satisfactory adjustment through the gratifications of work and being economically independent. When her mother-in-law left a few weeks following the baby's birth, she became steadily more depressed.

We have found, as did Sampson and his associates, that the marital couple is often drawn more closely together by the hospitalization experience. Not only can the daughter use the hospitalization for separating from her mother, but the mother is afforded new opportunities for disengagement. By treating the adult daughter as a wife and mother, the hospital fosters this growth, as does the joint admission experience by contributing to the increasing feelings of comfort in the mothering role a woman may come to experience.

In the other group, which Sampson et al. call "identification cases," the wives experienced difficulties in the two-party stage of marital life, particularly in the establishment of an appropriate identity which would promote and sustain intimate heterosexual relations and feminine role performance. These difficulties seemed to be associated not with leaving mother but with *being* mother, or at least being some aspect of their internalized mother image.

An example of an identification case is Mrs. R [discussed above in connection with an attempted joint admission], whose relationship with her mother was of great importance during her hospitalization. She was a twenty-three-year-old nurse admitted in a schizophrenic turmoil three weeks after the birth of her daughter. During her nursing training her mother had visited her and was admitted with involutional melancholia to the psychiatric ward where Mrs. R was working. Mrs. R went home with her mother to take care of her after discharge and had difficulty in avoiding being delegated responsibility for the care of her mother's house. She did, however, complete her nursing training in a hospital nearer home. When she later became pregnant, things progressed well until the last month, when her mother came to help her. This so upset her that the mother was sent home, and the maternal grandmother came to assist. As might be expected from this history, the issues of "being a daughter and having a daughter—having a mother and being a mother" were the central focus of therapeutic work during the hospitalization.

The patient's mother is important both in a practical sense as the usual surrogate caretaker and in a dynamic sense as a person on whom the patient may be unusually dependent, or from whom she may be estranged. Either overdependence or rebellious estrangement are likely to make effective surrogate mothering difficult. In these cases, therefore, it has been invaluable to offer these grandmothers additional social casework support when possible. The casework is oriented toward ameliorating the dysfunctional relationship. In the overdependent situation, the grandmother is helped to allow her grown daughter become independent and to care for her own child in her own way. On the other hand, in the rebellious cases, we have been able to help the grandmother reestablish satisfactory relations with a daughter whose exaggerated rebellion left a legacy of mutual hostility. It is always in the best interests of the child that the surrogate caretaker be supported by the hospital in this unexpected, although not always unwelcome, task, and, when the surrogate mother is the maternal grandmother, that her relationship with her grandchild be free of the burdens of past antagonisms.

## EVALUATING THE ALTERNATIVES TO JOINT ADMISSION

In our first joint admission case it was apparent that the decision about bringing in the child required that the alternatives be considered. The reader may recall that early in the patient's hospitalization her husband had been caring for Bobby at night and a neighbor was with him during the day. However, this was a short-term plan which had many disadvantages in terms of the dynamics of the marriage and the patient's illness. The couple felt that their only alternative was to send the child to live with the patient's mother, more than a thousand miles away, and their reluctance to do this was helpful in making the joint admission decision.

It is important to keep in mind that joint admission planning and decision making almost always involve *relative* rather than *absolute* judgments. The ward staff, the patient, and the family must always evaluate the advantages and disadvantages of this treatment adjunct by comparing it with actually available alternatives for the care of the child or children. The choice should be directed toward the best interests of the mother and the child.

Little systematic attention has been given to the disposition of the children of mothers hospitalized for mental illness. Rice, Ekdahl, and Millor (1971) have reported on an extensive investigation of some aspects of the problem. Rice and her associates have thoroughly documented the fact that when a mother is hospitalized for emotional disorder, families make their own arrangements for child care with essentially no help either offered by hospitals or sought by the families. Their data discount the widely held view that services are better utilized if the individual is motivated to seek them out and actually applies for help. In a demonstration phase in which assistance was offered, they found most families receptive, and their referrals to community agencies for help with child care problems were followed up with gratitude. These investigators have also found, as might be expected, that disruption of the family and inadequate child care are far more frequent when the mother is hospitalized than when the ill parent is the father, and that youngest children are most subject to dislocation and disruption. (We have summarized here only a small fraction of this comprehensive study. The reader is referred to the original source for a great deal of valuable information.)

*The Massachusetts Mental Health Center Home Visit Study.* In our own project, a home visit study was concerned with the question of surrogate care of children during the mother's hospitalization (Fasman, Grunebaum, and Weiss, 1967). It differed considerably from the large-scale investigations of Rice and her associates. Mrs. Jean Fasman, our research social worker, selected twenty consecutive admissions who were mothers of children under two years of age, and made two visits to the home where the youngest child in each family was being cared for. The first visit was made shortly after the mother entered the hospital, before it was known whether there would be a joint admission. Five of the cases later involved joint admission, while in the remaining fifteen the children were cared for by others during the entire hospitalization period. The second visit followed six to nine months after the mother's discharge, depending on when she had "regained the care of the home and children." Using unstructured and informal methods of interviewing and observation, Fasman sought to gather data concerning three questions: (1) What happens to the baby when the mother goes into the hospital? To what extent does the surrogate care meet the needs of the child, and how does the quality of the emotional and physical care provided by the surrogate mother differ from that given by the child's own mother? (2) What changes occur in the family during the mother's hospitalization? (3) What differences are found between those mothers who brought their babies into the hospital and those who did not?

*Initial Home Visit Findings.* Analysis of the initial home visit data showed that, in every case but one, the family had made arrangements for the baby's care without asking for advice or assistance from the hospital or any other agency. Eleven children were being cared for in their own homes, eight were in relatives' homes, and the one exception was in a foster home by court order. The maternal grandmother was most frequently chosen to be the mother substitute. Although relatives were initially willing to take the baby during the crisis of the mother's hospital admission, they were not always able or willing to keep the child after this emergency. Of the twenty babies visited, fourteen had had one mother surrogate, and six, two or more. In some instances, the baby was moved from one home to another to be cared for by a different person, and in others, housekeepers were changed while the baby stayed at home.

The modal hospital stay for the twenty mothers was three months. Patients who had their babies with them stayed an average of five and a half months, while those who did not stayed only three and a half months. Joint admission could certainly affect a psychiatrist's decision about when to discharge a patient. If the mother provided adequately for her baby in the hospital, there was less pressure either from her or from her family for her discharge. She was also less likely to insist on a discharge against medical advice, as happened in three of the non-joint admission cases.

What happens to the older siblings in the family while the mother is in the hospital? Of the twenty families studied, eight were one-child families. Five of the remaining twelve, including one family with ten children, kept the children at home and together. One family held together until the baby joined his mother in the hospital and then scattered. In seven cases where the children left home and were separated, all were under school age.

The following cases illustrate minimal and maximal care given by relatives.

Mrs. B's baby received minimal care from the patient's sister, Mrs. D, a white woman married to a Negro and mother of one child. When visited, she was about to adopt a Negro child and was fostering two little girls in addition to the patient's daughter. Mrs. D felt that she had been rejected by her family because of her marriage. There had always been a great deal of friction between the two sisters, including physical fights.

During the home visit, it was observed that Mrs. B's six-week-old baby was abnormal. Mrs. D seemed aware of this, though she could not express it directly. The baby had never been seen by a doctor, due, said Mrs. D, to the father's refusal to consent. The baby had a cold and was lying in her dirty carriage near the lighted gas stove. She was sweating and had a facial rash. The research social worker felt that Mrs. D, while taking a "serves you right" attitude toward her sister, was unable to face her directly with the baby's disability. Her generally bitter feelings caused by her family's rejection prevented her from giving any of the children in her care the love they needed. Mrs. D claimed that she had taken the baby as a favor to her sister, but revealed an underlying need to prove to her family that she was the healthy sister who could take over despite her family's feelings that she was "crazy" and a "tramp" because she had married a Negro. There was little physical comfort for the children, but they were made to conform to rigid standards of behavior.

In contrast, another patient, Mrs. O, left her son with her husband's cousin, Mrs. P, who was providing excellent care. Mrs. P had three boys of her own and was a competent, maternal, happily married woman who, although she hardly knew the patient, felt sorry for her. Mr. O also stayed with her, and she cheerfully shouldered the burdens of an extra man and newborn baby.

Since the surrogate mothers were chosen by the families primarily for their willingness, rather than their ability, to care for the baby, the results were often not ideal. If a close relative of the child, the substitute mother could be influenced by feelings of guilt toward the patient and by a sense of responsibility for the hospitalization. The mother substitute's own unresolved personal problems must also affect the quality of her mothering. The following are examples of the problems the foster mothers had, and how such problems influenced care of the child.

One foster mother, Mrs. A, was desperately eager to have a child of her own, having had four miscarriages. She was the patient's sister-in-law. She was deeply attached to the three-month-old baby boy but felt unable to care for the patient's other child, a two-and-a-half-year-old girl, although she had the room and the time to do so. Although she gave the baby excellent care, the idea of eventually returning the baby to his mother very much upset Mrs. A and resulted in tense, possessive handling of the baby. She was overly concerned with his development. She worried if he awoke at night; his cradle was kept right next to her bed so that she could hear every sound; she kept count of the number of teaspoons of solids he ate each day, and changed his diapers constantly. Mrs. A was overtly antagonistic toward her brother-in-law and believed his wife's illness was all his fault. But her criticism of him reflected her indirect hostility toward her sister-in-law; for example: "It's not her fault that her apartment's a mess. Her husband won't let her buy any decent furniture."

Mrs. A said that her family kept reminding her that the baby was not hers, and she, too, had to keep telling herself this. She obviously felt herself a far superior mother to her sister-in-law and resisted returning the baby, who had finally almost to be wrested from her. A total rift in the family developed, and though the patient remained in need of much help, she never sought it from her sister-in-law, preferring her husband and neighbors.

In another family, where the patient's husband took charge, the social worker felt that the child was receiving better care than the mother would have given her even if well. The unemployed father enjoyed caring for the home and children and was a patient, loving, mother substitute. The mother, on the other hand, was masculine and ambitious and was anxious only to resume her teaching career. She was extremely impatient with her children and resented being tied down by them. Having the children's father care for them suited the mother, who recognized that she could cope adequately in other ways only if pressure to fill the maternal role was lifted.

*Data from Follow-up Visits.* The follow-up visits permitted a comparison of child care by the substitute mothers and by the psychotic mothers after discharge from the hospital. Since some of the patients visited had participated in joint admission and others had not, these two groups could also be compared.

For various reasons, only sixteen of the twenty could be visited. Twelve of these were found to have moved since the original home visit. The mothers seemed to feel that making a fresh start on discharge from the hospital involved moving or, as in seven cases, having another baby. Five of the sixteen mothers both moved and had another child.

On the basis of observations during the first and second visits, each surrogate and each mother was rated on three five-point scales in the following areas: (1) physical condition of the child and home; (2) interaction of the child with the mothering person; and (3) mental status of the mothering person.

Analysis of the results showed ratings of physical condition of child and home to be quite similar for the mothers and the surrogate mothers. On the other hand, the surrogates were scored on the average significantly higher than the mothers in their interaction with the children and somewhat higher in their mental status. This may have been due to the ages of the children or the timing of the home visit; or it may have reflected real differences indicating that mothers discharged from a mental hospital need additional support and assistance because they continue to be disturbed both in their mental status and in their interactions with their children.

Comparison of scores for the five joint admission and eleven non-joint admission mothers revealed little difference in the way mothers in each group kept their homes and little difference in their relationships with their children. One would have expected that the former group, provided with greater opportunities in the hospital to develop a relationship with their babies, would later have related better to their children. Possibly one home visit provided insufficient evidence about this.

However, there was a striking difference between the two groups in the ratings of their mental status. The joint admission mothers seemed to have been able to work through their interpersonal problems more satisfactorily than did the non-joint admissions, and none of the former either showed significant memory loss or were living primarily a fantasy life. This was not true of the non-joint admission mothers, five of whom showed severe disturbances. Several others had realistic problems in relation to husband or parents, or financial worries.

Why was it that the mothers who brought their babies into the hospital with them were in better mental health at the time of later follow-up than those who did not? Possibly the psychiatrists chose for joint admission only those women with a good prognosis, but there are many other issues, including some psychiatrists' and nurses' ambivalence to the procedure. It was our impression that some patients who did not bring their babies in with them might have done so satisfactorily if either the family or the ward staff had been more encouraging of such a plan.

There were other factors which might help to account for the higher degree of mental health shown by the joint admission mothers. As research subjects they had a great deal of extra attention in the hospital, including daily visits from the research nurse, regular pediatric and psychological examinations of the baby in which the mother participated; and, perhaps most important, the mother acquired great prestige on the ward. The extra attention could well increase a woman's self-esteem, so that a child originally seen as a threat became a means for her to feel superior and to enjoy the envy of other patients.

After discharge from the Massachusetts Mental Health Center, patients routinely return for treatment with a psychiatrist, but otherwise have little contact with the hospital. The joint admission mothers, however, had continuing and strong support. The research psychiatric nurse made routine home visits, at first as often as every two weeks. The mothers brought their babies back for periodic psychological and pediatric examinations. All these factors combined to make them feel important as mothers. Particularly with primiparae, the baby became a status symbol. Whereas the arrival of the child may have been a threat to the mother's own infantile needs and marked the end of adolescent freedom, now the baby was seen as a key which unlocked the world of motherhood.

In Fasman's judgment there was a great need for follow-up social work among these discharged mothers, yet only one of the non-joint admission patients was receiving such aid. Four asked for further help with their problems, and three indicated indirectly they would like it. A further eight were judged to need on-going casework—four of these, urgently so.

*Overview of the Home Visit Study.* We briefly summarize the home visit study in terms of the questions which it sought to explore.

1. "What happens to a baby when his mother enters a mental

hospital?" Of the twenty families studied, nineteen made their own arrangements for surrogate care, usually from a grandmother or close relative. Half the babies stayed at home, half went to relatives until joining their mothers in the hospital or after discharge. The substitute mothers had only somewhat better mental health than the patients but probably responded better to the needs of the babies than the mothers did on their return home, in view of the fact that these babies were now toddlers making active demands.

2. "What happens when the mother comes home from the hospital?" A partial answer is that many of the families felt the need for some dramatic change. Two-thirds moved to a different home and almost one-half of the mothers had another baby, some doing both. There was one divorce and there were no deaths. The mothers were giving the babies approximately the same physical care as that which the surrogates had provided, but were experiencing more difficulties in the area of mother-child interaction.

3. "What are the differences between those mothers who brought their babies into the hospital and those who did not?" There was little difference in cleanliness and mother-child interaction as far as could be judged, but there was considerable difference in their rated mental health. The joint admission mothers had fewer problems in family relationships and were much better oriented to reality than were the non-joint admission mothers. This was attributed to the greater support the joint admission mothers received from members of the research project.

*Evaluating the Available Sources of Child Care.* The clinical implications of our observations will be examined with regard to two stages of hospitalization: at the time the patient's admission is being arranged, and at the time a joint admission is being considered.

The studies of Rice and of Fasman and their associates have clearly documented the fact that families make their own provisions for surrogate care of the children when a mother is hospitalized, and that in many cases these initial arrangements are of short duration and less than adequate. If the hospital staff wishes to be of help to the entering patient and her family in this matter, it can do so by including in its standard operating procedure, at the time of the first contact, an inquiry into their plans for the care of the children. Even if an immediate change is unnecessary or impossible, the inquiry is likely to elicit to some degree whatever reservations, ambivalence, or disagreement there may be about the plans the family has made. Since these plans are often made in a crisis, they are typically decided upon, especially in cases of first admission, with a feeling that "this is the only thing we can do." Asking about child care right at the start will accomplish two further gains: it will convey the staff's interest in the family's well-being, and it will initiate or facilitate the idea that alternatives are available. From a therapeutic standpoint, it is *always* helpful to have the feeling that one has genuine choices and alternatives, that one is not "boxed in" or forced to follow an undesired course. The following brief case note shows this to be true both for the patient and for the hospital staff.

Mrs. V, mother of a three-year-old son, was admitted in a depressed state of moderate severity. She expressed interest in caring for her son on the ward but was doubtful about her ability to provide for his needs immediately. On the other hand, leaving him at home in the care of the maternal grandmother, a chronic alcoholic whose relationship with her daughter was chaotic and hostile, was appealing neither to the patient nor to the staff. On advice of a consultant, an appropriate social agency was contacted and arrangements were made for foster care *as a backup* in the event that the mother could not sustain her joint admission responsibilities. This seemed to take the pressure off everyone.

In most cases the optimal initial arrangement is one in which the children are cared for in their own home by one responsible and willing relative whom they know and like. This is obviously not always possible or feasible, and the next best solution may be for them to be cared for either by a homemaker in their own home or by a relative familiar to the children in that person's home. For older children the latter solution may mean separating from friends and even changing schools if the hospitalization is lengthy; for younger children there are equivalent losses of environmental security which may be harder to detect if they cannot be verbalized.

Families rarely have any idea how long a hospitalization they may face, so that plans are often made which are appropriate for a few days but which simply will not work if the hospitalization lasts weeks or months. Helping the family to make plans which take into account the available relatives, the likely length of the hospitalization, and the needs of the children of different ages would seem a necessary first step. Clearly, a family which has been assisted to plan for the children from the day of admission will be more receptive to future planning for the children, and especially to the proposal of a joint admission.

In the normal (and recommended) course of events, joint admission will be proposed when the mother is better prepared to consider it than she was on admission: her feelings of helplessness, anxiety, rage, and guilt are within controllable limits; she has recovered from a regressive phase to some degree and feels she has something to give; and her reality testing, at least with regard to the question of mothering, is improved. She is now in a position to consider with greater objectivity her own capacities and wishes and also those of the surrogate mother. She is now able to react to the indication that the hospital staff finds her to be closer to the point of readiness to resume her responsibilities.

## CONCLUSION

We have suggested that planning the treatment of the psychotic mother involves a careful assessment of the patient and her interpersonal relationships both at home and in the hospital. The principles and methods involved in reaching a descriptive and psychodynamic diagnosis for such a patient are essentially the same as for any other patient. Treatment decisions about the use of drugs or electro-convulsive treatment and the individual psychotherapeutic approach to the patient are to a considerable degree based on clinical assessment of the patient herself.

However, we have examined those special aspects of evaluation which are relevant to assisting the mother to resume care of her child in the hospital. We found that the interpersonal realities, resources, and resistances of the patient, her family, and the hospital staff are central factors in the success or failure of a joint admission. Each of these individuals will influence the patient's decision to resume the care of her child in the hospital.

Ambivalence, uncertainty, or mere compliance on the part of any of these individuals will influence adversely the course of the mother-child relationship in the hospital.

Because the decision to have a mother care for her child in the hospital must be weighed against other available alternatives, we have discussed surrogate selection and the need for casework assistance to the surrogate mother, usually the maternal grandmother.

The one participant in the joint admission who, depending upon age, has little or nothing to say about it is the child. Our first "baby," Bobby, was a delightful, outgoing, and independent sixteen-month-old who rapidly made his surroundings the happiest place on the ward. He created a good feeling not only toward himself but toward the joint admission program. Tense, colicky, and unhappy babies are not pleasant for either the mother or the ward. However, such babies make hospital staff and the parents painfully aware that only a mature commitment can accomplish the tasks of caring for a child and helping a mother to do so successfully.

# References to Part 1

Baker, A. A.; Morison, M.; Game, J. A.; and Thorpe, J. G. 1961. Admitting schizophrenic mothers with their babies. *Lancet* 2: 237–39.

Bakwin, H. 1942. Loneliness in infants. *American Journal of Diseases of Children* 63: 30–40.

Bardon, D.; Glaser, Y. I. M.; Prothero, D.; and Weston, D. H. 1968. Mother and baby unit: Psychiatric survey of 115 cases. *British Medical Journal* 2: 755–58.

Bowlby, J. 1951. *Maternal care and mental health.* Geneva: World Health Organization Monograph No. 2.

Douglas, G. 1956. Psychotic mothers. *Lancet* 1: 124–25.

Dupont, R. L.; Grunebaum, H. U.; and Ryder, R. 1971. An unexpected result of psychosis in marriage. Paper presented at Annual Meeting, American Psychological Association, Washington, D.C.

Fasman, J.; Grunebaum, H. U.; and Weiss, J. L. 1967. Who cares for the children of psychotic mothers? *British Journal of Psychiatry and Social Work* 9, no. 2: 84–89.

Fowler, D. B., and Brandon, R. E. 1965. A psychiatric mother and baby unit. *Lancet* 1: 160–61.

Freud, A., and Burlingham, D. T. 1942. *War and children.* New York: International Universities Press.

Glaser, Y. I. M. 1962. A unit for mothers and babies in a psychiatric hospital. *Journal of Child Psychology and Psychiatry* 3: 53–60.

Grunebaum, H. U., and Weiss, J. L. 1971. Psychotic mothers and their children. *American Journal of Psychiatry* 119: 10.

Grunebaum, H. U.; Weiss, J. L.; Hirsch, L. L.; and Barrett, J. E., Jr. 1963. The baby on the ward. *Psychiatry: Journal for the Study of Interpersonal Processes* 26, no. 1: 39–53.

Lidz, T.; Cornelison, A. R.; Fleck, S.; and Terry, D. 1957. The intrafamilial environment of schizophrenic patients: II. Marital schism and marital skew. *American Journal of Psychiatry* 114: 241–48.

Main, T. F. 1958. Mothers with children in a psychiatric hospital. *Lancet* 2: 845–47.

Mitchell, N., and Turton, C. 1966. Children under five in an adult psychiatric ward. *British Journal of Psychiatry* 112: 1117–18.

Pao, P. 1960. Young schizophrenic mothers' initial posthospital adjustment at home. *Archives of General Psychiatry* 2: 512–20.

Pugh, T. F.; Jerath, B. K.; Schmidt, W. M.; and Reed, R. B. 1963. Rates of mental disease related to childbearing. *New England Journal of Medicine* 268: 1224–28.

Rice, E. P.; Ekdahl, M. C.; and Miller, L. 1971. *Children of mentally ill parents: Problems in child care.* New York: Behavioral Publications.

Sampson, H.; Messinger, S.; and Towne, R. 1964. *Schizophrenic women: Studies in marital crisis.* New York: Atherton Press, Prentice-Hall.

Sobel, D. E. 1961. Children of schizophrenic patients: Preliminary observations on early development. *American Journal of Psychiatry* 118: 512–17.

Spitz, R., and Wolff, K. M. 1946. Anaclitic depression: An inquiry into the genesis of psychiatric conditions in early childhood. *Psychoanalytic Study of the Child* 2: 313–42.

Van Der Walde, P. H.; Meeks, D.; Grunebaum, H. U.; and Weiss, J. L. 1968. Joint admission of mothers and children to a state hospital. *Archives of General Psychiatry* 18: 706–11.

Weiss, J. L.; Grunebaum, H. U.; and Schell, R. E. 1964. Psychotic mothers and their children: II. Psychological studies of mothers caring for their infants and young children in a psychiatric hospital. *Archives of General Psychiatry* 11: 90–98.

# part 2

## psychiatric nursing perspectives

*Carol R. Hartman*

# Introduction to Part 2

In part 1 we have attempted to convey to the reader by means of the case study method our initial efforts toward the twin objectives of learning about and being of help to hospitalized psychotic mothers of young children. We have followed our first mother in some detail, to be sure, but the case study had a broader focus. It was concerned with the hospital administration, the ward staff, and other patients as well—the entire milieu into which the concept of joint, mother-child admission was introduced. We then moved to a consideration of what we had learned about planning for a joint admission after varied experiences with different mothers, children, families, and ward staffs. The primary intent of this presentation was to provide the reader with pragmatic assistance, first, in introducing joint admission to an institution as a therapeutic modality, and second, in selection and planning for individual cases.

Part 2 takes us from there into the heart of the therapeutic process of joint admission. The nature of emotional breakdowns in mothers following childbirth or in the early stages of mothering is examined, and the problem is formulated in terms of a crisis in normal maturation. This formulation then evolves into a framework within which the entire course of the mother's—and child's—stay in the hospital and the progression of therapeutic staff work may be understood and evaluated. In our setting the maternally-oriented work with the mothers was done by psychiatric nurses, for reasons which are discussed in the text. However, there is no reason why the concepts and methods discussed here could not be equally well applied by any member of the staff with appropriate motivation and knowledge.

In the last two chapters of part 2, the post-hospital adjustment period is described. Observation of mother-child interaction in the home and therapeutic work with the mother in that setting appear to be a natural means for assisting patient and family to return, as far as possible and more adaptively, if possible, to where they were before the hospitalization became necessary.

Recent shifts in the pattern of mental health care have a direct bearing on the matters presented in this section. More frequent treatment of serious emotional disorders in the community rather than in the hospital, together with decreased length of hospitalization, lead to the expectation that maternally-oriented therapeutic programs of the kind we have described will increasingly take place in the home. The sequence of stages presented below will be different in certain aspects if there is no hospitalization, or if the mother is only briefly an inpatient, but the basic issues for her will remain essentially unchanged. She will still need to come to terms with herself as a person who has decompensated and requires assistance, to decide when and how she will engage or reengage herself in the tasks of motherhood, and to work out her relationships with other members of her family.

# 3

# Treating the Mother in the Hospital

A woman who chooses to become a mother must make significant emotional and psychological adjustments to her new role. In particular, she must be capable of making the shifts necessary in identifying herself as distinct from her child. She also must be aware of and able to respond to her child's attempts at communicating. When a woman cannot make these adjustments to motherhood, the result may be a maturational crisis. The term we give this crisis in our study is puerperal breakdown.

The acute disequilibrium which characterizes the crisis is expressed in the mother's attitudes toward and treatment of her family. The new relationship between mother and infant is particularly vulnerable to the mother's sense of dissatisfaction and failure in other aspects of her life. Withdrawal, emotional detachment, intense involvement marked by inconsistency and impulsiveness, poor judgment in evaluating the baby's needs, and seemingly irreconcilable conscious or unconscious negative feelings toward the baby—one or several of these elements may characterize the mother's behavior during her breakdown. Underscoring these reactions is her conscious awareness of extreme and inexplicable displeasure in caring for her baby; she senses her failure.

Widely differing types of research and clinical appraisals of mothers have suggested that puerperal breakdown is dependent upon many factors. Most useful for our purposes are findings which link breakdown to social and psychological stresses in pregnancy and marriage and hypotheses which link breakdown to historical factors relevant to the mother's development into womanhood. Such studies lend strong support to a clinical approach which recognizes that the maturational tasks involved in mothering crystallize past and present dimensions of the mother's life.

Successful working through of the conflicts encountered in becoming a mother holds significant potential for improved mental health. Failure to deal with the maturational tasks of motherhood may bring a woman into the hospital, but the accomplishment of those tasks will facilitate her more mature development. With the help of the hospital staff a mother can learn to modify many long-standing and unsuccessful ways of dealing with conflicts which have made her vulnerable to her immediate crisis. Within an interactive framework focusing on the tasks she is currently attempting, a mother can achieve new equilibrium.

Joint admission of mother and baby to the hospital ward permits the mother to experience her difficulties in mothering in an environment where she can work out her problems *as they occur*. Furthermore, since the treating staff is able to observe her behavior directly, they can suggest and support responses which appear to be most effective. We believe that focusing attention upon the maturational crisis in this manner helps to prevent further withdrawal from mothering with attendant loss of self-esteem. We also believe this method of treatment helps to change some of the manifest behavior which may have a deleterious effect on the baby.

Our own work with the joint admission process attempted, first, to focus on the specific pragmatic problems in the immediate life situation of the mother who has to some degree withdrawn emotionally and, perhaps, physically from mothering; and second, to place this focus within a context of maximal therapeutic interaction with staff. Because the nurse is an environmental constant, immediately present with the important people in the mother's life when interactions take place, she can act as a catalyst for the exploration of the mother's immediate problems and conflicts in facing the task of motherhood. (The term "nurse" will be used in the singular throughout the text, although the material presented should be useful to all staff who have daily contact with the mother—attendants, aides, licensed practical nurses, registered nurses, etc.)

The primary aim of the nurse-mother-baby interaction is to help free the mother of negative influences in her personality and experience which prevent adaptation to the needs of her baby. Subsequent satisfaction in attending to those needs occurs as conflict in mothering is reduced. Reduction of stress in the mother-child relationship enhances the mother's self-esteem, giving her needed energy to obtain gratification in other important relationships.

## CONCEPTS AND GOALS

As we worked with the mothers who were deciding whether to care for their children on the ward and with those whose children had already joined them, certain themes arose repeatedly in the context of treating them. These themes, which we call "maternal issues," seemed to arise in a phase-specific order. When discussion of an issue resulted in a mother's attaining a reasonable solution, she felt more comfortable and exhibited more self-control. The themes were to a greater or lesser extent verbalized by all the study mothers, and so can be viewed as a way of organizing and thinking about our work with the mother. They were not developed prior to the study or derived through a research method, but are the product of a clinician's observations organized for the purpose of teaching and explaining care to other nurses. Furthermore, these maternal issues provide an opportunity to investigate certain correlates of nursing care, such as the extent to which the mother's ability to work through an issue correlates with her clinical improvement.

Close observation of mother-baby interaction on the ward revealed two quite different kinds of responses in mothers. We have named them "distant mothering" (type I) and "involved mothering" (type II). These mothering styles differ in two important respects: first, how the mother accepts her own needs and is able to maintain self control while tending her baby, and second, how the mother approaches the maternal issues from the outset of her hospitalization. We found this concept particularly useful during the joint admission period, or phase III.

Three main goals have directed our study. We sought first to conceptualize the crucial pragmatic problems which confront a mother entering a psychiatric hospital and eventually caring for her baby as part of her treatment. We wished to use these conceptualized problems as a guide for nursing intervention during hospitalization. Second, we sought to use the developed concepts in a systematic investigation of nursing intervention so that we could relate the intervention to the outcome of treatment and determine predictive characteristics and sub-groups of patients. Our third objective was to apply the formulations used during the hospital course to the period when mother and baby return to home, family and community.

## PHASES AND ISSUES

Joint admission as a treatment method involves two dimensions: a temporal one dividing hospitalization into three phases, and a substantive one consisting of the maternal issues confronting the mother during each of the three phases. The manner in which each mother deals with the issues as they arise determines to a large degree the efficacy of her treatment. Thus, to provide optimal care one must first understand how these issues function in the mother's immediate crisis and how the mother confronts them. The next step is to help the mother reach a reasonable resolution of the issues. The staff encourages the mother not to avoid them or minimize their importance by arriving at irrational conclusions.

Using mother-nurse interactive data to focus on the core issues confronting the mother in all phases, we evaluated her performance by the degree to which she either explored or avoided the issues. Her response to nursing intervention can be judged as more or less workable according to her defensiveness.

An example of a mother with a workable response would be one who can communicate the upsetting feelings she has toward her children but who then terminates any exploration by directing the discussion to her current physical symptoms. In doing so she fails to make any link between these troubling physical symptoms and the disturbing feelings that she first mentioned in connection with her children.

Definitions, clinical excerpts, and statements of rationale follow. In order to present a chronological outline of the joint admission process and to furnish procedural nursing guidelines within our working framework, we present for each of the three phases a general description of the phase, definitions of the maternal issues of that phase, examples from the interactive data to illustrate either workable or unworkable responses to each issue, and discussion of the recommended nursing intervention.

*Phase I: Initial Orientation.* When the mother enters the hospital, she needs to acknowledge the fact that she has left her family and that she requires special assistance from strangers in an unfamiliar environment. The nurse, through her daily contacts with the mother plus her knowledge of the mother's family, can help to assess the factors which favor or contra-indicate inviting the mother to care for her baby as part of her treatment. During this period in particular, it is most important that information be shared among the mother's physician, social worker, and other personnel directly involved in her treatment. *The staff must arrive at a consensus, taking all data into account, before asking the mother and family if they wish to participate in the joint admission treatment plan.* Any doubts, hesitancies, or staff difficulties should be worked through before the mother is approached.

During phase I, the mother must deal primarily with maternal issues inherent in being a *patient.* The most immediate of these is separation from her family. Concomitant issues include: dealing with the fact that certain thoughts and feelings, as well as behaviors, are symptoms of emotional illness; gaining control over self-destructive behavior; reconciling her need for help from strangers; and becoming oriented to and involved with the ward environment and the various approaches.

*Maternal issue I: Orientation to treatment staff and patients.* The manner in which the mother relates to staff and patients and accepts their help is the focus for evaluating clinical data. An example of an unworkable approach would be one in which the patient is divorced from reality:

Mrs. G: "I know all about this psychiatry business. I'm in here for a rest. At X hospital they asked me to be on the staff. After all, I'm a professional too."

In a workable approach the patient may well resort both to acting-out and to regressive behavior, but in doing so she verbally acknowledges her need and desire for help. For example:

Mrs. C was in the dayroom playing cards with a group of adolescents. She set fire to some paper in an ash tray. The nurse said, "What's going on?" Mrs. C laughed. "I just wanted you to know I was here." The nurse: "There are other ways...." Mrs. C: "Ha-ha, just don't forget I'm around."

*Maternal issue 2: Orientation to separation from family.* The mother's leaving her family and abdicating her role as wife and mother activates tremendous anxiety, guilt, and loss of self-esteem. At the same time the mother experiences a deep depression. Each mother attempts to justify her separation as a means for resolving her conflicted feelings. Workable and unworkable responses would be defined as in the first issue.

*Maternal issue 3: Orientation to emotional upset and symptoms.* After some time in the hospital, a mother can acknowledge the initial confusion created by aberrant physical and psychic experiences. The extent to which she evaluates these experiences as strange and unjustified when compared with what is actually occurring is directly related to her capacity to acknowledge concerns she has about herself and her relationships with other people and events in her life. The focus for judging her performance is the degree to which symptoms dominate the clarification of the concerns and conflicts.

Mrs. E demonstrates an unworkable approach to this issue. Three days of nursing notes reported her as "weaving" down the hall between periods of playing cards with the other patients, occasionally asking the nurse for an aspirin.

*Maternal issue 4: Orientation to treatment methods.* Treatment approaches vary in the amount of participation and responsibility the mother must take. Response is usually characterized by one of two extreme positions: passive compliance with, or antagonism and resentment toward, anything done or suggested. Both positions may be underscored with the conviction that whatever is done from the outside has some type of magical quality. The antagonistic mother may fear poisoning or depletion of her power, while the passive, compliant mother may be expecting some type of magical cure from whatever is recommended. There are times when the mother may be quite right about a treatment approach that is not helpful to her. The extent to which a mother views treatment methods as punishment, as attempts to render her helpless, as magical potions, or as opportunities for regaining health, provide focus for evaluating how she is coping with this issue. Mrs. D demonstrates a workable approach to this issue:

"I cleaned the lounge today—it was as if it had never been cleaned. I don't feel better—how is this supposed to get me well?" Nurse: "Just doesn't make sense." Mrs. D smiles: "Well, at least I'm doing something even though I feel I don't want to—it's better than crying all day."

*Discussion of phase I.* Our clinical experience and process data suggest that despite the chronic nature of a mother's psychopathology and family difficulties, the repudiation of motherhood is the crucial element leading to her admission to the hospital. Separation from her baby is the most difficult issue for the mother to deal with. She experiences this separation as her rejection of her identity as a mother. In order to suppress these painful feelings, she tenaciously emphasizes immediate, external solutions to her plight, while failing to come to terms with the underlying problems which precipitated it. Pursuit of external solutions—one unworkable approach to the core issues—is characterized in phase I by the mother's tendency to focus complaints on her baby and husband, either overtly or covertly; by denying illness and attempting to return home without treatment; and by attempts to rid herself of people. Divorce, giving up the baby, and trying to resign herself to permanent hospitalization are the most common solutions verbalized.

Concurrently, the mother's behavior during this period is characterized by many ostensible paradoxes. For example, a mother may claim she is ready to go, be dressed neatly, and appear coherent, only to ask in a fleeting manner about the magnetized property of the bedside table. Or she will say that she has overcome her difficulties but will flounder when pressed for details concerning her plans. The nurse must remember that these inconsistencies do not occur in reality in this manner. Mothers are extremely guarded. It is important to note that in the mother's immediate prehospitalization period she has tended to act on, not to verbalize, her psychic turmoil. Commonly, the precipitating factor for admission has been a suicidal gesture or threatening behavior toward the child. Until this acute manifestation of her illness, she had maintained, however marginally, the care of her baby, and the family became aware of the necessity for help only when she acted to disrupt or threaten her maternal responsibilities.

This pattern naturally transfers into the hospital. A mother tends to comply with ward (that is, external) requirements, but manifests great difficulty in accepting help through interpersonal relationships. Although she talks about factors leading to her hospitalization and other seemingly reality-based concerns, she finds effective ways of keeping people at a distance, and her discussion avoids exploration of underlying feelings. Just as the family had assumed she was working out her care of the baby, the nurse and doctor may assume she has engaged herself in treatment. When a mother seems actively involved with "real" concerns and, in addition, offers "possible solutions," it is not unusual for the staff to miscalculate the depth of psychic disturbance. Careful listening reveals, however, that the mother is attempting to explain and justify selected events to herself. The treating staff should be especially alert to apparently compliant language and behavior which may mask unrevealed confusion.

The following example of mother-nurse interaction demonstrates these points.

Mrs. J was acutely psychotic after the birth of her second child. She vacillated during the first week of hospitalization between being helpless, dependent, and disorganized and being neat and quiet. A nurse assigned to work with her met with the patient at an arranged time. Mrs. J was well groomed and intent on maintaining self-control. She talked for over an hour, giving a complete history of events leading to her hospitalization and the dominating symptoms. She then took little cognizance of the nurse and seemed to be solely engaged in talking to herself. The next morning she was disheveled, confused, and disorganized. The nurse interrupted Mrs. J's rambling and commented that she seemed to be talking to herself. The vagueness in Mrs. J's eyes cleared, and she directed her attention to the nurse, saying it was just the way she felt. The nurse commented on the day before; and Mrs. J said that she felt that if she dressed up, people assumed she felt better when in fact she didn't. The nurse told Mrs. J that if she dressed up, she (the nurse) would not assume she felt well.

Within the next two days Mrs. J gave up her disheveled appearance and cried a great deal, saying that she would never get well and would have to leave her husband and children and be hospitalized for the rest of her life. The nurse noted how this approach was also a means of keeping their relationship distant. More importantly, however, her compliance with a neat appearance and the ruminative quality of her complaints tended to mask the expression of totally bizarre thoughts. Although the nurse was fully aware of this, she failed to communicate it emphatically to the staff. They felt the mother was better, as did the doctor, who reduced her medication. Within an hour she ran screaming down the hall, brandishing a razor.

Guilt that is aroused by separation from home and socially defined duties, compounded by an upsurge of infantile wants and wishes, leaves the mother feeling helpless. Because she is fearful of revealing what she is experiencing, she goes to great lengths to hide her disorganized thinking. Her helpless, isolated state must not be underestimated because of the socially desirable or comprehensible behavior she is able to demonstrate when so motivated. Mothers tend to avoid or minimize the conflicts inherent in the issues confronting them upon admission.

When the mother begins to accept the need for treatment as a means of helping herself to return eventually to her family— and, in some instances, begins to recognize that treatment is an opportunity for her to clarify long-standing doubts about herself—she experiences a growing awareness that she "didn't just become ill." At this point workable approaches to and reasonable resolutions of the maternal issues become possible.

Usually a mother will settle on a workable approach, making a compromise between her realistic insights into her difficulties and her pathological defenses. She will register some awareness of long-standing factors contributing to her difficulties, but will emphasize aspects of her immediate situation which bypass exploration of the conflicts from which her problems stem. She may accept hospitalization as a form of protection from outside stresses; she may seek an alliance with treating personnel so that they will intercede in her behalf and on her terms. However, when the mother's quest for external solutions is accepted by the nurse and doctor, she becomes irritable or depressed, and it becomes clear that she has compromised her investigation of conflicted feelings in the issue at hand. The following is an example of a mother's pursuit of external solutions.

Upon admission, Mrs. G was diagnosed as a paranoid schizophrenic. For several years prior to admission, she had manifested increased suspiciousness and irritability toward her husband. Two months after the birth of the second child, her increased accusations, irritability, and neglect of her baby necessitated hospitalization. She maintained that she was going to divorce her husband. She never commented on how she felt about being away from her children except to say she needed a rest and it was now a matter of "I" before "you." She became angry at any investigation of her solution and accused the doctor and nurse of constantly trying to save her marriage. She felt that no one was interested in treating her because they did not believe in divorce; yet she, herself, took no steps to seek legal counsel. When this was broached, she became very depressed and tearful, complaining that the doctor and nurses were trying to make her sick.

Mrs. G attempted to seek help but was unable to establish an alliance. At the same time, she avoided recognizing that her behavior indicated her emotional illness and need of hospitalization. When attempts were made to focus on the details of her solution, her irrationality was revealed, and she became defensive and angry.

We have found that, since most mothers will make some

compromise in exploring the maternal issues, the extent of the compromise must be evaluated. The greater the mother's efforts to minimize or frankly deny the basic issues confronting her during the period of orientation to the hospital, the less successful will be her ability to make a firm decision about bringing in her baby.

*Phase II: Deciding Whether to Bring in the Baby.* The mother, husband, and family must now decide whether they want the mother to care for the baby in the hospital. The mother is engaged in the process of making a decision. The nurse is concentrating on the two interrelated aspects of providing optimal care: recognizing and supporting the mother's efforts, and evaluating the basis and the manner by which the mother arrives at her decision. Nursing goals for this phase are therefore concerned with facilitating a rational decision and fostering arrangements suitable to the needs of the mother and baby on the ward.

The staff should expect to devote time to conferences with family members for consideration of several mutual concerns. First, the husband and family will want to have a clear idea of the benefits that joint admission may have for both mother and baby. The mother's participation in these discussions is advisable, so that everyone concerned can deal directly with misapprehensions and avoid disruptive differences, whether real or imagined, within and between staff and family. Second, both the mother and the family will be concerned that the baby might be harmed. While this concern may be initially verbalized as fear of dangerous *other* patients on the ward, the underlying fear is that the mother will in some way harm the baby. Although potential danger from the mother is first mentioned with guilt and anxiety by mother, husband, and others, frank discussion has been found to alleviate much anxiety.

Before encouraging the mother to bring in her baby, the staff will have to deal with extreme forms of anger, suspicion, fear, and evasive, noncooperative behavior evinced by the family toward the mother's illness and hospitalization. A strong negative reaction on the part of the husband and family will foster a defiant decision rather than a reasoned one. It is better to delay the admission of the baby under these circumstances.

If there has never been a joint admission on the ward, or if considerable time has elapsed since the last one, the doctor and nurse should spend time introducing the idea to other patients. Patients will be as concerned with their own welfare as with the baby's. For example, they will worry that the baby's arrival will result in their receiving less attention from the staff. Understanding each mother's relationship with other patients on the ward has been found helpful. Strong antagonism and resentment between patients and mother should be dealt with before the baby arrives. The most frequent problems are with single women who are jealous of a particular mother, and with other mothers who feel guilty about not taking care of their own children. Most frequently, however, these reactions are compensated for by an oversolicitous attitude toward the mother. Problems from the patient population are generally the least difficult to handle.

The nurse's responsibility to the mother and baby should be made quite clear. The mother, husband, and family should be informed that the mother is expected to take care of her baby and that the staff will assist but not take over. The nurse has much opportunity to assess how the mother is managing, and can specify on what basis she will arrange for the baby's care— for example, when the mother has other commitments or when in the process of working through a problem she becomes momentarily too upset to care for her baby. (Some nurses have estimated that forty-eight to seventy-two hours is the maximum time the ward staff can commit itself to care of the child during a crisis with the mother.) Only when a mother, given this kind of leeway, is still unable to care for her child, will she be asked to return him to a surrogate until she decides she can resume responsibility for him. It is especially important that both mother and husband be assured that treatment will be continued and that the mother's return to health is not dependent upon her caring for the baby in the hospital.

During phase II the nurse also discusses with the husband the ways in which he can assist his wife and baby while continuing to meet his other responsibilities. Fathers can, for example, help by arranging for baby food, diaper service, baby equipment, and pediatric services, and by bringing in the baby. Staff can help the father by permitting unlimited visiting time, except when contraindicated. The nurse's aim is to assist the husband but not to usurp, or engage in, decisions to be worked out between husband and wife. She tactfully redirects these prerogatives to the couple.

The process of reaching a decision reveals a multitude of dynamic factors. While the mother, husband, and family are ostensibly deciding about the baby, they are also working on problems which have resulted in the current family crisis and disruption of family unity. Asking a mother to decide to care for her baby also confronts her with her relationship to her husband and other family members.

The maternal issues of this period involve the various separate decisions the mother must make, and the successful working through of one is sometimes closely related to success with others. A mother must consider to what extent she will discuss with the nurse and others certain intimate concerns she has about being a mother; whether she can accept the limited responsibility of others (nurses in particular) for her behavior toward the baby; to what extent she will talk about other people who play a part in her decision to have the baby come in; to what extent she will cooperate with her family and the staff in arranging for equipment and space for tending the baby, given the limits of facilities and people with other commitments. And finally, in consultation with her husband and the nurse, she must decide on a date for the arrival of the baby.

We believe that the bond between mother and baby becomes increasingly fragile when it is made the focus of other conflicted relationships. Therefore the resolution of the maternal issues during this phase requires that the mother explore the influences of these relationships. Our clinical experience, however, suggests that often the mother avoids detailed examination of her desires to be a mother precisely at the time she is deciding whether or not to bring in her baby. This exploration is admittedly complex, and mother and staff should expect that her commitment to mothering will tend to be unstable.

*Maternal issue 1: Deciding to work with the nurse on specific problems concerning motherhood.* The question here is whether or not the mother is able to acknowledge and discuss the feelings and thoughts she has about being a mother. What she thinks and feels about marriage, pregnancy, and her baby is noted, and her ability to explore these concerns with the nurse and to arrive at a mutual understanding of what some of the problems are, is evaluated.

*Maternal issue 2: Deciding to care or not to care for her baby in the hospital—making an initial commitment to the baby.* The emphasis in this issue is on the mother's reasons for deciding to assume the care of her baby and the degree to which those reasons are based on her relationships with other people, her fears and symptoms, as opposed to an open appraisal of her own desires of wanting her baby and wanting to take care of him at this time. What is evaluated is whether or not the mother accepts investigation of her reasons and arrives at an independent decision without undue anxiety and guilt.

*Maternal issue 3: Deciding on and arranging for the cooperation of staff, family, and patients for basic equipment, space, and the time for the baby to arrive.* As the mother implements her decision to bring her baby into the hospital, she must enlist the cooperation of others and tolerate obstacles which may arise in the process of carrying out the arrangements. She will have to anticipate the needs of the baby and his care in order to make decisions about what she needs. The focus for evaluation is the mother's willingness to address herself to these matters.

*Discussion of phase II.* In varying degrees, the mothers in our study evaded coming to terms with their mixed feelings about taking care of their babies and therefore failed to arrive at confident assessments of their own desires to be mothers. This was true of mothers who made affirmative, as well as negative, decisions to bring in their babies. Thus, despite the anxiety aroused by the baby, thorough exploration of maternal issues during phase II did not occur. What the mother usually determined, initially, was that she *wanted* her baby, not that she wanted to take care of him. Only in the context of *caring* for her baby did she work through her ambivalence.

The following clinical excerpt portrays how one mother dealt with her difficulties in this area. This excerpt also illustrates her inability to accept the fact that the staff could not control her behavior.

Mrs. C, diagnosed as a borderline schizophrenic, experienced severe problems in her relationship with her twenty-two-month-old daughter and found herself impulsively abusive toward the child. She decided on joint admission because she needed help with her destructive outbursts. She asked the nurse to assist her by being around and preventing this behavior. The nurse made it clear that she could not control or anticipate Mrs. C's loss of control, but would be available, as would other nurses and doctors, when the mother felt she needed help. Mrs. C proceeded to recount tearfully numerous situations in which she lost control with her baby, and manifested much guilt and shame.

However, during the next several days she refrained from discussing her decision, despite the nurse's attempts to talk about the fact that no one could always be present to control the mother's behavior. Mrs. C's evasiveness was climaxed by suicidal threats and the concealment of pills, which were reported to the physician. Mrs. C complained that she felt pressured when talking to the nurse about making arrangements. So she and the nurse arrived at a mutual understanding that the mother would decide when she wanted to consult with the nurse concerning bringing in the baby, and that the nurse would be available. Mrs. C expressed the worry that the nurse was offended, but the nurse assured her that this was not the case and that she remained available to discuss any other concerns Mrs. C might have.

Two weeks later, Mrs. C said very casually that she was going to bring in her baby, and avoided any discussion except what was necessary to complete basic arrangements.

Mrs. C and the nurse worked together through some trying periods with the baby, including the mother's neglect in care and supervision of the active child and failure to set limits for the child's behavior.

After discharge from the hospital, Mrs. C confirmed conclusions made by the nurse about critical events in the hospital which moved her toward a commitment to motherhood. She revealed that she wanted her daughter with her because she felt it was the "last chance" she had to "straighten things out." When, during a highly excited period, Mrs. C pushed her child across the room in the presence of the nurse, she realized that she was the only one who had control over what she did, and that she did *not* want to relinquish care of her child to anyone else. She felt tremendous shame over this incident, as well as about those that had occurred previously, but—and this is most critical—accepted the act *as her own*. She was able to reestablish her rapport with her daughter within hours of the incident.

The decision phase permits the nurse to evaluate the extent to which a mother circumvents her own desires when deciding to bring in her child. The evaluation is a necessary step, for the mother's behavior is directly related to the degree of difficulty she will experience when she cares for her baby. For example, Mrs. C freely described her impulsive behavior toward her baby, but became anxious and angry when denied the assurance that the nurse could control that behavior. While refusing to discuss her fear and anger, she revealed both emotions in acting-out behavior (threats and pills).

Thus Mrs. C was initially blocked from making a decision for joint admission because she felt that having her child admitted represented her "last chance to get well." She also believed that her hostility toward the child would render the joint admission a failure. She reasoned that without the nurse to curb her hostile behavior, she would fail in caring for her child and thereby fail in her "last chance to get well."

Our experience with Mrs. C showed us clearly that a decision either by mother or by staff often reflects an underlying wish that the baby will cure the mother. This point is important. The staff must be alert to the fact that the "baby as cure" is frequently a mother's unstated reason for deciding to bring in her baby. Naturally then, profound depression will be associated with negative decisions, depression which sometimes reaches suicidal proportions because the mother feels that she not only has withdrawn from her baby but also has rejected a "chance to get well." It is imperative that the nurse explore the mother's decision with her to be sure she is quite clear that taking care of her baby is *not a cure*, and that *continuation of treatment is not dependent on her agreeing to have the baby with her*.

Mrs. C's eventual decision to have her child on the ward and her reaction to that decision illustrates the point that an affirmative response to joint admission carries pressure as well. A mother who agrees to joint admission often experiences anxiety and exacerbation of symptoms as she prepares to bring her baby in. She may expect to be "well" either immediately after making her decision or at least as soon as the baby comes on the ward. Therefore, the nurse must be prepared to deal with the anxious mother who has agreed to bring in her baby as well as the guilty and depressed mother who has refused. Either decision will be followed by one or the other reaction. The intensity of these reactions and the emphasis on the baby as a cure-all will be greatest in mothers who substitute a rapid decision for exploration of the maternal issues.

The nurse will find it profitable, both for herself and for the mother, to talk with the mother about the overall intention of joint admission. The mother is thus helped to understand what is expected of her and what she can expect from the nurse. Beginning with statements such as, "Mothers seem to have the least amount of problems in learning to do things for their babies; most mothers experience difficulty in what they *feel* and what they *think* about being the *one who has to do* for the baby," the nurse can help the mother distinguish between some of the basic factors that create apprehension when she begins to care for her child. The mother needs to know that time is available for talks about her thoughts and feelings bearing on her decision to bring in her baby, and that the nurse can provide information concerning practical arrangements.

The decision to work on the problems concerned with mothering (maternal issue 1) during phase II raises conflicts that are similar to, though broader in scope than, those found in working through the issue of separation during phase I. Further exploration of a mother's feelings about separation from her baby recurs at this time and is necessary for several reasons. Through such discussion the nurse can begin to assess the degree to which the mother's decision about joint admission is influenced by guilt feelings or other factors. These discussions help the mother to examine her relationships with the important people (husband, baby, relatives, doctors, nurses, patients, herself) in her life, and to see how she perceives the nature of their influence upon her. In addition, the mother usually reviews her pregnancy and delivery, thus initiating clarification of some of her most intimate and troubling thoughts and feelings about her baby and motherhood. The details of what the mother brings up and the feelings she manifests often forewarn the nurse of shifts the mother may make in accepting responsibility for her decision. The degree to which a mother feels supported or blamed by others is important, as is the degree to which she appears to be intimidated by their criticism, threats, or abandonment.

When a mother attempts to avoid consideration of joint admission by threatening suicide, severe complications are indicated, which must be dealt with before the mother can make her decision. Often the mother experiences her own desire to decide as a demand from the nurse, doctor, or husband, to say yes. Avoidance, confusion, negative reactions to the nurse, are signals to reexamine responses to the maternal issues and to try to locate the source of the difficulty.

Problems in phase II can be traced to unworkable approaches to, or avoidance of, maternal issues in phase I, indicating that nurse and mother have not established a constructive relationship. Our experience suggests that nurse and mother will engage in mutual avoidance when problems reside in the alliance between them. Mothers who are inclined to be extremely hostile, suspicious, and evasive are the most difficult for the nurse to work with. Frequently a mother's disaffiliating maneuvers block the nurse, so that she cannot assist the mother to clarify fundamental issues. Only when the mother feels confident that the nurse understands her dilemma can she share her feelings about taking care of her baby or providing substitute care. Phase III, the joint admission period, is negatively affected when the maternal issues in the previous phase are not dealt with constructively.

The decision phase foreshadows the mother's basic dilemma in the joint admission phase, that is, the conflict of gratifying her own needs when confronted with the needs and demands of the helpless infant. Workable approaches to, and resolution of, the issues during phase II are largely dependent upon the mother's learning to tolerate delay, to modify her expectations of others, and to sort out her immediate problems. She must learn these behaviors without experiencing a real or fantasied withdrawal of help from those important to her as she weighs reasons for and against bringing in her baby.

*Phase III: Joint Admission.* In phase III, the mother works to establish and maintain a mutually satisfactory pattern of physical and emotional care for her baby while both reside in the hospital. Tension accompanies the baby's arrival. Then the mother often experiences excitement and euphoria for about a week or so. Other patients evince great curiosity and interest, and both mother and baby become a ward focal point. At the beginning the nurse will need to intercede to protect mother and baby from exhausting hyperactivity and interruption.

The nurse, doctor, and mother should meet during the first week of the baby's arrival to share information on the vicissitudes of taking care of the baby on the ward, so that the mother knows her progress is observed and the staff is available for assistance. The meetings can help her cope with the intense concern she has about being criticized and judged. The nurse should be alert to and prepared to investigate manifestations of mistrust, excessive sensitivity, fear, and anxiety as these arise in numerous situations, particularly those centering on baby care and maintaining the treatment schedule.

Reasonableness in the nurse's expectations for herself and the mother make it easier to accept a degree of disorganization, negligence, and awkwardness as the mother establishes her mothering style. Since the nurse has invested much time with the mother, she tends to think that the plan has failed when upsets occur. The disappointments of mother, nurse, doctor, and husband can reach unreasonable proportions. Sometimes the baby will be removed prematurely from the mother's care. Removal of the baby under these circumstances leads to hurt, guilt, and anger within the mother, often reaching suicidal proportions. *The mother's upsets in caring for her baby mean that major therapeutic tasks are at hand, and not that the baby ought to be removed.*

The maternal issues during this phase of joint residence focus on the mother's maintaining and establishing relationships and patterns of interaction which can enhance her treatment and unite her with life outside the hospital.

*Maternal issue 1: Maintaining a relationship with the nurse while caring for the baby.* The mother must address herself to the baby's needs while simultaneously expressing her own wishes, desires, and needs to the staff. She must learn to recognize and accept the premise that the staff, and particularly the nurse, are there both to help her and to oversee the care of her baby.

*Maternal issue 2: Establishing and maintaining a pattern of maternal care commensurate with the needs of the baby.* The focus of this issue is on the mother's instituting and maintaining a pattern of maternal care that is mutually satisfactory for mother and child. The mother's ability to note or modify inconsistent and inappropriate behavior in caring for her baby and her ability to take into account other people's observations are evaluated. This issue involves interaction between mother and baby such as feeding, changing, playing, or setting limits as well as interaction between mother and nurse.

*Maternal issue 3: Maintaining relationships with the other patients while caring for the baby.* The mother is concerned about other patients' reactions to the kind of care she gives her baby. She must come to grips with their involvement in what she is doing, set limits on unwelcome and unhelpful intervention, but also accept help and not misinterpret other patients' constructive interest. The mother's ability to address herself to these matters in a constructive manner that is helpful for her and her baby is evaluated. The following are examples of unworkable and workable approaches to this issue.

*Unworkable:* Georgie was in the play pen, crying, while his mother was in a group meeting. A male patient took him out of the pen and was consoling him when his mother came out of the meeting. She stormed the dayroom: "Put him down—it won't hurt him to cry—mind your own business."

*Workable:* Mrs. B had put a sign on her door three days after her baby arrived on the ward. It read: "PLEASE GET ME WHEN THE BABY CRIES." Returning from another section of the ward, she heard the baby crying and found a female patient holding the baby. She thanked the woman, took the baby, and then asked if, in the future, it would be possible to contact her first.

*Maternal issue 4: Working through commitment to the baby and motherhood.* Here the mother focuses on whether or not she wants to care for her baby. While she may tangentially address herself to this issue in discussing various aspects of physically caring for her child, to confront the question she must go beyond material considerations to her fundamental concern: Can she accept the responsibilities inherent in being a mother? What is evaluated is the manner in which the mother applies herself to this issue, taking into account antecedent views of her own relationship with her mother, husband, and others. Again Mrs. G (Georgie's mother) illustrates an unworkable approach to this issue.

Mrs. G: "It's I before you. I don't wrap myself up in my kids." Nurse: "Feel this is different from most women?" Mrs. G: "Look, it's the way I said. I don't even care to discuss it." Nurse: "You sure get on guard and scrappy about it." Mrs. G: "Ha-ha—none of that analyzing bit."

A workable approach involves recognition of conflicts and some ability to verbalize them.

Mrs. K was talking to the nurse about how terrible she felt and how sloppy she was; not interested in anything, concluding that it was very hard for her to get to the hospital in the morning (she was on the day program). Mrs. K said that she was quite concerned that she could not take care of the baby, that it was all she could do to keep her head above water. The nurse said: "I guess you just feel that depressed." Mrs. K: "That's it precisely—how I feel." Sober pause. Nurse: "It's difficult having such mixed feelings toward the baby, wanting to take care of him, not wanting to take care of him." Mrs. K said it was most upsetting to her and she began to cry. The nurse asked Mrs. K about her pregnancy. At this point, Mrs. K talked at length about how frightened she was during her pregnancy both for herself and the baby because she was in her forties. She went on to talk about how she hadn't expected any more babies and was just beginning to live for herself again—children grown, etc. Now she doesn't know if the baby is a blessing or not. She added she was scared of future pregnancies, yet was upset when the doctor recommended tubal ligation, which she refused. She ended saying that she was confused as to why she should be in a slump now.

*Maternal issue 5: Maintaining self-control while caring for the baby and dealing with other problems.* Here the mother addresses herself to volitional acts, learning to understand their development in relation to internal and external stress factors. She must develop a capacity to assess disruptions in her functioning and become aware of long-standing patterns of either dominating or being dominated by others. The mother's ability to address herself to problems of self-control and the effects of her behavior on her baby are evaluated.

*Maternal issue 6: Preparing to leave the hospital and reestablish herself with her baby in her home.* Throughout her hospitalization the mother has assessed her capacities and her desire to return home. What is evaluated is how realistically the mother approaches this matter. Mrs. G demonstrates an unworkable approach:

Mrs. G was angry with her doctor for scheduling couple's therapy sessions. She had decided this was against her best interest and planned to sign herself out. The nurse asked what she had in mind. Mrs. G replied, "What difference does it make? I can take care of myself. Nobody is going to keep me a prisoner here. Look, I don't need any of this psychiatry business. Perhaps I'll take my baby with me and I'll do something. I don't want to talk about it. Nobody is going to talk me out of it." Nurse: "The decision is yours—but why do you get so angry about reasonable plans?" Mrs. G, with a bit of fear and perplexity, "Well, I'm not mad at you. I just feel I have to get out of here— can't get dependent on the place."

A workable approach to this issue is illustrated by an example from Mrs. E's case.

Mrs. E spent one and a half hours talking with two of the nurses about what had helped her during her hospitalization and what had not. She particularly emphasized that it was not clear to her whether the nurses were there to help her with her problems with the baby or whether they were there to "keep watch" over her. She said that when one of the nurses asked her one day "was she or wasn't she going to take care of her baby," she realized the nurse was trying to help her, not trying to judge her. She said she had felt scared of leaving the people in the hospital who understood her, but she felt she knew she wanted to take care of her children and that this helped a great deal.

*Discussion of phase III.* Establishing a rewarding pattern of maternal care is the dominant issue of phase III. When a mother loses control during this phase, it is often because she is conflicted about what she has to do for her child and what she wants to do and can do. By encouraging her to verbalize her fears and needs, the nurse helps the mother to differentiate her own needs from those of her baby. Thus the mother is enabled to clarify issues, arrive at reasonable decisions, and take appropriate actions. As the mother is assisted in these tasks, she begins to experience a sense of mastery. Her increased self-esteem enhances her relationship with her baby and fosters her further collaboration in this approach. However, critical determinants of the mother's receptivity to this work are her capacity to give and take, and the degree of defensiveness she manifests in revealing her real or imagined inadequacies to others and in becoming aware of them herself.

## DISTANT VERSUS INVOLVED MOTHERING

It is in phase III that the concept of distant versus involved mothering becomes useful in understanding and anticipating different mothers' responses to the nurse and to their children. The following typology outlines the two mothering styles, first in relation to the nurse, and second in relation to the baby.

| *Type I: Distant Mothering* | *Type II: Involved Mothering* |
|---|---|
| 1. *Mother-Nurse Relationship* | |
| Type I tends: | Type II tends: |
| 1. To deny need for assistance and to appear grossly ashamed and defeated when openly revealing her needs. | 1. To claim helplessness as a way of asking for the nurse's help. |
| 2. To be defensive and to push the nurse away with anger, sarcasm, or aloofness. | 2. To be highly self-critical and guilty about her needs or wishes. |
| 3. To be incredulous about the nurse's sincerity, and to interpret her aid as the nurse's maneuver to manipulate the mother. | 3. To say that nothing will help or gratify her. |

4. To be unable to wait, and to interpret the nurse's delay or hesitancy as an expression of dislike.

5. To bargain with the nurse when the nurse makes a request.

6. To appear depressed when receiving or giving, and to respond with very brief expressions of satisfaction. (The nurse, experiencing a sense of emptiness and sadness, often feels that she has not done enough for the mother.)

4. To be unable to remind anyone that she has made a request.

5. To acquiesce to the nurse's request even if it is impractical or unreasonable.

6. To appear grateful when things are given to her, but to belittle her own attempts to give. (The nurse may doubt the mother's pleasure in what is given to her or taken from her; she often experiences frustration and irritation in doing for the mother.)

## 2. Mother-Baby Relationship

Type I tends:

1. Rarely to acknowledge that the stress of motherhood was instrumental in causing her breakdown.

2. To be rigid and defensive in the routine care she gives her baby; to disregard the child's reactions.

3. To appear organized until the baby reacts negatively to her inconsistent and inadequate care.

4. To respond with distress and irritability to the baby's crying, stating that the baby must get used to things on his own; by her anger to ward off profound depression and guilt triggered by baby's crying; to feel she has done something wrong.

Type II tends:

1. Frequently to state fears of motherhood, and sometimes to blame the baby and/or motherhood for her breakdown.

2. To vacillate between being highly involved in the baby's care and being distant; to be hypercritical of the care she provides.

3. To provide a generally acceptable level of physical care for the baby, but to be inadequate in any other contact with her child.

4. To view baby's crying as an indication that she has disappointed the baby, and is inadequate; to be anxious about anger and guilt associated with thoughts, feelings, and possible reactions to baby.

5. Rarely to relate the baby's mood or behavior to her own, but, when she does, to project her own anger and aggression onto her child; to avoid comments about the baby's need for love, protection, etc.

5. Frequently to associate the baby's mood and behavior to her own, particularly the baby's need for people, attention, love, and protection, and to view this negatively; to avoid comments about aggressive behavior or cries of protest from the baby.

6. To handle separation from the baby in a stark, aloof manner, avoiding the protests of the baby when she leaves; to inhibit joy or curiosity about the baby when she returns.

6. To avoid the reactions of the baby to her separation, often minimizing the baby's attachment to her; to respond with joy or anxious fondling on return; covertly or overtly to seek information about baby's reaction to her absence.

7. To take pleasure in identifying positive physical characteristics in the baby as similar to herself, and to be at a loss when unable to do so.

7. To avoid remarking on the baby's physical characteristics, but, when she does, to express anxiety that the baby will resemble her in some way she views as a defect; to view the baby as "perfect," better than herself, fragile.

8. To institute early discipline (limits) over a large range of the baby's behavior; to use a sharp, threatening voice; to slap.

8. To be inconsistent in disciplining (limiting) baby; to be impulsive and physically abusive; to use excessive talking and reasoning beyond the baby's comprehension.

9. Rarely to play with the baby; if she does, to play in quiet, not highly stimulating manner; to ignore the baby's initiatives and to be upset and concerned about others' playing with him.

9. To be physical and highly stimulating to the baby when playing; to push or force the baby to coo, giggle, laugh; to be disappointed he does not do so; abruptly to drop her interest in playing and to become irritated if the baby wants to continue; to enjoy showing off the baby.

The type I mother tends to care for her baby in a way that reflects her own hostility to the external world, which she perceives as filled with deprivation and as ultimately unsatisfying. She tries not "to let other people get the best" of her, and she reflects this attitude in caring for her child. Because she cannot perceive the helpless, dependent nature of her infant, she tends to interpret his pleas for nurture and physical sustenance as aggressive behavior. Thus she sets inappropriate limits on a broad range of the baby's behavior and is excessively harsh. Although failing to recognize the baby's need for love and attention, the mother provides his basic physical needs, often when they are not indicated, which results in an unenjoyable experience for both. The mother is unable to enjoy loving her baby and applies a harsh adult reality in considering what is in store for him. She tends to minimize her contacts with her baby.

The type II mother tends to care for her baby in a manner which reflects her extreme ambivalence toward being a mature woman. She vacillates between a state of impulsivity, irresponsibility, and helpless confusion. This mother's conception of the world is similar to that of the type I mother, but her reactions are consciously defeatist. Unlike the distant mother, the involved mother accepts her role as a condemned weakling in a hostile and aggressive environment. She transfers this attitude to caring for her child and thus finds it hard to take any initiative and often behaves as if the infant controlled her. Her attempts at disciplining her child therefore tend to be impulsive and inconsistent. This mother often registers disgust and anger toward her infant's dependent state and expresses fear that her child will be as helpless as she is. At the same time, she often ignores or curtails assertiveness in the baby. She tends to be involved frenetically with her baby, and then to separate abruptly from him.

The classification of mothers on the basis of mothering styles indicates that the manner of resolving the maternal issues *prior* to the baby's admission may have predictive value as to positive and negative factors influencing the mother-baby unit *during* joint admission.

Because the mothering styles are based on differing maternal responses, expressing different "need orientations," they, in turn, suggest two different modes of maternal nursing care. The following statements of nursing care illustrate, in a highly abstract and sequential manner, how the nurse, through her relationship with the mother, deals with pertinent factors bearing on particular needs, and how the nurse's approach to these needs and to the mother's mode of negotiating them affect the mother-child relationship.

*Distant Mothering and Nursing Care.* In dealing with type I patients, the nurse focuses on assisting the mother to clarify her own wants and needs before concentrating on mother-baby interaction. In this way the nurse helps the mother to define herself as a separate entity from her child. Anticipating the mother's need for distance and the baby's need for care, the nurse can initially assign staff to care for the baby when the mother needs time for herself. The nurse also should clearly state her own availability to the mother's needs and questions.

As it becomes apparent that the mother avoids asking for help or appears distressed when it is offered, the nurse will begin to discuss with the mother her impressions of the existence and manifestations of this problem. Even if the mother is not at first irritated when dealing with this question, she will be later. If, however, the mother is able to discuss the reason for her irritation, and it diminishes, the nurse may continue exploration in this area. If the mother cannot discuss it, the nurse can indicate that she is aware of the irritation, respects the mother's right to manifest it and to discuss it at her own pace, and accepts the mother's inability to focus on her defensive anger. It is important that the nurse continue contact and foster positive interchanges to the best of her ability. In this way she widens the base of understanding and respect between the patient and herself.

As the baby's demands become more specific, the nurse can anticipate more demands and criticism from the mother. Distinguishing between the mother's manifest anger and her underlying feelings of disappointment and frustration becomes a crucial therapeutic task at this point. Focus on anger intensifies the mother's negative perception of herself, whereas focus on disappointment uncovers depression which can be tolerated to a limited degree, provided it is related to present situations.

This is a critical period because the mother wants gratification from important people. Becoming acutely aware of her own thoughts and feelings of helplessness and her longings for dependence, she finds it very difficult to give to and provide for her baby. For while her child's demands for infantile care and attention have increased, so has her awareness of her own childlike needs for care and protection. Anger and distortion of the intentions of others will arise at this time, and again the nurse can assist the mother in clarifying the situations in which negative affect arises until she is more comfortable with the pain associated with talking about how much she feels she wants and needs for herself.

Until the mother differentiates her own needs for psychiatric help from her baby's need for care, she can be expected to withdraw from her baby. A mother may have to send her baby home at this time if she feels she can provide only very limited care and requires more time for herself. Her depression and sense of confusion can be reduced if she is helped to realize that arranging for the baby's care is another way of providing care and, at the same time, of helping herself get well.

More often, however, a distant mother will continue to care for her child in the hospital. Even when she becomes exasperated with his demands, she will try to hide her resentment for fear that the nurse will criticize her and their relationship will be jeopardized. If, however, the mother and nurse have worked through earlier crises, the nurse can now deal with the mother's attempts to suppress her anger and resentment at her child. She can also help the mother see that her extreme concern with the nurse's reaction to her irritation only serves to exacerbate that irritation. The mother then begins to see that her anger is a way of distancing herself as a defense against losing positive relationships. Anger is not, as she thought, an indication that she lacks "feeling" or is incapable of positive affective responses. When the mother can accept this premise, she will be less defensive in talking about herself and she will be able to tend her baby more comfortably. A reduction in her defensive anger and a more positive response to her child's infantile needs naturally enhances the mother-child relationship. In turn, the baby's positive responses to his mother's efforts encourage her to be increasingly flexible.

*Involved Mothering and Nursing Care.* With patients evidencing an involved mothering style, the nurse deals with multiple shifts from the mother's relationship with her baby to her relationship with adults immediately important to her. Initially, the mother is apt to focus on her own thoughts and feelings toward the baby, which express the general theme that the baby has interfered with pleasurable pursuits or does not elicit a sense of pleasure.

Mother and baby should not be separated when the mother states as her need for separation her own fancied inadequacies. Separation under mutually pleasurable circumstances, however, should be supported. When the mother is under stress and needs to be separated, the nurse should actively support the mother's maintaining control over separation by having her make arrangements for the baby's care.

Since the type II mother is rather articulate about her relationship to her baby, the nurse can encourage her to be as explicit as possible about pleasures and dissatisfactions in actual care. The mother may claim that nothing pleases her or that she knows it is ridiculous to blame the baby. The nurse then focuses on how the mother's blaming herself or the baby leads to feelings of shame and disappointment. At this point, there is a subtle shift: the mother now turns from concern about her child to concern about her relationship with the nurse.

The mother's concern about the nurse's impressions and expectations of her are tested and tried in many ways. The mother may attempt to please the nurse for a time, but soon irritation breaks through and the mother will again return to picking on the baby or herself. By this time the nurse has witnessed the mother's efforts to provide for her baby and has seen moments of pleasure or satisfaction the mother has had in caring for him. As the nurse points to the paradoxical relationship between the mother's internal state and her positive actions with the baby, the mother indicates with sadness and sympathy that the baby is "perfect," "good," and that she is "imperfect," "bad." A critical point is now reached as the nurse engages the mother in considering her need to belittle herself when her behavior indicates concern for her baby. Therapeutic attention is then addressed to the question of why the mother cannot be pleased by her own productive efforts.

The mother may retreat by shifting her focus to other relationships—to her doctor, husband, or nurse—in which conflicts and criticisms also center on pleasing or being pleased, doing or being done for. In varying ways the mother demonstrates how she is the loser in these situations, always succumbing to the superior will of others. Her care of the baby may be haphazard at this time, and the nurse can help her to recognize that her difficulty in being self-assertive is registered in her relationship to and care of her baby. The nurse and mother can investigate the manner in which the mother asks the nurse for help, or responds to a difference of opinion between herself and the nurse. The mother's wish for dependency leads to expressions of guilt and shame. She now confronts the nurse with her dilemma: How can she function as an adult woman when she wants to be and feels she is a "baby" herself? The mother's struggle between adult strivings and dependent, childlike expectations is now clearly illuminated. As she has finally verbalized her central dilemma, she can now also state her fear that she has failed to be a loving and giving person. For although she takes care of her baby, and may do it well, she does it with a deep feeling that she really does not want to. She is tearful and perplexed because she *wants* to want to be a mother and wife but does not *feel* this way. She may now stress her desire to be single and may become particularly envious of the unmarried nurse or of the nurse she believes capable of being a better wife and mother than she. At the same time, she jeopardizes her relationship with her baby by insisting that she is unfit as a woman and mother.

The nurse can encourage detailed discussions of why the mother wants to be a baby, why she wants to be single, and why she thinks the nurse superior. The mother begins to show more awareness that she is not a baby, even though, like her child, she experiences helplessness and dependency and wants love and attention. At this point the nurse can help the mother to understand that these feelings do not make her a baby but are indeed an adult woman's wants and needs and can be gratified through active participation in the adult world.

As the mother reflects on her desires to be single, an unmarried state seems to her to be a compromise between being a baby and being a mature, responsible woman. It becomes apparent that she is attempting to rid herself of other people to achieve a sense of self-sufficiency which she is unable to experience in being a mother and wife. At this time the mother may have a deep sense of dissatisfaction with others, provoking intense hurt and anger, which are muted by fear of desertion and abandonment. She becomes querulous with the important adults in her life, indicating that if they changed she would feel better. The hurt and anger she feels result in great anxiety, and she may become very concerned about the emotional state of her baby, fearful that she is adversely influencing it, thus focusing again on her child.

The nurse can point out to the mother that even though the mother is upset, the baby is not. The mother may indicate displeasure at this and feel guilty that she is envious of her baby's capacity to enjoy himself. It is imperative at this time for the mother to recognize that she would be upset if it were otherwise, and that perhaps her envy is directed more toward the adults in her life who seem to be able to enjoy things when she cannot. At this point the mother and nurse are able to deal more directly with the mother's tendency to rely on pleasing adults and appealing for their help, rather than on participating as an equal with them.

It is particularly important that mother and nurse reach an understanding of the extreme fear of abandonment which motivates much of the mother's obsequious behavior. This is crucial if the mother is to be free to commit herself to motherhood and the care of her baby. The involved mother must come to realize that being able to function in a responsible way with her baby will not deny her the assistance she now needs in negotiating her adult relationships in a more meaningful and self-enhancing way. When she is able to accept help in achieving satisfaction in other problem areas in her life, inconsistencies in her maternal care will be reduced. Her concern over the baby's infantile needs will decrease; she will be less anxious about her reactions to his assertive behavior and more able to recognize his growth with some pride.

## SOURCES OF MALADAPTIVE BEHAVIOR

The more the mother-baby unit is divorced from the mother's generalized patterns of maladaptive behavior—as outlined in the typology of mothering styles—the greater will be the mother's ability to exercise judgment and self-control in her relationship with her baby.

Maladaptive behavior resulting in crises in the mother-baby unit appears to arise from four sources. The first is the mother's displacement of conflicts she has with other important people in her present life situation onto her relationship with her baby. Nursing care can help the mother to clarify the true basis of her reaction. The second source is the mother's reenactment of primary traumatic events in her own life. In the hospital, the maladaptive behavior arising from this source may be the mother's attempt to abandon the baby in some way, such as impulsively pushing him away. The mother may complain bitterly and be perplexed as to her motivation. She may even acknowledge, intellectually, that she does not want to treat her child as she was treated. When these repetitive, negative patterns occur, the mother should be helped to describe her feelings in detail. The third source of disruption is a transient confusion of identity between mother and baby, when the mother's own wants, wishes, and impulse life prevent her from viewing herself as separate from her baby. For example, the mother may inform the nurse that she is not sure whether it is she or the baby who is crying. When this occurs, the nurse assists the mother to test the reality of the situation. The fourth source appears to be a long-standing impairment in negotiating interpersonal relationships. The mother will manifest gross ignorance concerning what is appropriate for her child, given his age and reactions, and does not seem able to learn from trial and error. One mother was very much upset when her eighteen-month-old daughter had a temper tantrum on a shopping trip. Numerous coats had been tried on the child, but the mother could not understand the child's unruly behavior. The nurse can help the mother correctly to appraise a given situation and to modify her own behavior through understanding her child.

The nursing care for both mothering styles should take these four sources of maladaptive behavior into account. Of paramount importance is the recognition by staff, mother, and her family that during hospitalization the mother only begins to work out difficulties in accepting motherhood. The similarities in both types of women—problems in giving and taking, problems in expressing emotions of positive and negative import, fears of depending on and being depended upon, dominance of a depressive state—are rooted in deep feelings of inadequacy and insecurity. Since these feelings are often experienced as physical symptoms, the mother assumes them to be constitutional. In this context then, helping a mother to express concerns about her body's imperfections and how her concerns affect her feelings toward her baby has been found to be valuable regardless of the mothering style a woman may tend to approximate. The specific time at which a mother will bring up these concerns varies, but their importance cannot be overstated. They may be uncovered in the course of talking about the birth and delivery of the baby, breast-feeding, the physical and behavioral growth of the baby, and illnesses that the baby may have or that the mother may anticipate.

We do not feel that the mother's involvement in or avoidance of the health and development of her baby reflects "unconscious hostility toward the baby." Rather, anger, irritability, overconcern, or avoidance may be viewed more fruitfully as expressions of the mother's deep fear that she has transmitted constitutional weaknesses to her baby and is culpable for the ways in which her child develops. Her thoughts say, "I have always suspected that there has been something gravely wrong with me; knowing this, I married and conceived when I shouldn't have. Therefore, if there is anything wrong with the baby, I am responsible." A mother may surmise that she is physically weak because she was "afraid of delivery and the pain." Sources of illness on her side of the family may make her fearful that she has been "contaminated." When a mother has had a difficult delivery or postpartum complications, a miscarriage or stillbirth prior to her most recent conception, her fantasies of vulnerability are supported by her reality experience. Any physical deviation from the norm in either mother or baby is a reality, and thus can open a Pandora's box of doubts.

## DISCHARGE PLANNING

When the mother and child have achieved a stable relationship, the mother must decide whether she is ready to return home, where she will focus primarily on clarifying problems and working out solutions with her family and friends with less immediate support from professionals. As the nurse reviews with the mother aspects of her relationships with the hospital personnel who helped her to function, many disproportionate concerns about returning home will be lessened. Problems which can be worked out only at home can be identified, and the mother can begin to arrange for their solution by talking with her doctor or with her husband or with both. She can plan a gradual return home to see whether the problems are as overwhelming as she first thought. In some instances, arrangements can be made for a nurse to visit the home once a week for a month or so, gradually reducing the visits over a period of six to ten weeks.

When discharge planning is handled in this manner, the mother does not misconstrue hospitalization as a cure; she is given support in accepting the fact that problems in living are not solved by residing in a hospital but by participating in the world outside of the hospital. Unless the nurse acknowledges this fact with the mother before discharge, the mother will face great disappointment and a total sense of failure when she returns home only to find she still has problems. A sense of failure seems to be one of the most important causes of a mother's depression upon separation from the hospital. The complexities of home life often overwhelm her, leading her to believe that she can function only in a hospital setting. If old symptoms recur at this time, she becomes doubly burdened and often returns to the hospital. However, when she is given time to adjust to the realization that in returning home she will still be confronted with moments of great panic, anxiety, and stress, her self-confidence is less vulnerable and she is more able to work out these moments on her own.

Next we shall follow eight of these mothers back into their homes with their families, and we shall see the shifting influences of past and present on the mothers' behavior. Visiting and working with them and their families in their homes revealed to us many rich and diverse elements not fully taken into account during the earlier stages of the mothers' crises.

# 4

# Treating the Mother after Discharge

After leaving the hospital, a mother makes what seems to her a drastic move. She shifts from an environment which sanctions her dependency and extends protection to an environment in which suddenly *she* must reassume responsibility for the decisive nurturing and protective functions. As the mother assumes increased responsibility to her children and husband, many factors in her relationships with others will determine her success in interaction with her own family.

Of the eleven study mothers, eight were followed after hospital discharge through home visits. The remaining three mothers, all in the "unsuccessful outcome of hospitalization" group, withdrew from treatment and from the research project. In the hospital, all mothers had individual psychiatrists. Upon discharge, individual psychiatric treatment was offered by the hospital to all mothers and their husbands. Two mothers terminated with their psychiatrists under unfavorable conditions shortly after discharge, but they agreed to the home visits. Attempts had been made during hospitalization to engage all couples in couples therapy; only two couples accepted. Periodic nurse-psychiatrist conferences reviewed the progress of each mother.

Visiting the mother in her own home is both instructive for the nurse and helpful to the mother. The mother has an opportunity to share with a professional person her on-going life experiences in a natural setting. The nurse can help the mother appraise those experiences and can thus help her cope during a stressful period so that she will not have to return to the hospital.

In our study, home visits were agreed upon before the mother's discharge. A gradually diminishing schedule was established with each mother: six to eight weekly visits; five to eight biweekly visits; four to eight monthly visits; and one visit every three months until termination. The visits ranged in length from one to two hours over a period of one to three years. This schedule proved to cover the critical periods in the mother's stabilization in her home and gave sufficient time for her to clarify her most pressing concerns. Two mothers who lived at a considerable distance were visited once every two weeks for approximately fifteen visits before a reduction to monthly visits.

The clinical data were recorded from notes made immediately after each visit. Repeated review of the nursing notes, including a mother-to-mother comparison, yielded three broad components which appear critical to the mother's successfully reintegrating herself in life outside the hospital. This chapter details the components with supportive examples and incorporates a guide for the mother's nursing care after hospital discharge.

The first component is the resolution of a series of maternal issues unique to the post-discharge period. The second is the mother's relationship with her nurse, which can be divided into three phases. These three phases serve as a procedural guide for the visiting nurse. The third is reflected in the nature of the interest and support given to the mother and her husband by their extended family. This factor seems of such major significance that we have examined levels and degrees of interest in terms of (1) the outcome of hospitalization and (2) mothering styles.

## MATERNAL ISSUES OF THE POST-HOSPITAL PERIOD

The maternal issues of the post-hospital period are as follows:
(1) The mother must integrate her illness and hospital experience as part of the process of separating from the hospital.
(2) The mother must integrate herself into her family in

appropriate mother- and wife-roles on affective and instrumental levels. (3) The mother must identify herself as a member
of her neighborhood and community, reinstitute herself in
former friendships, and make new friends.

*Maternal issue 1.* To integrate her illness and hospital experience
as part of the process of separating from the hospital, the
mother must accept her illness and hospitalization as part of her
life experience. All mothers in our study stated that they found
the nurse's visits in the home to be especially beneficial because
they needed to talk about their experiences but felt that their
husbands, family, or friends would not wish them to do so.

In the early home visits, the successful (S) mother tends to
reflect upon the dependent, safe position she occupied within
the hospital. She gradually engages in a more constructively
critical exploration of those facets of hospitalization which were
more, and less, helpful to her. During this analysis of the
hospitalization, the mother reviews her breakdown and symptoms and draws some reasonable conclusions about what led to
her hospitalization. For the S mother, talking about her hospital
experiences appears to afford several specific gains.

1. Much latent anxiety is discharged. Freedom from the
hospital and the concomitant release from the threat of
permanent institutionalization gives the mother both opportunity and impetus to face the reality of her breakdown.

2. The mother can now question the many unrealities she has
experienced and express her concern for her image in the world
of "other people." She becomes particularly interested in the
whole phenomenon of mental illness.

3. As the mother begins to recognize that other people
manifest equally disturbed behavior, have disorganized life
situations, but, unlike herself, fail to seek psychiatric help, she
develops self-confidence and pride in her efforts to gain more
understanding and ability to change undesirable situations.

4. As the mother's self-confidence increases, she becomes
articulate in her criticisms of experiences within the hospital
setting, accepting the human limitations of the treatment staff
and placing more realistic value upon positive experiences.

In contrast, the unsuccessful (U) mother spends more time
discussing negative hospital experiences than the history of her

illness and how she felt about being home. Because the hospital staff and the U mother have often been in conflict, this mother has very difficult and negative situations to work through. These delayed reactions to hospital experiences often negate the doctor's post-discharge psychotherapeutic efforts. The mother makes many attempts to devalue and/or to discontinue treatment. Frequently, the physician assumes that the conflicts in the treatment relationship are due to emergent transference problems. Nurse-psychiatrist consultation concerning the discussions during home visits may establish, for example, that the mother has been deeply hurt and is "carrying a grudge." Thus she is interpreting her experience of loss associated with discharge from the hospital as a sign of further rejection and anger by the treating staff.

At the start of home visits with the U mother, the nurse must make an effort to negotiate a constructive alliance between the mother and herself and to support the positive efforts of the treatment staff during the recent hospitalization. The nurse deemphasizes negative experiences. Often a mother's hypercritical attitude masks a need to find a constructive point in her experiences. For if the nurse supports the complaints, the mother's fears will be confirmed; she *is* an incorrigible person who is *rightfully* rejected by everyone. The nurse must recognize, after a reasonable period of discussion of the negative aspects of hospitalization, that the mother's continued emphasis on the subject is a manifestation of her alienating tactics. That is, she is attempting to avoid leaving her illness. When this is pointed out to the U mother, she usually begins to make the same progress as the S mother.

The moderately successful (MS) mother handles the hospitalization issue in much the same manner as the S mother, but with greater emphasis on its negative events. Her stress on negative events arises not from a desire to avoid giving up her psychosis but from loss of self-esteem due to regression during her psychotic episodes. This mother is extremely doubtful of ever becoming free of her psychotic symptoms. The symptom she most fears is estrangement from reality. She may reveal that she purposely misled the staff and physician to believe that she was improved when, in truth, she had symptoms at the time of discharge. She presents this information to the nurse in the manner of a confession, for the added stress of being alone at home without the structure of the hospital makes the mother fearful that she has left too soon and will have to be readmitted.

Mothers in this group tend to have spent less total time in the hospital than either successful or unsuccessful mothers, though their orientation period was the longest.

In working with the MS mother, the nurse should encourage her to let her physician know that she can function in the home even though she is plagued by symptoms. The mother can be helped to discuss the reasons for hesitating to let him know. She should understand that hospitalization is not necessary just because one has symptoms, and that continued clarification of her problems will help to reduce those symptoms. The nurse also urges the mother to pay particular heed to those events which lead to an intensification of the symptoms. This maneuver reaffirms the therapeutic commitment to the mother, gives her assurance that she will not be abandoned, and meets her needs for help on a level which does not intensify her concerns and guilt about repeating the regression which overwhelmed her in the hospital.

*Maternal issue 2.* Integration of self into family in appropriate mother- and wife-roles on emotional and instrumental levels is the most critical and complex issue of the rehabilitative process. Within the conjugal family and the extended family, the mother must establish reciprocal relationships which provide for sustaining positive affective gains, more mature functioning, and a reasonable division of responsibility necessary for the care of the children and the household. Deficient interpersonal relationships within the total family complex before the hospitalization may have significant bearing on the nature of the mother's functioning after she is discharged. The stages of the mother-nurse relationship and the effect of the marital relationship upon parental behavior have distinct bearing on the resolution of this issue.

Maternal issue 2 is comprised of several critical decisions to be made independently by the mother about her adult relationships in the family in order to sustain a productive family life. These are: (a) to achieve a preliminary level of functioning; (b) to decide to retain or to alter pre-hospital modes of coping with deficiencies; (c) to clarify and apply new modes of coping with such deficiencies; and (d) to integrate more mature levels of functioning within the family complex.

The reactions of the mother and her family to her recent hospitalization are major elements of the emotional climate in the home when the mother returns. Her return allays the doubts and fears held by both herself and her family that she may be incurably insane. They all now feel relief, pleasure, and hope. Their behavior may reflect attitudes that "the worst is over" and "now everything will be all right."

The quasi-cure effect that "all is well" is related, in part, to the degree of the mother's self-confidence in being able to manage her household and the child. The mother who is insecure about her abilities in this direction tends to focus her energies on functioning, and she interprets her success in managing as an indication that she is now free of the problems which led to her hospitalization. Most often, this mother has the least help from her extended family. In contrast, the mother with moderate-to-good extended family support is less optimistic about her cure, because she promptly encounters the old problems between self and family. This woman, because of her past capabilities, is not unsure of her ability to function: her main concern is whether there has been a change in the attitudes and behavior of family members toward her.

It is important to recognize that a satisfactory preliminary level of functioning is not a resolution of maternal issue 2. The precarious nature of the preliminary level of functioning becomes particularly clear by the end of six weeks. By then, the mother finds herself falling into those familiar relationships which were dissatisfying prior to hospitalization.

The second decision confronting the mother is whether to retain or to alter pre-hospital modes of coping with the dissatisfying relationships. No mother in our study completely accepted the pre-hospital status. The mother with the least support from her extended family tends to move into prior marital patterns only to find her stabilization in the home eventually threatened by a resurgence of symptoms and a deterioration of her level of functioning. The mother with moderate-to-good extended family support tends to work harder to change her relationships within the family, particularly those she views as dominating.

Perhaps because of its intimate bearing on a woman's attitudes toward herself, marriage, and motherhood, the one relationship which consistently comes into consideration in dealing with decision *b* is the woman's relationship with her own mother. In many ways, the mother's mother becomes a focal person for blame. She is the most readily discussed and the most specifically identified as having deprived the patient of important experiences which would have prevented her present suffering. The maternal father seldom reaps the criticism that the mother does. The focus on the mother's mother in our study appears to have been an important factor in stabilizing the preliminary level of functioning when it was deteriorating at the end of six weeks.

The nurse must recognize the mother's ambivalence as she acknowledges deficiencies in such important relationships as that with her mother. If the assumption is made that a mother should sever her relations with either parent, because of apparent ill effects, the issue is evaded. The nurse must recognize that the mother's basic identification remains rooted in her relationship with her parents despite her negative experiences with them. Positive, idealized perceptions of womanhood and motherhood are part of a woman's identification with her parents and are essential to her efforts to attain fulfillment. If the treatment supports the negative attitudes which a mother holds toward her own parents, the therapist is, in effect, asking the mother to disregard important aspects of her own personality. The mother's investigation of her perceptions of, and difficulties with, her parents increases her understanding of her own attitudes and behavior toward them. She is thus enabled to broaden her perception of her parents from one confined by the past perceived deprivations to one which includes new and mature interactions.

When this step has been taken, a third decision must be faced. The woman must now devote her energies to clarifying and applying new modes of coping with deficiencies in family relationships. It is not unusual for her to make her first attempts at more appropriate and acceptable ways of dealing with adults in interaction with her parents, especially her mother perhaps because she no longer lives intimately with them. However, if the woman has severed her contacts with her parents, this opportunity is not available to her. That Mrs. G's parents were dead might well account for her less stable adjustment at home than other women whose parents were living. For example, Mrs. F's parents were alive and available. She came to perceive that, although they had never sought psychiatric care, her parents were mentally ill. This new knowledge gave an entirely different perspective to Mrs. F's assumption that they did not love her. She could now see that her mother refused to care for her grandson because she felt totally inadequate to do so and not because she disliked or was angry with her daughter.

Improved relations with their parents seem to be the pivotal point for the mothers' eventual assault upon their marital problems. Case material indicates that a woman takes a calculated risk when she attempts new modes of working through differences within the family complex. The other members may respond in negative ways, causing the mother to retreat from her efforts; or they may respond positively, requiring her to relinquish immature patterns of behaving.

The mother must now evaluate her gains (more mature levels of functioning in adult relationships) and the energy required to maintain them within the family constellation against the reciprocal alteration from other family members (decision c). At this point, marriage becomes the focal point. When the marital pattern is deeply rooted in the prehospital interpersonal deviations of the couple, the mother's attempted changes may upset the balance in the couple's primary relationship. If the husband is unable to reciprocate to positive change, the mother must decide how valuable her gains are to her and must choose between several options. She can either continue her level of functioning without expectation of reciprocity, dissolve the frustrating relationship, or relinquish her gains and succomb to her illness.

In helping a mother with these four decisions, the nurse must repeatedly evaluate the mother's status in the process of rehabilitation as it is related to the resolution of the total issue of family integration. She will thus time her intervention according to the mother's status rather than to her own expectations.

*Maternal issue 3.* In the mother's identification with neighborhood and community, in her taking up again with former friends and making new friends, four factors determine how deeply and how quickly she becomes involved: (a) the amount of involvement a mother has had with people outside her family before her breakdown; (b) the mother's acceptance of her illness and recuperation; (c) her reduction of her alienating behavior patterns; and (d) her need to compensate for lack of extended family support through nonfamily adult relationships.

*Amount of prior involvement.* All of the study mothers tended to have few friendships prior to hospitalization. They thought of their homes as either physically or as otherwise restricting their efforts to make friends. Lack of friends and/or sense of community is most evident in the U mother. Initially she attributes the absence of friends to each spouse's rejection of the other's friends. MS and S mothers do have some friends outside the family but view these as being primarily fostered by their husbands and associated with their husbands' vocational interests.

The U mother usually denies that she has problems in establishing friendships; the MS and S mothers are less defensive in acknowledging that they have few friends and have problems in making friends. A mother's difficulty in making friends may be revealed to her when she recognizes that she is tenaciously clinging to friendships she has established with patients in the hospital. Upon discharge, one U mother in our study needed and valued the friendship of the hospital friend more than she was needed by the friend, while the more successful women were sought out by patient friends still in the hospital or recently discharged.

Regardless of the kind and number of friendships held prior to hospitalization, when they returned home, all of the study mothers exhibited a marked need to seek friends and establish community ties. It is postulated that the hospital experience, which stresses the importance of affective attachments within the hospital setting and acknowledges the ward as a community of people living together, operates within the individual patient as a positive model in patterning her adjustment after discharge. Mothers who had more friends outside the family prior to hospitalization more quickly take steps to reestablish a circle of friends and soon drop their close association with patients.

For the mother with the least prior experience, most often the

U mother and the type I mother, the transition is longer, more complicated, and more painful. Her relationship with the nurse becomes exceedingly important to this mother as a means of relating to other adults and of filling her need for friends and a sense of belonging.

*Acceptance by a mother of her illness and recuperation.* Reluctance to move away from the illness seems to maintain a mother's attachment to the hospital and people in it. If it is accepted that a particular aspect of treatment makes the mother acutely aware of her need for friends and a sense of belonging, it is reasonable to assume that she will adhere to her illness until she begins to have fulfilling experiences in the realm of non-illness. If the nurse helps the mother to see that viewing herself as ill binds her in certain relationships in order to satisfy her desires for friends and a sense of belonging, the mother can then drop aspects of the patient-role which impede her progress in establishing herself outside of the hospital.

*Reduction of alienation behavior patterns.* In the S and MS involved mothers, distance with nonfamily members is most often traced to the mother's guilt feelings about being mentally ill and her fears that other people will not like her. The first post-hospital contacts are often with neighbors and old friends who know of the hospitalization. Initially, these people offer sympathetic understanding, and the mother tends to trade on these relationships in a far more dependent manner than ordinarily expected in friendship. The mother soon begins to feel that this type of dependency is restrictive to her own desires to be spontaneous in the relationships. Much of the conversation in these contacts centers on child rearing and housekeeping. The mother finds she differs with her friends but is hesitant to express her opinion. Irritation followed by withdrawal is the only technique the mother employs to handle the situation of difference of opinion. In mother-nurse explorations, it becomes apparent that the mother lacks the confidence to be direct because she feels inferior on account of her mental disturbance. When she can scrutinize her faulty assumptions, she begins to be more assertive in her relationships; she learns to tolerate differences of opinion and the expressed irritable feelings of others toward her without needing to terminate her relationship with them.

The U and MS distant mothers have more difficulty. Their hostile, defensive maneuvers and need to keep secret their desires for sympathy, dependency, and understanding tend to restrict the possibility of friendships. These mothers usually have no access to old friends or neighbors who know of the illness. Since communications with past acquaintances have never been close or detailed, renewed contacts require the mother to decide whether or not to mention her illness. Consequently, she most often attempts to establish a mutually reciprocal relationship from the beginning. Her concept of friendship, however, is very rigid and based on the premise that "if I do for you, you do for me, in like manner, according to my unspoken expectation."

The expectations of the mother are usually unrealistic, and she may withdraw from an embryonic friendship with bitter complaints and grievances. After openly expressing these thoughts to the "friend," she ceases to receive overtures from the friend. This hurts her; she becomes angry and frequently decides that people are prejudiced against her because of her illness. When her reactions are clarified in terms of the realities of the interaction, she usually understands that the people involved were not as committed to the acquaintanceship as she was, that they did not know of her illness, and that they were not as aware of her anger as she had thought. After such exploration, the mother finds that she can resume the relationship. Gradually she begins to alter her expectations and to diminish her angry responses to the behavior she has previously interpreted as a personal affront and sign of rejection.

*The need to compensate for a lack of family support through nonfamily adult relationships.* A mother who does not have extended family support tends to become involved early with people outside her family. But barriers to compatible relationships continue to impede her. Nursing intervention assists her to work through obstacles and encourages her to establish friendships.

Our experience with psychotic mothers indicates that correcting the misconceptions which thwart a mother's desire for a sense of community with others outside her family *is not sufficient.* The mother also needs an undetermined period of time for experimentation with new modes of behavior. When an organized structure of human interaction has not been a recognized part of a mother's life before admission to the hospital, she needs time to develop such organization within the context of what is available and what is of value to her. The nurse does not tell the mother how to live but becomes sensitive to the stages a mother will pass through as she achieves a network of relationships supportive of her efforts for more mature functioning as mother, wife, and member of her community.

## STAGES OF THE NURSE-MOTHER RELATIONSHIP

The three stages of the mother-nurse relationship following discharge provide criteria upon which to base a decision to terminate the relationship. Mothers may differ in the length of time required for each stage.

*Stage I: Immediate Adjustment.* Stage I is the time during which the mother must make an active commitment to the nurse to discuss what transpires in her household. She must integrate her illness and the hospital experience as part of the process of separating from the hospital, and must confront her reactions and those of her family to her recent separation. Responses to separation, which determine patterns of family interaction, will become the major focus of the mother and the nurse. Fear, guilt, and anger in conjunction with some pleasure will be the dominating emotions in all interactions.

The mother tends to withdraw from the nurse during this time because she wants to hide her thoughts and feelings associated with her anger and guilt concerning her family's demands. The mother's ability to cope with these demands will, in part, be dependent upon her willingness to acknowledge that the family has negative feelings toward her for her absence and her illness. When children other than the child she cared for in the hospital are in the home, her withdrawal is even more marked. In talks with the nurse, the mother may recount physical symptoms instead of facing the obvious dilemma she is experiencing. At this time she will make many demands upon the nurse to view her as helpless and ill. If the nurse responds only to the symptoms, ignoring current events and their bearing on the symptoms, the mother is likely to cut short her relationship with the nurse by having to be readmitted to the hospital.

On the other hand, if the nurse explores with the mother her reliance on the nurse and her doubts concerning her own ability to function, the relationship is clarified so that the mother can willingly decide to maintain it.

The mother makes her dependency appeals to the nurse in two ways. In one, the mother will await the nurse's visit and will expect that the nurse has prior knowledge of the problems and will solve them. The mother may have prepared refreshments but will manifest withdrawal from her participation in the home by having the house in disorder and the child somewhat neglected. She may claim that she forgot that the nurse was coming. She will not remark on the obvious disorder and will wait for the nurse to comment upon it.

The second type of appeal is more active. The house may or may not be in disorder, yet the mother will be excessively critical of herself and openly complain that she is not well and cannot manage. While the mother may be very articulate and voluble, she will concentrate on her personal inabilities to manage, and will ignore, or fail to recognize, the household events which create her intense feelings of being ill.

The nurse should make it clear to the mother that she fully understands the mother's difficulty in running her family and house. At the same time the nurse should show that she understands the mother's inability to discuss this difficulty or her doubts that the nurse can help. Now a beginning step is made in acquainting the mother with the use of the nurse's visits. Her resistance to taking an active part in, and responsibility for, clarifying the present situation decreases. The mother may deny the value of talking about daily events. The nurse will have to be patient, encouraging the mother to talk in detail about the day-by-day happenings in the home. The mother tends increasingly to deny the value of talking as she comes closer to revealing the incidents which she and the family are unable to handle satisfactorily.

When the mother recognizes that she is avoiding the trouble spots, the decision to deal with them in greater detail is left to her. Investigating her reluctance most frequently uncovers feelings of guilt arising from her sense that her difficulty is related to the family's feeling of anger and shame toward her for being ill.

Less frequently, a mother takes a heavy hand upon her return home and attempts to exploit the guilt feelings of her family as a means of avoiding their anger. In this situation, family members attempt to arrange everything for the mother and, at the same time, avoid her because of her hostility. The mother becomes increasingly upset and dictatorial because she cannot tolerate the withdrawal of the family members. It is not unusual for this mother to direct a great deal of hostility toward the nurse during this time, with many premature attempts to terminate the relationship. Attempts by the nurse to appease her will result in a "cat and mouse" relationship, which intensifies the mother's anger and her unspoken despair and guilt. An attempt by the nurse to mask her own anger by submitting to the mother's initial request to terminate the relationship coincides with the pattern of withdrawal manifested by the rest of the family.

The nurse must deal directly with the mother's angry assaults while preserving her right to meet her professional obligations. That is, the mother has the right to terminate her relationship with the nurse, but the nurse has the professional responsibility to handle termination in a particular manner. A requirement that three visits must be made to work out the termination is usually agreeable to the mother.

By the next visit, the mother's anger has abated, and she may have decided against terminating. The nurse now attempts to explore some of the reasons for the mother's anger, but she should not be discouraged if little progress is made. Perhaps the most beneficial thing she does for the mother is not to be driven off by the anger; her perseverance apparently relieves the pressure the mother is feeling from the family's reaction to her. The waves of rancor about the separation, emanating from the family toward the mother and from the mother toward the family, subside with little exploration. The mother begins to function more effectively in the home, and she can control her irritability in more positive ways.

Again the mother may wish to terminate, and the nurse will note that the mother brings up termination without the previous antipathy. Two or three visits give the mother plenty of opportunity to decide whether there are matters she wishes to discuss more fully. If she decides there are none, the relationship should be terminated at this stage, but the mother should, if feasible, have the option to contact the nurse in the future.

Other mothers, however, having worked through this stage of their adjustment by actively investigating the family interactions, are prepared to continue to stage II.

*Stage II: Change.* During stage II, long-standing difficulties within the mother's family are alleviated. The mother must work through the sense of shame and guilt which restrict her from discussing current situations pinpointing these difficulties. She gives up her dependent relationship with the nurse as well as with members of her family as she implements new and positive behavior patterns and ways of handling her problems.

Inability to establish a pattern of intimacy with her husband and inability to meet her child's dependency and need for love are related to the mother's earlier problems in achieving satisfactory states with her own parents. To progress, she must give up her infantile wish to recapture what she feels she lacked, and must find advantage in her present adult relationships. Confrontations with long-standing problems within current life happenings constantly frustrate the mother's childlike hopes to regain her lost and idealized youth. By the way she acts, she may indicate that she is avoiding the opportunity to be independent. This behavior may surface in the following ways: petulance and irritability with the nurse; unexpected and incongruous claims that all her problems are solved just as she has revealed a critical difficulty in relating to her child, husband, or parents; and claims of a recurrence of symptoms. In the face of this kind of regression, the nurse may be tempted to respond in an authoritarian or parental manner. She should avoid doing so.

It is imperative that the nurse constantly convey her respect for the more mature capabilities of the mother. The nurse notes the anger directed toward incongruities, but waits until the mother decides to investigate them. She should approach manifestation of symptoms with strong emphasis on how they are related to thoughts, feelings, and situations the mother is reluctant to talk about.

The nurse must be prepared for increased demands, requests for guidance, and requests for solutions to problems. If, during this period, a family crisis occurs, she should be prepared to intervene directly. The mother's demands on the nurse often indicate that the nurse has taken too directive and involved an approach to problems presented by the mother and has strayed from the task of having the mother clarify her problems and arrive at her own style of dealing with them. The nurse may find herself in this position when the mother is reluctant to face problems in her marital relationship or other adult relationships and is using the nurse, rather than husband, family, or friend, to work out arrangements necessary for the functioning of the family.

The later part of stage II will be marked by more freedom in the mother-nurse relationship and more initiative on the part of the mother. The mother will seek suggestions from the nurse with the full intention of evaluating them, not feeling obligated to follow them but not feeling defensive if she does.

Termination during stages I or II, if it does occur, must be arranged so that the mother is left with positive feelings about her final separation from her nurse and the knowledge that, should she need it, help is available. When this step toward separation is taken on the mother's initiative, stage III evolves naturally.

*Stage III: Termination.* As the patient approaches termination, she will experience a resurgence of dependency. Both mother and nurse must understand this as the mother's attempt to cope with loss. The nurse's assumption of any responsibility which is rightfully the mother's will only serve to extend this stage and perhaps undermine the mother's prior efforts at achieving maturity. It must be emphasized that dependency bids are related to the mother's sadness in separating from her nurse. They do *not* suggest failure in the mother-nurse relationship. The nurse need not be surprised if the mother shows anger. Nor need she be surprised at some of her own responses in which she avoids the matter of termination. Missed visits, tardy visits, changes in visits, visits turned into social occasions, are indications that the nurse too feels sad about parting.

Viewing termination as loss gives insight into the accompanying feelings and reactions. Termination may recall previous important separations, such as the death of a parent, absence because of illness, separation from the family of origin for marriage. Reluctant to face termination, the mother uses avoidance or anger as a means of defending against sadness associated with past changes in relationships.

Sufficient time and effort should be allotted to working through these aspects of ending the mother-nurse relationship. It is not unusual for the mother to manifest her unwillingness to part in her treatment of her children. For example, she may revert to child neglect as an expression of her fear that the nurse, in leaving her, is neglecting her. It may be useful at this time to help the mother make an analogy between her dependence on the nurse and her child's dependence on her. For she sees that her child is growing up and becoming more independent and separate from her, and her reaction is a dual one. She experiences both sadness and pride. Once she recognizes the analogy, she can acknowledge that she too is an individual, needing to grow and separate from her nurse. The nurse can encourage her by making her see the progress she has made since she was first admitted to the hospital.

One of the mother's fears about termination is that the nurse will simply forget her. This fear appears to be related to the mother's passage through the emotional aspects of termination to her realization of the professional nature of the relationship between herself and the nurse. By assuring the mother that she is interested in hearing from her, the nurse conveys the idea that she regards the mother as a person in her own right, not just as a patient.

## POST-HOSPITAL ADJUSTMENT AND THE MARITAL RELATIONSHIP

The importance of the marital relationship—on which the life of the family depends—may be obscured by concerns with the mother's illness, disturbing child behavior, and conficts with the extended family. But one must bear in mind that a close husband-wife relationship can provide a major source of encouragement to the wife as she attempts to separate her behavior toward her child from other neurotic behavior patterns. Ironically, difficulties with her husband are among the last issues the mother will discuss. In the context of our study this fact is significant, because the outcome of hospitalization, as we evaluated it, did not determine how quickly a couple would begin to confront and work through their marital difficulties.

Some of the study mothers, including those who had a successful outcome, discussed relationships with parents and family or proposals to return to work long before approaching problems relating to their husbands. They did not deny the emptiness in their marital relations, but they did not view this emptiness as a possible source of their unhappiness and illness. When mothers postponed acknowledging and working through their marital problems, we found that difficulties in the mother-child relationship were also prolonged. Conversely, as husband and wife achieved greater understanding of their relationship, or as the mother found other adult activities which provided partial compensation for gratifications lacking in her marriage, inappropriate mother-child responses were reduced.

Recognition that the achievement of intimacy in the marital relationship has great bearing on the mother's responses to her child directs the nurse's attention to the quality of the marriage from its inception and to disruptive events which remain unresolved. This does not exclude the importance of those early events in an individual's life which influence his ability to relate to another person as an adult, but it places the focus on the relationship between unresolved family crises and pathological responses.

The characteristics of the marital relationship after discharge and the concurrent parent-child interactions are summarized for each family in our study to demonstrate that a reduction of tensions between the parents serves the welfare of the children. The mothers are grouped as to "outcome of hospitalization" and "extended family interest."

*The Unsuccessful Mother with No Extended Family Interest.* Two mothers were in this group. For both, the immediate period of adjustment was difficult and marked by minimal involvement of the husbands; the fathers had little contact with their children. At discharge, the babies were beginning to crawl. Both babies were cautious when approaching their mothers, showed a preference for strangers (such as pediatrician or nurse) in the presence of their mothers, and frequently cried when separated from the stranger. Mrs. F represents mothers in this category.

Mrs. F returned home with her baby son, whose care she had resumed only a few weeks before hospital discharge. In a pattern characteristic of the pre-hospital marital relationship, Mrs. F took all of the necessary steps in obtaining an apartment and setting up the household. Her husband participated little and made no objections to his wife's arrangements not to return to their home but to rent and subsequently sell it. Mrs. F was very bitter that her husband left all arrangements to her. She insisted that talking with him was useless because he responded with perplexity and hurt feelings, claiming he could not understand why she was upset. In addition, Mrs. F complained that earlier problems in the sexual relationship continued; during the first two years of married life the marriage had not been consummated, and when she returned home, they did not engage in sexual intercourse.

While Mrs. F showed exceptional capability in arranging an attractive home, she remained depressed and complained of a lack of interest and pleasure in her activities. The bizarre, strange experiences associated with her psychosis had not completely abated.

Mrs. F related to her son in a rather rigid, routinized pattern, and, as he grew, she had difficulty in making appropriate shifts in her care of him, leading to minor crises in their relationship. For example, when he refused, at the age of nine months, to allow his mother to spoon-feed him, she responded by withholding solid foods and giving only the bottle, in order to maintain her control. She was hurt and distressed that the child responded openly to strangers and appeared to prefer them to her. However, she rarely initiated affectionate behavior toward him, nor did she respond to his attempted verbalizations and physical approaches to her; the boy's pseudo-adult affect both attracted and perplexed her.

As Mrs. F was able to realize that the child's verbalizations and his infantile behavior were attempts to engage her and to convey meaning, she became sensitive to the words he was trying to use. Increasingly successful in understanding the child, she became correspondingly more flexible, and the child began to respond to her with some of the spontaneity he exhibited toward strangers. Mrs. F soon spent more time with him and became less eager to put him aside for naps. She encouraged other children to play with the boy and soon was taking the group to a nearby playground.

This development of interest was not observed in the father.

Mr. F was content to come from work, eat dinner, watch television, and retire. Upon the father's arrival at home, the child manifested excitement and toddled toward his father, only to be ignored. After a time, the child no longer approached the father. Mrs. F was upset by her husband's behavior but felt guilt because she had demanded the pregnancy when her husband had not wanted to have a child.

As the mother developed a very close (for her) relationship with her son, she became frightened that she was depending upon him too much for affection. She felt the need for adult interaction. When the child was two, she left him in the care of a competent neighbor and returned to work. Work provided sanctioned competitive activity, and she achieved several promotions. However, with each success she became increasingly concerned that she was behaving more like the man in the family. Her husband, whom she frequently belittled, was content with his unskilled job despite the encouragement of his employer to undertake more skilled work. Mrs. F's discontent continued as she became increasingly tired of the double role of earning money to provide the standard of living she desired and caring for the child. The child was upset by the long day's separation from his mother and by the tension which grew between the parents in the evening.

A crisis emerged when Mrs. F purchased a home. Her husband was openly petulant and fearful of assuming responsibility, and this behavior contradicted his apparent pleasure in having a home. Mrs. F then had a period of increased suspiciousness, uncontrollable rage reactions and tantrums, and physical fights with her husband.

The acting out of the dilemma ended when the couple agreed to seek psychiatric assistance to work on their marital problems. During Mrs. F's participation in individual therapy, offers to treat the couple together were refused. Individual treatment was difficult because the marital problems were central to Mrs. F's adjustment. She had attempted to terminate treatment many times, and finally did so in a positive manner. At the time of termination she knew that both had to face their difficulties but decided that neither was ready. About seven months after termination of individual treatment, the couple took steps to try to improve their marriage through psychological counseling.

Home visits focused on assisting Mrs. F in increasing her sensitivity to her child, in dealing with the guilt she felt in leaving him to go to work, and in unraveling those reactions to her work situation or to her child which were the result of her feelings of frustration in the marital relationship. During Mrs. F's critical period of extreme anger, the nurse used the positive aspects of the mother's relationship with her to explore the painful aspects of her marriage. Mrs. F related that in the year prior to coming to grips with the marriage, she had set up small, achievable goals before being able to face the "real problem."

*The Moderately Successful and the Successful Mother with Minimal Extended Family Interest.* Mrs. I had a two-year-old daughter and the infant daughter to care for upon her return home; Mrs. C and Mrs. D each had one child. The husbands of these mothers were outstanding in their lack of involvement with their children, in contrast to the close relationship between the children and their mothers. All of the children demonstrated open distress when separated from their mothers. How each mother confronted and dealt with the lack of marital intimacy and the husband's distance and noninvolvement with his children led to different situations, each stressful, for the children. Mrs. C is here the prototype.

The situation of Mr. and Mrs. C was volatile. This may partly be accounted for by their attempts to face marital problems while Mrs. C was hospitalized. Mr. C started, and soon discontinued, individual therapy, and the couple did not seriously attempt to understand each other until the influence of the extended family was curtailed through several crises. During a period one and one-half to two years after the hospitalization, Mrs. C's mother became seriously ill, Mr. C's parents divorced, and his mother remarried.

Mrs. C's mother, after partially recuperating, assisted the couple financially, thus modifying her long-standing position against marriage and family life. At the time of her divorce and remarriage, Mr. C's mother ended the hostile alliance she was establishing with her daughter-in-law against her son. Mrs. C became aware of the tenderness she felt for her husband as she witnessed the cruel behavior of his parents. With a decrease in his wife's antagonism, Mr. C returned to therapy, clearly recognizing that he was doing this on his own behalf.

Before the major family events resulting in the changes in the marital relationship, the couple's little girl had lived in a very tense environment. Mrs. C was extremely irritated with her husband because he did not take an active part in the household and in the care of their two-and-one-half-year-old daughter. In retaliation, Mrs. C repeatedly left the child in the care of her unwilling husband after arguments over household matters. Then, against his expressed wishes, she took an evening job. Leaving the daughter with her angry father was obviously upsetting to the child, who responded with regressive behavior and precocious sexual concerns.

The nurse, in discussing the situation with Mrs. C, pointed out that she was using force to involve her husband with his child. As Mrs. C began to explore the situation, she began to realize that while she had had an opportunity to work out many of her feelings about being a mother, her husband had not been able to work through his feelings about being a father. This was the only productive route at that time, for Mrs. C refused to consider her reasons for working in the evenings. She was consciously convinced that her husband was not motivated to work out conflicts in their marriage. Mrs. C reflected at length upon her feelings of worthlessness and helplessness, and said that working created in her a feeling of independence. She acknowledged that her husband was successful in his work, but believed that they were so dependent upon each other that they could not afford to settle their problems until each had more self-confidence. The nurse reminded Mrs. C of the insights that she had gained in establishing a close and relatively understanding and sensitive relationship with her daughter. Gradually Mrs. C became less hostile toward her husband's efforts and more considerate of what he was doing with their child.

As his wife's expressed hostility decreased, Mr. C sensed that her need to work was not a reaction to him but of much more deep-seated origin. He then became a little less defensive and less teasing and provocative toward his child. He began to take part voluntarily in putting her to bed, reading her stories, and tucking her in. For the first time in his life, he began to enjoy her. The child responded by resuming certain mature behaviors she had transiently ceased.

The nursing intervention was based on evaluation of the core intrapersonal conflicts Mrs. C was attempting to resolve. Mrs. C was correct in her belief that she and her husband were bound together by dependent needs so deep that they could not face their problems in achieving intimacy until each felt more confident. Mrs. C did not know who she was; in many ways she appeared adolescent. She had not wanted to have a baby, particularly so soon after marriage. She and her husband were two lonely students who married upon discovering that they were spending most of their time together; each had few friends. When they married, they shared an apartment with another newlywed couple; the two men were inseparable friends, and the couples lived together as in a cooperative dormitory. When the baby arrived, they had not yet lived independently as man and wife.

The nurse's relationship with Mrs. C was a pivot around which the mother could explore her more mature, yet nascent attitudes toward parenthood and married life. This relationship was in direct contrast to her friendships with adolescent girls who had been fellow patients. As time progressed, Mrs. C adopted a maternal attitude toward the adolescent girls and later broke off her relationship with them.

During this time, Mr. C was cast as the outsider to his wife and child. The nurse was most careful, despite Mrs. C's annoyance, not to respond to the many subtle bids by Mrs. C to have the nurse support her negative attitudes toward her husband; these attitudes reflected much of what Mrs. C perceived as her own mother's attitudes toward men. At the same time, the nurse did support Mrs. C's effort to be like her productive, career-oriented mother. The nurse helped Mrs. C to realize that the roles of wife and mother and of intellectual career woman were not mutually exclusive.

As Mrs. C began to integrate employment with housekeeping, her undercutting sarcasm and hostility toward her husband subsided. Simultaneously, Mr. C began to develop a meaningful relationship with his child. The crises in the extended family tended to bring the couple closer and allow them to see that their parents felt positively about their marriage.

*The Successful Mother with Moderate Extended Family Interest.* Mrs. E exemplifies this category.

At the time of discharge, Mr. and Mrs. E had a very complicated relationship, which clearly affected the lives of their children. The couple had decided to separate, and Mrs. E was discharged to her parents' home, taking with her the two youngest children, including the baby who had been in joint admission. She then arranged to have the two older children join her on weekends and holidays until the end of the school term. The older children responded with aggressive and regressive behavior to the tensions which had grown during the many years of marital discord, separation due to illness, and the mother's family's reaction to the divorce. The parents' efforts to spare their children pain were ineffective, but a major achievement occurred when the parents clarified to the children their own acceptance and understanding of the children's fright and anger about the separation. Subsequently, most of the children's reactions were openly directed toward the parents. The older children responded at times with extreme guilt, and the seven-and-one-half-year-old boy particularly was convinced that he was responsible for all that had happened.

When Mrs. E moved with her children to a separate dwelling, near her parents, much of the tension was temporarily reduced. But the grandparents were intolerant and insensitive to the children's loss of their father; they wished to restrict his visits because they were upsetting to the children. This was little help to Mrs. E as she attempted to help the children deal with their feelings while she herself was experiencing strong emotional reaction to the loss of her husband.

As Mrs. E faced her mixed feelings about divorcing her husband, and as Mr. E, who was initially insistent that his wife divorce him, faced his mixed feelings, the children were tormented by their parents' vacillation. The older boy's sense of being responsible became increasingly unbearable to him, and he requested psychiatric help. Mrs. E, an involved mother, then began to examine her reaction toward the boy and noted that she often turned to him as if he were an adult. This pattern had started before the hospitalization and was a measure of the marital discord. The crossing of generational boundaries was most apparent in this family and became a focal point in the nursing intervention. The numerous upsets and family crises frequently were the results of interaction in which Mrs. E abdicated her maternal role, or in which the older children were forced into roles beyond their years and inappropriate for their positions within the family.

Conflicts with the children and inability to set appropriate limits for them, characteristic of the involved mother, were paralleled by tension in Mrs. E's relationship with her own parents. While the parents wanted Mrs. E to respond as a mature, independent adult, their attitudes and behavior toward her were those of omniscient authorities. They could not reevaluate their advice, and withdrew when their daughter did not comply. With no one else to turn to, Mrs. E was thus forced to respond to her parents in a pattern reminiscent of her childhood. Similarly, when Mrs. E asserted herself, she was fearful of parental withdrawal and tended to negate her more mature efforts and responses. As Mrs. E was able to confront her parents with this dilemma, a degree of understanding was achieved; interactions with the children became calmer.

Nursing intervention was directed at supporting Mrs. E in working through differences of opinion with her parents and in gaining some objectivity so that she could avoid being intimidated by their withdrawal from her. Mr. and Mrs. E. made arrangements for long-term counseling to assist them through the various stages of their separation and divorce, in addition to seeking help for their son. Both parents became more aware of the behavior and attitudes which were disrupting to their children and attempted to take steps to avoid perpetuation of these conflicts in their relationships with their children. Mrs. E's relationship with the younger children was more rational from the outset. She said that the joint admission was most important because she knew that she had much to straighten out with the older children and that this would have been impossible to do had she not gained self-confidence through establishing a less conflict-ridden relationship with her infant son while in the hospital.

*The Moderately Successful Mother with Good Extended Family Interest.* Parents in this category were very much involved with their children, and there was much open conflict between the parents in matters of child rearing. The parental behavior and attitudes acted upon clearly reflect the differing life experiences of the mates and their manner of relating and defending themselves in their relationships with people.

Mr. and Mrs. J were newlyweds. The early arrival of the child and Mrs. J's psychotic episode proved to be the base upon which the young couple's relationships with their families were altered to constructive ends. Without a realignment of relationships, neither would have had an opportunity to develop more mature attitudes toward their child.

Mr. J was struggling to assert himself as head of the household and was obviously threatened by the involvement of in-laws and other adults in his family life. He resented the psychiatrist and forbade his wife to continue treatment despite her desire to do so. Her "sneaked visits" to the psychiatrist created mounting distrust in the marital relationship. As a compromise, Mr. J did allow the nurse to visit. It soon became apparent that the visits provided Mr. J an opportunity to clarify some of his own concerns, when he wished, but did not require him to make a commitment to treatment.

After discharge, Mrs. J was able to gain her mother's counsel and support, which had not been given her when she married. Mrs. J's father, his son-in-law's badgering and threatening employer, withdrew from the couple's life and affairs when his daughter was hospitalized. Mr. J came to feel less threatened by his mother-in-law as she showed sensitivity to the adjustment problems of the newlyweds.

The Js' household atmosphere appeared demanding and tense for their child. Mrs. J, who had been rather rigid and distant in her relationship with her child in the hospital, seemed, however, to be gaining in awareness of the child's needs. She recognized that many of the accomplishments she expected were not yet appropriate to the little girl's age and abilities. Nevertheless, despite the growing awareness, Mrs. J persisted in carrying out inappropriate activities, such as an insistence on toilet training the nine-month-old child. When the nurse attempted to discover the origins of pressure on Mrs. J, she found that Mrs. J was engaged in a disagreement with a family member but was too fearful to face it and also too fearful to proceed in accordance with her own judgment. This conflict was shared with the nurse when Mr. J requested that she visit at lunch, before he left for work.

While the adults were eating, their nine-month-old child sat in her high chair, insisting upon feeding herself. Her young father became irritated with her behavior because she made a mess; he was harsh and scolded her sharply, insisting that she let him feed her. When the child began to cry, the father became angrier, reprimanded the child for crying, and commanded that she stop. The baby controlled her sobbing and tried to eat what her father fed her. Mrs. J was visibly upset by her husband's behavior. She said she felt the baby was too young for such harsh discipline, and the father's rage would make his daughter fear him. She turned to the nurse and appeared to seek confirmation for her conclusions. Mr. J retorted that he did not want his child to grow up to be "a spoiled brat like her mother." He asked the nurse directly if she did not believe that children needed discipline to "learn they could not have their way all of the time." The nurse pointed out that it seemed that he and his wife were not in disagreement about the fact that discipline was needed but about the kind of discipline appropriate for a nine-month-old child.

Not taking sides, but instead restating the issue, proved an effective approach. Mr. J opened up and described his own father's methods of discipline, in which he punched Mr. J, as a child, across the kitchen table. Mr. J then sat in silence, appearing surprised at what he had revealed. The nurse asked what he thought of this kind of discipline, and whether he wanted to repeat it with his own child. The father, obviously depressed, replied, "No." The nurse, noting that Mrs. J was watching her intently, commented in a general way that parents have to learn how to raise their own children and often their only guide is their own childhood, but that when they reflect on these experiences they come to understand that this is not what they want for their children. The nurse also remarked that the difficulty for new parents is increased by the unsolved problems between them—problems placed in the background of awareness, yet somehow becoming tangled in the arguments about the child. The nurse then asked Mr. J if he had had an opportunity to talk about his wife's illness and what the whole episode meant to him as a husband and father.

Mr. J began to relate in a spontaneous and moving manner how frightened and guilty he felt when his wife became ill, and how he became the brunt of her family's anger and his own family's anger. They blamed him for what had happened. As he revealed that he was struggling not to blame himself, he began to see that he was trying to handle these emotions by blaming his wife and insisting on harshly disciplining their child.

This encounter provided a substantial basis for Mrs. J to begin to evaluate her own, and her husband's, relationship with their daughter. Gradually the couple began to talk to each other about differences involving the child. Gradually Mrs. J's need to be protective of the child decreased, and Mr. J became less reticent in his tender feelings toward his daughter.

However, a second pregnancy triggered many of the deeper difficulties basic to the marital adjustment. While there was much concern over Mrs. J's becoming ill again, the real issue, which resulted in an exacerbation of symptoms in Mrs. J, had to do with their sexual adjustment. As Mrs. J progressed in her pregnancy, her needs for tenderness and warmth from her husband increased. He was upset by her demands and became more demanding of his wife and very harsh with his daughter. Fearful of seeming disloyal, but driven by her situation and the pressure of demoralizing thoughts and feelings, Mrs. J revealed to the nurse the nature of her sexual maladjustment with her husband. She was sensitive and responsive to his unspoken cues for various types of sexual stimulation but was bewildered that he rejected her requests for tenderness, such as a kiss before leaving for work, or sitting closely together while watching television.

Of initial importance was the nurse's assurance that Mrs. J's sexual willingness was that of a young and healthy woman. When Mrs. J gained this support, she was able to understand how frightened, guilty, and doubtful her husband was of his own sexual feelings and feelings of tenderness. Regaining her self-confidence, Mrs. J talked with her husband about aspects of their sexual relationship. Mr. J became less harsh with his child and began to involve himself fully in the pregnancy. Mrs. J was particularly astute about her husband's reactions. Both became more at ease in sharing with each other their fantasies and their concerns. The degree of intimacy they achieved was sufficient to carry Mrs. J through her pregnancy. She delivered her child by natural childbirth, and her husband was very proud of her.

The impact of the marital relationship on the parental inter-action can be seen to reach back beyond the immediate happenings within the family to long-standing problems of the father and mother in their individual self-concepts. These problems are clearly seen in newlyweds who have not had years in which to construct complicated schemes of grievances which obscure the problems of achieving intimacy, and this may account for the Js' rapid appraisal of their marriage. Mr. and Mrs. J's struggles underscore the precariousness of each person's self-esteem when he or she engages in searching out barriers to intimacy.

## MOTHERING STYLE AND MARITAL AND FAMILY PROBLEMS

Clinical assessment of the post-hospital data suggests that type I mothering is associated with lack of intimacy in the marital relationship, and that type II mothering reflects a selective capacity to achieve intimacy but failure to maintain it on a mature level.

The type I mother who has no or minimal extended family interest tends to maintain excessive control over her child's behavior. Few family members are involved with the child, and often child care is provided by strangers. The child tends to be quiet and obedient, inhibited in aggressive behavior, and less apt to respond with overt distress when left with a stranger. He frequently initiates, toward adults, social contact which appears precocious because of the pseudo-adult quality of the overture. It appears that these children are forced to adopt adult mannerisms in order to maintain contact with their parents, since the parents initiate little communication commensurate to the developmental level of the child.

The child of a type II mother who has minimal parental support tends to have an exceedingly close relationship with his mother and is openly upset when separated from her. He manifests marked negativism of a subdued nature, with eventual submission to the will of his mother. This child is open in his demands for his mother's attention, and the mother is apt to respond to these demands, if not to anticipate them; nevertheless, she immediately seeks to control his aggressive, autonomous bids.

The child of the type II mother with moderate-to-good parental interest tends to be hyperactive, impulsive, demanding, stubborn, provocative, and reckless. The mother may be openly perplexed and irritated by her child's behavior, as well as amused and delighted by it. The child is involved with siblings and other family members. The mother finds difficulty in setting limits for the child and is often angered that the child, failing to exercise his own self-control, requires adult intervention.

The child of the type I mother with good parental interest alternates from hyperactive, seemingly irrelevant activity to subdued, withdrawn behavior. The father and maternal grandfather were observed in play with the child of one such study mother. The men stimulated the child to attempt feats of motor activity beyond her capacities; they encouraged the child to box and wrestle, suddenly interrupting their activity with abrupt commands and irritation when the child became overly excited and began to cry. They teased and reprimanded. The mother had exhibited similar behavior with her child in the joint admission but, upon return home, began to assess the situation and to intervene on the child's behalf. She did not readily relate her irritation and confusion to the assertive demands of the child; she reflected a pervasive control over the behavior of the child, similar to that of the type I mother with none-to-minimal support.

## MALADAPTIVE BEHAVIOR IN MOTHERING

This brief clinical appraisal of the impact of the mothering style on the behavior of the child suggests that the mother-child pair continues to mirror, after discharge, the style of mothering associated with the mother during her hospitalization. Conclusions drawn from the survey of a study population of eight are necessarily limited to suggestion and speculation in the formulation of a framework through which the nurse visiting in the home can function. The formulations derived during the mother's hospitalization were incorporated into the post-discharge nursing approach and proved to be useful in intervening in disruptions between children and mothers of either type.

With type I mothers, continued clarification of the helping nature of the nurse's relationship with the mother is needed. Only when that clarification is achieved can the mother face problems with her child. Until then, problems of mistrust in the mother-nurse relationship persist.

Most frequently, disruption between mother and child results from the mother's poorly developed or impaired capacities for exploring and understanding human needs and relationships. The postulation that the type I mother has had limited positive experience in interpersonal relationships is confirmed by her family history and by negative involvement of the extended family upon the mother's discharge. This deficit is further increased by her psychosis. The nurse does best to attend to specific situations between child and mother, reinforcing the mother's ability to notice and comprehend the infant's verbal and nonverbal signals. The mother is unable to do this alone. Helping the mother to appraise her child's developmental steps increases her understanding of him. And, as the mother attends to the child's verbalizations, mutuality is increased.

The second most frequent source of disruption arises from

conflicts involving current relationships. The nurse can assist the mother to review situations in which she is displacing conflicts with others onto her relationship with her child.

The third source of disruption originates in conflicts involving earlier relationships and experiences. The mother unknowingly reenacts traumatic events in her own life, or behaves in accordance with roles and feelings which may once have been, but no longer are, appropriate. In our study, the nurse observed an incongruity in the mother-child interaction which suggested that the mother had abdicated her parental role and had become a child responding to a child. Denying the child's bids for attention or pushing the child away were frequent occurrences, stimulating the mother to say that this was the way she had been treated and that she was unable to avoid responding similarly. Nursing intervention focuses on the past event in the mother's life so that it can be explored in reference to the mother's behavior toward her child.

With type II mothers, a continuing appeal to, and support of, the more mature strivings of the mother, distinguishes the mother-nurse relationship. The mother's tendency to abdicate her position of authority and responsibility persists beyond hospitalization, particularly when she is under stress.

The disruption in this mother-child unit arises most frequently from conflicts involving current relationships; then from conflicts involving earlier relationships and experiences; and then from her poorly developed and currently impaired capacities for exploring and understanding human needs and relationships. Least frequently, disruption is related to symptomatic states.

It is proposed that the typologies of mothering styles are related to a preliminary scheme of psychological barriers to mothering. Nursing intervention should take account of these typologies in approaching mothers. The formulations deserve further clinical observation and objective measurement. Nevertheless, the clinical experience with mothers at home supports the conclusion that the nursing intervention, as set forth here, will constructively influence the mother's adjustment in her home and her relationship with her child.

## NURSING PRINCIPLES FOR HOME VISITS

All eight study mothers were able to integrate their illnesses and hospital experiences, to adjust to immediate affective and instrumental requirements of their families, and to seek adequate medical assistance for the physical and emotional health needs of themselves and their children. Seven mothers were able to progress through all three stages of the mother-nurse relationship to an effective termination. They went beyond immediate stabilization with the family to work through long-standing difficulties in their marital and parental relationships and to modify various psychological barriers to effective mothering. Two mothers and their husbands sought separation and divorce.

Certain nursing measures of intervention were found to be universally effective in the care of the study population. These principles, basic to the treatment of the joint admission mother upon her return home, are stated as directives to the nurse.

Deal with the mother's feelings of guilt due to her recent separation from the family, and help the mother to unravel her reactions from those of other family members.

Shift the focus from the mother as an individual to the mother as a member of the total family complex.

Support the husband in adjusting to his parental and marital roles.

Refrain from assuming responsibilities which rightly belong to family members.

Assist the mother in recognizing and altering behavior which perpetuates cross-generational alliances within the family, nullifies age-appropriate roles, and contributes to disruptive tension and intrapersonal disorganization, i.e., a mother's reliance on her child to fulfill emotional deficiencies experienced in her marriage.

Assist the mother in working through psychological barriers to mothering. Guide the mother in understanding normal developmental changes in the child. Help her to become sensitive to the autonomous behavior of the child, to appropriate discipline for his level of development, to his attempted verbal and nonverbal communications, to the mother's displacement of conflicts upon her relationship with her child, and to the reenactment from her own childhood of adult-child interactions which have a negative influence on her child.

Help the mother to understand her responsibilities for the emotional support of other family members, especially her husband.

Support the mother's attempts at new levels of behavior when these are frustrated or obstructed by family members.

Evaluate and alter behavior in response to the status of the mother. Slow progress and differing rates of change among mothers necessitate patience on the part of the nurse in allowing the mother time for reflection, decision, and experimentation.

Select and interpret aspects of the mother's intra- and interpersonal experiences which have the most immediate bearing on the resolution of current issues.

Select approaches suitable to the problems and to the mother's ability to cope with anxiety and depression. This should be a supportive approach, in which the nurse allies herself with the experiences of the mother and assists her in recognizing the mixed feelings and motivations with a lessening of discomfort and confusion. Interested listening is crucial. Also useful are (1) an investigative approach which assists the mother in specifying the details of a situation, in making relevant connections between events, feelings, and actions, and in considering alternative interpretations and actions; (2) an informative approach (including demonstration of procedure) which provides the mother with the opportunity to question suggestions, express alternate opinions, and decide freely whether to use the information; and (3) a directive approach which conveys the nurse's professional responsibilities and obligations to the mother and family when their welfare is jeopardized and an emergency exists.

Permit the mother to use the mother-nurse relationship in her experimentation with new modes of relating to adults and, primarily, to an adult female.

Give assurance and direction when assisting the mother in differentiating "normal" from "psychotic" states. This requires that the nurse have sensitivity to the existential experiences of a psychotic mother and not withdraw from the implicit terror of the mother; the nurse must relate to the mother and her state, helping her to reengage herself in reality.

Convey respect for the mother's growing maturity, reviewing with her her achievements.

Avoid being driven off by the mother's negative behavior. Recognizing that nurse-directed anger is the mother's attempt to avoid her most pressing conflicts, the nurse seeks to help the mother to acknowledge her conflicts and to change alienating patterns of behavior.

Maintain constant awareness of one's own feelings and motivations in relation to the mother, the family members, and the family's style of living. Strong feelings of liking and disliking, sympathy and condemnation, avoidance and overinvolvement will be reflected in specific nurse behaviors. Strong negative feelings may be evidenced by frequent changes in visit appointments, failure to keep records, anxiety before visits, desire to terminate, and inability to focus on the mother's urgent concerns; overconcern may be manifested by excessively long visits, assumption of functions and responsibilities of members of the family, preoccupation with worries about the mother and family, and overemphasis on the fantasy life of the mother and sexual aspects of her conflicts. Restricting emotional reactions and involvement on the part of the nurse will be further manifested by a breakdown of communication with other professional persons working with the mother, by anxiety and omission of relevant material when reviewing the case with a supervisor, and by an avoidance of supervision and consultation.

# 5

# Eleven Hospitalized Mothers: Research Design and Findings

Our investigation was limited to data concerning the first eleven mothers who agreed to participate in the research project. Obviously under these circumstances the researcher did not control patient selection or participation.

The nursing staff, in all but one situation, requested that the investigator take the dominant nursing role with the mother so that they might learn from her. As time progressed, staff nurses indicated an increased willingness to take more active responsibility with the investigator and to use her primarily as a consultant. This meant that she had clinical responsibilities for mothers selected by the medical and nursing staffs, while they maintained a general clinical responsibility to the mother and ultimate administrative authority.

Although a wide range of diagnoses was applied to the mothers, most were described as psychotic, with either schizophrenic or depressive features. In all, the immediate precipitating stress was considered to be the birth of their youngest child and subsequent pressures they experienced in caring for him. The time lapse between the baby's birth and the mother's psychiatric hospital admission varied from three days to twenty two months. The study women represented various social classes, nationalities, and religions. They were admitted to an urban, general, state psychiatric hospital devoted primarily to teaching and research (see chapter 1).

153

## DATA COLLECTION

The raw data in this study consist of notes recorded either by the author or by nurses on the ward. The investigator obtained most of her material in her clinical role as participant-observer. Treatment sessions with each mother varied in length from fifteen minutes to over an hour and in frequency from three to five times per week. The sessions covered a wide range of situations, activities, and arrangements.

The investigator's observations emphasized chronology and attention to detail. Several mothers and their babies were observed simultaneously by the project research psychologist. On these occasions, the notes of the respective workers were found to be similar in sequence and content. No attempts beyond this were made to establish the reliability of the investigator's nursing observations.

*Typologies of Mothering Styles.* Nine characterizing statements depicting the mother's care of her baby in the presence of the nurse were developed from the recorded nursing observations and interactions of phase III, the joint admission period (see chapter 3). Evaluating the mother's behavior by the way she approached the various maternal issues, the investigator decided whether a mother was better described by statements from type I (distant) or type II (involved) of the typology (see chapter 3). She assigned a mother to the mothering style in which 75 percent or more of the characterizing statements were applicable to her.

*Outcome of Hospitalization.* An evaluation, which we have named "outcome of hospitalization," was made of how the mother was caring for her baby at the time of her discharge from the hospital. The investigator made her evaluation according to the three criteria described below. A consulting psychiatrist, using the same criteria, made an independent evaluation. The agreement was 100 percent.

1. *Successful joint admission.* The successful (S) mother kept her baby despite periodic upsets and periods of separation. When discharged from the hospital, she could discuss difficulties in caring for her child and in being a mother. Thus, she was able to alter her care of the baby without feeling

overburdened. She verbalized a change in her feelings toward the baby and manifested pleasure in him and in caring for him.

2. *Moderately successful joint admission.* The moderately successful (MS) mother kept her baby despite upsets and periods of separation. She was less involved with nurses and doctors in openly discussing problems of child care and in being a mother. However, she did maintain care in accordance with the baby's needs. Although she did not verbalize an awareness of change in her thoughts and feelings toward the baby, she did demonstrate more tolerance of and pleasure in him. She manifested this change by spending more time with him when he was distressed or when he wanted to play.

3. *Unsuccessful joint admission.* The unsuccessful (U) mother did not keep her baby with her and terminated medical treatment against advice and in anger; or she kept the baby but evidenced little alteration in her thoughts and feelings toward him. She manifested gross inconsistencies in her behavior toward the baby, and he showed obvious distress in his behavior. She remained highly defensive whenever discussing problems in mothering and in being a mother; she discussed these problems infrequently.

*Historical Data.* For each of the eleven study mothers, eighteen items of background information were tabulated from the hospital records. They are presented in table 1.

*Process of Data Analysis.* Rules and criteria were established for coding the recorded nursing notes with regard to the thirteen maternal issues. Examples of the issues, definitions for classifying the theme content as an issue, and the criteria for rating the mother's solutions to the issues as either workable or unworkable were given in chapter 3. The content unit was that amount of data which represented a theme falling under one of the thirteen issues. Since the data were sequential, a theme arising a second time in one observation was coded a second time. When content reflected several themes, each theme was coded as to the maternal issue represented. Thus, some units were subjected to multiple coding In all, 2,864 theme units were coded into maternal issues.

*Reliability.* To determine reliability in the classification of

TABLE 1. BACKGROUND AND HISTORY OF ELEVEN STUDY MOTHERS

| Subject | Age | Class | Number of Previous Children | Delivery Complications | Previous Hospitalization for Mental Illness | Admission Diagnosis | Age of Baby at Mother's Admission | Age of Baby When Joint Admission Began |
|---|---|---|---|---|---|---|---|---|
| Mrs. C | 24 | I | 0 | 0 | + | Borderline schizophrenia | 22 mo. | 23½ mo. |
| Mrs. D | 28 | IV | 0 | 0 | 0 | Postpartum psychotic depression | 3 wk. | 3 mo. |
| Mrs. E | 29 | I | 3 | 0 | 0 | Borderline schizophrenia | 7 mo. | 8 mo. |
| Mrs. H | 30 | I | 2 | 0 | 0 | Postpartum anxiety reaction | 5 mo. | 6 mo. |
| Mrs. I | 24 | II | 1 | 0 | 0 | Acute schizophrenic reaction | 4 wk. | 2½ mo. |
| Mrs. J | 18 | IV | 0 | 0 | 0 | Postpartum psychosis | 15 days | 3 mo. |
| Mrs. A | 28 | IV | 2 | 0 | + | Schizophrenic reaction paranoid chronic | 23 mo. | 24 mo. |
| Mrs. B | 28 | III | 2 | + | 0 | Postpartum psychotic depression | 3 wk. | 2 wk. |
| Mrs. F | 23 | IV | 0 | + | 0 | Paranoid schizophrenic reaction postpartum | 3 wk. | 2½ wk. |
| Mrs. G | 28 | I | 1 | + | 0 | Paranoid schizophrenia | 2½ mo. | 5 mo. |
| Mrs. K | 43 | III | 4 | 0 | + | Borderline schizophrenia | 3 mo. | 3 mo. |

clinical data as to specific maternal issues, and in the rating of the solutions to maternal issues, three expert judges made independent ratings of a sampling of the clinical excerpts. A judging manual was constructed, following the rules used by the investigator. Each excerpt of clinical data, selected and identified by the investigator as falling under a particular maternal issue, was typed on a card. Only the phase was identified; this identification seemed permissible since the phase is determined by time and specific events which require no judgments. Seventy-one excerpts, in which multiple coding would not be required, were submitted to the judges.

The judges, using only the manual, classified each excerpt as a specific maternal issue, and rated each as to the mother's solution (workable or unworkable approach) of the issue

TABLE 1 (continued)

| Sex of Baby | Emotional Illness in Maternal Parents | Mother's Parental Preference | Patient's Opinion of Husband | Private Psychotherapy before Admission | Years Married | Length of This Hospitalization | Post Discharge Follow-up | Hospital Outcome | Mothering Style |
|---|---|---|---|---|---|---|---|---|---|
| F | 0 | Mo | More intelligent but passive | + | 3 | 5 mo. | 2 yr. | S | II |
| F | Mo | Fa | More intelligent, decision maker | 0 | 7 | 4 mo. | 2½ yr. | S | II |
| M | Mo | Fa | Superior in all aspects | + | 9 | 11 mo. | 2½ yr. | S | II |
| F | 0 | Mo | More intelligent, successful | + | 8 | 2½ mo. | 2½ yr. | MS | II |
| F | 0 | Mo | Sensitive, creative | 0 | 2 | 3½ mo. | 2½ yr. | MS | I |
| F | Mo | Fa | Dominant, unsure, selfish | 0 | ⅓ | 3 mo. | 2½ yr. | MS | I |
| M | Mo/Fa | 0 | Deserted her but she still loves him | 0 | 9 | 5 mo. | 0 | U | I |
| M | Fa | Mo | Domineering; she is afraid of him | 0 | 7 | 2 mo. | 0 | U | II |
| M | 0 | 0 | Passive, a failure | 0 | 3 | 10 mo. | 2½ yr. | U | I |
| M | Fa | 0 | Passive, tied to mother | 0 | 7 | 7 mo. | 1 yr. | U | I |
| M | Mo/Fa | 0 | Indifferent | 0 | 20 | 3 mo. | 0 | U | I |

identified. The judges had no training sessions or previous contact with the clinical data; they did not compare their judgments.

To determine the degree of agreement between investigator and judges, a comparison was made between the judges' classifications and ratings and those of the investigator, which had been completed before the judging. After familiarizing themselves with the manual, the judges obtained an average reliability figure of 77 percent across the three phases.

## DATA ANALYSIS AND FINDINGS

Mothers were grouped first according to "outcome of hospitalization" and second according to "mothering style."

The number of theme units coded under each maternal issue was recorded for each mother, and the frequency of ratings on the issues was recorded.

For each outcome group (S, MS, U), the recorded raw scores were converted to percentages based on the total number of theme units for each phase. The result was a percentage distribution of theme units and a percentage distribution of the "workable/unworkable" ratings of these units. The three outcome groups were then compared as to the percentage of responses under each issue and the percentage of "workable/unworkable" ratings.

For each of the two mothering style groups, the frequencies of themes and ratings under each maternal issue for each phase were converted into percentages, and the two groups were compared to determine which group showed more workable solutions.

To maximize the possibility of generating useful hypotheses in our discussion of the results, we have employed an arbitrary rule of thumb, such that a difference of ten or more percentage points between groups (in tables 2 and 3) have been interpreted as meaningful, although no formal test of statistical significance has been applied.

*Outcome and Selected Historical Data.* Associated with unsuccessful outcome of hospitalization are an initial diagnostic statement of paranoid tendencies, the masculine sex of the baby, and complications of delivery. Furthermore, U mothers, with one exception, had no parental preference and viewed their husbands less favorably than did S and MS mothers. S and MS mothers most often themselves had emotionally ill mothers, whereas both parents of U mothers were often mentally ill. We shall refer to these relationships in our further discussion of the findings.

*Outcome and Sex or Birth Complications.* Findings related to the sex of the baby and complications at the time of delivery gain interest when tied into other clinical knowledge. U mothers, in general, were especially desirous of having this particular baby. The sex of the baby was of great importance to them, in contrast to the S and MS mothers, who claimed more mixed feelings about their pregnancies or who had not wanted to be pregnant. Three of the five U mothers had boys but wanted girls. Expectations were that a girl could receive all the pretty clothes and attention from the mother that she had not had from her own mother. Also, these mothers felt a need for an alliance "against" all the males in the family. For the two U mothers who had boys and had wished for a boy, expectations, although different, were extremely high. The U mothers felt that they must be "something special" to their sons and they would be "most responsible" for how their sons "turned out."

Within the group of U mothers, expectations during pregnancy reached such rigid and narcissistic proportions that they bore no relation to reality. Knowing this fact and knowing also how these same mothers responded to their deliveries, one is deeply touched by their disappointment. Two of the U mothers required Caesarean section, and the third, after a long, strenuous delivery and sudden onset of alopecia totalis (baldness) was found to have a bicornate uterus. Without exception, these three women felt that their bodies had failed them and that they were constitutionally inferior as women. When they found themselves withdrawing and failing as mothers, they were depressed and bitter.

*Outcome and Diagnosis.* There is strong evidence that the U mothers tended to have a less stable life style, barren of meaningful relationships. Repeatedly, staff statements concerning these mothers focused on their hostile, blaming, and critical behavior toward the nurses, the treating physicians, and their own families. Regression and confusion upon admission were not as operant in the U mothers as in the S and MS mothers. It is curious that the U mothers did not demonstrate hallucinations or bizarre delusions, whereas MS mothers, in particular, did. One MS mother, fearing that she was to be a victim of "the strangler," converted this thought to the idea that the "communists are taking over the country." This idea remained with her after discharge from the hospital. The U mothers were more often diagnosed as paranoid schizophrenic.

These data suggest that diagnosis may not be the relevant factor in predicting outcome of hospitalization. Rather, the mothers' ways of relating to other people, compounded by profound disappointment in their present lives, led to conflict between these mothers and the staff. Additional support for this proposition emerges as we examine the data relevant to the maternal issues and mothering styles.

*Outcome and Duration of Phases.* The total number of days spent in all three phases is not identical with the total length of hospitalization, for some mothers remained on the wards after their babies were sent from the hospital. The MS group had an average hospital stay of three months; the S group stayed longest with a mean of six months; and the U group stayed 5.4 months.

The three groups differed in the average number of days spent in each of the three phases which encompass the thirteen maternal issues. The S mother (N = 3) averaged 31 days in phase I (orientation), 19 days in phase II (decision), and 117 days in phase III (joint admission). Thus the S group was involved in phase III for 70 percent of its total time in all phases. By contrast, MS mothers (N = 3) averaged 26, 8, and 31 days, respectively, in the phases. MS mothers spent 40 percent of their time in phase I, distinctly more than S and U groups. U mothers (N = 5) averaged 12, 22, and 56 days, respectively, in the three phases. Of the three groups, U mothers had the shortest phase I (13 percent of their time in phases) and the longest phase II (24 percent of their time in phases). It should be noted that MS and U groups each included one mother who, by virtue of assuming care of the baby on admission, was scored zero days for phases I and II. In spite of this, S mothers still spent the most time in phase III.

In summary, S mothers spent 70 percent of their total time for all phases in phase III. MS mothers averaged 40 percent of their time in phase I, far exceeding the other groups. U mothers averaged 24 percent in phase II, more than twice each of the other groups.

*Outcome and Maternal Issues.* The total pool of 2,864 statements coded with regard to maternal issues was analyzed in terms of the frequency with which each issue (in phase) was represented in the process notes of patients in the three outcome groups. Table 2, last item, shows that 1,992 of the statements (almost

70 percent) pertain to phase III. S mothers have the highest frequency of phase II incidents, while MS mothers are slightly higher than the other groups in phase I, but considerably lower in phase III.

In table 2, for each outcome group, the frequency of each issue in each phase is expressed as a percentage of the total incidents in the phase. For example, in phase I, 33 percent of the theme content units of the process data for S mothers were classified as issue 3, "dealing with conflicts."

During phase II, S mothers tended to deal less frequently with equipment matters and more frequently with the other issues. In phase III, S mothers tended to have a higher percentage of incidents relating to the issue of motherhood.

TABLE 2. OUTCOME VERSUS FREQUENCY OF CODED MATERNAL ISSUES (Frequency for each issue is expressed as a percentage of the total for all issues within a phase.)

| | Outcome of Hospitalization | | |
|---|---|---|---|
| Phases and Issues | Successful | Moderately Successful | Unsuccessful |
| Phase I | | | |
| Issue 1. Relation to staff | 29% | 33% | 23% |
| Issue 2. Relation to family | 14 | 18 | 22 |
| Issue 3. Dealing with conflicts | 33 | 22 | 26 |
| Issue 4. Dealing with treatment | 24 | 27 | 29 |
| | 100% | 100% | 100% |
| Phase II | | | |
| Issue 1. Nurse | 45% | 36% | 43% |
| Issue 2. Baby | 47 | 32 | 37 |
| Issue 3. Equipment | 8 | 32 | 20 |
| | 100% | 100% | 100% |
| Phase III | | | |
| Issue 1. Nurse | 18% | 18% | 24% |
| Issue 2. Baby care | 23 | 23 | 26 |
| Issue 3. Patients | 8 | 8 | 8 |
| Issue 4. Motherhood | 23 | 16 | 10 |
| Issue 5. Self-control | 19 | 22 | 20 |
| Issue 6. Home | 9 | 13 | 12 |
| | 100% | 100% | 100% |

| Number of Coded Incidents per Phase | | | |
|---|---|---|---|
| | S | MS | U | Totals |
| Phase I | 141 | 165 | 133 | 439 |
| Phase II | 184 | 120 | 129 | 433 |
| Phase III | 871 | 319 | 802 | 1,992 |
| Totals | 1,196 | 604 | 1,064 | 2,864 |

Across all three outcome groups, table 3 indicates a relatively even distribution of frequencies for the issues within each phase, but it should be noted that four issues show a difference of at least 10 percent between the three groups: in phase I, issue 3, "dealing with conflicts"; in phase II, issue 2, "baby," and in issue 3, "equipment"; and in phase III, issue 4, "motherhood."

Table 3 compares the three outcome groups in terms of the percentage of incidents within each issue which were rated unworkable (Unw) and workable (W).

TABLE 3. OUTCOME VERSUS RATED APPROACH TO MATERNAL ISSUES (Approach is expressed as a percentage of unworkable and workable approaches to each issue for each outcome group.)

| | Successful | | Moderately Successful | | Unsuccessful | |
|---|---|---|---|---|---|---|
| Phases and Issues | Unw (%) | W (%) | Unw (%) | W (%) | Unw (%) | W (%) |
| Phase I | | | | | | |
| Issue 1. Relation to staff | 24 | 76 | 41 | 59 | 42 | 58 |
| Issue 2. Relation to family | 40 | 60 | 66 | 34 | 72 | 28 |
| Issue 3. Dealing with conflicts | 74 | 26 | 76 | 24 | 86 | 14 |
| Issue 4. Dealing with treatment | 33 | 67 | 44 | 56 | 71 | 21 |
| All issues, phase I | 45 | 55 | 54 | 46 | 71 | 29 |
| Phase II | | | | | | |
| Issue 1. Nurse | 47 | 53 | 56 | 44 | 40 | 60 |
| Issue 2. Baby | 48 | 52 | 63 | 37 | 77 | 23 |
| Issue 3. Equipment | 31 | 69 | 30 | 70 | 58 | 42 |
| All issues, phase II | 46 | 54 | 50 | 50 | 57 | 43 |
| Phase III | | | | | | |
| Issue 1. Nurse | 29 | 71 | 37 | 63 | 51 | 49 |
| Issue 2. Baby care | 44 | 56 | 47 | 53 | 52 | 48 |
| Issue 3. Patients | 40 | 60 | 44 | 56 | 61 | 39 |
| Issue 4. Motherhood | 42 | 58 | 38 | 62 | 55 | 45 |
| Issue 5. Self-control | 52 | 48 | 42 | 58 | 66 | 34 |
| Issue 6. Home | 50 | 50 | 45 | 55 | 60 | 40 |
| All issues, phase III | 44 | 56 | 42 | 58 | 56 | 44 |

Of the three groups, U mothers have the highest percentage of unworkable approaches in all phases. S mothers exceed MS mothers in percentage of workable approaches during phase I, but the two groups are similar in later phases. Intergroup differences on individual maternal issues will be discussed below.

*Maternal Issues in Phase I.* During all phases, the U mothers fared less well qualitatively and quantitatively on the maternal issues (table 2). The quantitative differences suggest that not only do the U mothers tend to move away from the nurse as well as away from the clarification of their differences, but that the nurse moves away from the mother.

In phase I this is clearly indicated by the paucity of process notes recorded about the U mothers, and by the notations that the mother had difficulty in dealing in a constructive manner with the issues (table 3). Exceptions to this were instances in which mothers needed special nurses because the acute psychosis manifested itself in confused and bizarre behavior; at these times, extensive notes were recorded. This does not mean that other mothers were not acutely psychotic. What it does reflect is that certain behavioral manifestations of psychotic states engaged the nurse more than did others. On the other hand, S mothers involved the nurses more than did U mothers, and these contacts tended to be more positive in terms of performances on maternal issues. What factors contribute to more frequent and more constructive mother-nurse relationships?

Since the whole concern of phase I is the orientation to the hospital and treatment personnel, family separation and problems, it is remarkable that the U mothers had the least amount of staff time spent with them before they were asked to bring in their babies. Very little effort was devoted by either the mother or the nursing staff to clarifying which member of the staff was available for what type of assistance. To a lesser extent, this was manifested in the S group of mothers. In the MS group, two mothers were acutely psychotic, and there was more mother-nurse interaction in which the nurse had clarified to some degree her position of assistance. The delineation of function in this case seemed to have been facilitated by the nature of the mother's condition; her confusion and difficulty in relating herself to her immediate surroundings were obvious, and the objectives of the nurse were more clearly understood and accepted. The nurse assisted the mother in maintaining self-control and orientation to time, place, and person. Rudimentary activities such as feeding, bathing, dressing, and administering medications were the major reasons for the nurse's contacts with the mother. These were the activities most familiar to the nurse, and she was quite prepared to adapt her behavior to the needs of the helpless, dependent mother.

As the acute turmoil subsided, the nurse was required to change to quite another level of interaction in order to assist the mother. Now she had to relate to the mother's more intimate problems of dealing with people. This required different skills and insights to direct her own behavior for the mother's welfare. It is very difficult to help a mother who both wants and recoils from assistance—even fighting treatment efforts. Analysis of the incidents dealing with the study mothers' orientation to and acceptance of the various treatment methods (phase I, issue 4) clearly indicates that the U mothers were less positive in their responses to treatment efforts. The mothers were often specific in criticizing the treating physician or the nursing staff. They belittled the staff's efforts to assist in clarifying problems, meeting with family members, or attending group meetings. Sometimes the denigration was general, accompanied by depression, the mother claiming that no one could help her or that she needed no help or that she needed only to return home. Sometimes a mother did not respond to any care given her and continued in a condition which was upsetting to the staff, necessitating some drastic measure such as electro-shock treatment. In these situations, a sense of futility and defeat dominated the nursing staff's attitude toward the mother. Interestingly enough, the nurses did not verbalize their private doubts and suspicion of the mother's capabilities, but they acted upon their feelings by avoiding her.

A similar sense of futility and defeat on the part of the treating physician was handled differently. The physicians of U mothers often expressed the opinion that their therapy sessions with a mother were "unproductive." If the mother brought her baby in, the doctor reasoned, she would have more to talk about in therapy. Thus the U mother was confronted sooner than the MS or S mother with the suggestion to bring the baby into the hospital. The treating staff, in this way, attempted to negotiate a crucial decision with a mother when no treatment alliance had been established. This was particularly difficult for the mothers. One must realize that the mother is overwhelmed by her fearful and hostile thoughts about her baby. She cannot verbalize and thus free herself of these disturbing fantasies unless she has confidence in the staff. She feels shame and guilt, but, most importantly, she feels that if her secrets are revealed she will be declared an unfit mother, incarcerated for the rest of her life, and her baby will be taken away.

Unlike the more successful mothers, the U mothers' orientation to being separated from their families was particularly stereotyped and negative. They expressed this in one of three positions: (1) they were passive, expressing abject hopelessness that the family would be reunited; (2) they expressed extreme guilt at being separated and felt pressed to return home; (3) they were totally opposed to returning home, blaming the families for their problems. This behavior contrasts sharply with that of the more successful mothers who expressed guilt and disappointment at being separated from their families and wanted to return, but realized they were ill and needed help. Similarly, the more successful mothers often acknowledged their symptoms, while the U mothers tended to deny or to keep secret very disturbing symptoms. Thus the U mothers were in no position to view the idea of bringing the baby into the hospital as particularly helpful, for hospitalization itself was not being experienced positively. In contrast, the more successful mothers had some positive experiences in their relationship with the staff and treatment methods. By the same token, the treating staff was more inspired by the positive effect of their efforts with the S mothers. It is not surprising that, during phases II and III, staff conflict was most often associated with the U. mothers.

Analysis of dominant characteristics in the U mothers' responses to maternal issues in phase I indicates that the crucial factor necessary for a positive mother-nurse relationship is that both sense that the treatment effort on the part of both physician and nurse is helpful.

As treatment progressed, we observed that an approach which was helpful in an earlier situation did not necessarily continue to be helpful or therapeutic. A staff nurse working with Mrs. F said, with deep disappointment, that she felt useful to Mrs. F when she was acutely psychotic; she could help her to recognize that she was misinterpreting events about her. But when the mother's behavior became less bizarre and she was attempting the care of her baby on the ward, she would not pay attention to the nurse or do as the nurse instructed. The nurse found she no longer enjoyed working with this mother. They disagreed and quarreled; the nurse felt that Mrs. F resented her presence. The nursing staff did not assess the consequences inherent in the initial type of assistance they were able to give this mother. Although the time came for Mrs. F to exercise more independence, the nursing staff continued to employ controlling techniques and approaches. The question of who was in control reached such seriousness that doctor, treating staff, and patient each demanded the right to determine the activities permitted the mother; one day, Mrs. F would be in command, the next, the treating staff would take charge. The result of this dilemma was a serious attempt by Mrs. F at suicide.

In contrast, Mrs. J, who was acutely psychotic, was attended by a staff nurse who was aware of the dominant role she herself needed to play at times when this mother lost her self-control. The nurse worked out a plan with Mrs. J whereby the mother gradually assumed the responsibility of seeking nursing staff when she needed assistance. The staff nurse assisted the mother in recognizing that the frightening aberrations she was experiencing were part of the illness and not a reality. She helped Mrs. J to develop other ways of handling her feelings toward her family when they visited, and she explored with her many aspects of the treatment methods. Mrs. J later recounted this period of her hospitalization and described her anger at those nurses who treated her "like a baby." She said she had a frightening desire to act "like a baby"; thus, when she encountered nurses who ordered her about like a child, she felt compelled to urinate on the floor and to go about nude, much to her own deep sense of shame and embarrassment.

The difficulties Mrs. F's nurse faced are not unusual. They can be partly avoided by recognizing that one has little control over another's behavior; that the one person a nurse can control is herself, and that she must exercise such control. In Mrs. J's case, the staff nurse gradually altered her own behavior to the end that the mother could reasonably exercise her own control. This was done deliberately and with the conviction that Mrs. J could eventually accomplish the goal of self-control.

*Nursing Propositions for Phase I.* The establishment of positive reciprocal relationships is inhibited when staff cannot recognize the defensive nature of disengaging behavior and therefore respond to it as if it were personal. All the U mothers were able, at times, to approach the maternal issues in a positive way. This observation is especially important because it indicates that the mothers did have some insight into their difficulties and did want some form of help. Operating from this assumption, the following propositions are found crucial to the nursing care in phase I.

1. The nurse's intentions and purposes must be well structured, and the mother must clearly understand them.

2. The nurse must not hesitate to state her professional responsibilities while simultaneously giving latitude to the mother's individual prerogatives. The nurse must tell the mother that her purpose is to assist in dealing with some aspects of the problems which have resulted in the mother's hospitalization, and that she has a right to make contact with the mother. By the same token, the mother has the right to make the decision as to what she wants to discuss and when.

3. The nurse must be able to differentiate those areas of ward living in which the mother has jurisdiction and those in which she does not.

4. The nurse must be prepared to evaluate and work through, when necessary, the mother's reactions to the latitude and to the restrictions of ward living.

5. The nurse must recognize her right and therapeutic responsibility to discuss with the mother matters under the maternal issues. At the same time, the nurse must learn to recognize the manner in which the mother attempts to avoid discussion. The defensive maneuvers must be made clear between mother and nurse, and efforts must be directed toward clarifying factors which elicit those responses.

6. The nurse must pay particular attention to her own reactions toward a mother. Withdrawal, disinterest, arguing, bullying, fear, disgust, or an excessive need to capitulate to the mother or to bargain with her, are indications that the therapeutic nature of the relationship is deteriorating and requires careful examination.

If these positions are not taken initially during the orientation period, particularly with those mothers who are adept at getting lost in a crowd, or those who can, with antagonism, intimidate people who intrude into the illness, phase II will be compounded by severe problems in the treatment alliance.

*Phase II.* The decision period is extremely important because it usually points out severe difficulties in the relations between mother and staff. The potentially unsuccessful mother and the nurse in our study both tended to concentrate their efforts on arranging for the baby's arrival. Continuing exploration of key factors during phase II particularizes the importance of the nurse in structuring situations in which the mother can talk about her baby without feeling the pressure of making a decison at a particular time. The focus of the exploration thus remains on the mother and what the baby means to her, and not a decision, which the mother may view as focusing more on the baby than on herself, or which she may view as more important to other people (the treating staff or her family) than to herself.

*Phase III.* The joint admission phase became the repository of the successes and failures of the first two phases. Even when previous difficulties had been worked through, the stress created by the baby's arrival reactivated the mother's earlier negative behaviors (suspicion, irritability, fear of the nurse's criticism, etc.), and she fell back into the pattern of defenses of the prior phases. A strong nurse-mother relationship during phase III became a central support upon which a mother was able to work through problems in relating to the baby or in caring for him, and to remobilize the gains she had made before the baby's admission. If the therapeutic alliance was weak or lacking, it became a point of intense antagonism from which a variety of struggles ensued (see table 3).

*Mothering Styles and Maternal Issues.* During phase III, as the mother attempted to establish and maintain the care of her child on the ward, two distinctive modes or patterns of maternal interaction become apparent—distant mothering and involved mothering. These groups were analyzed in relation to frequency and quality of performance on the maternal issues.

An almost equal number of mothers was assigned to each style: six to type I (distant) and five to type II (involved). The total number of coded incidents accrued by each of the two groups was almost identical: 1,444 for type I and 1,420 for type II.

In table 4 we see that, during phase I, type I mothers had the higher percentage of incidents coded as issue 4, but the lesser percentage in issue 3. During phase II, type I mothers had the higher percentage of incidents coded as issue 3 (deciding and arranging for the cooperation of family, staff, and patients for basic equipment, space, and the time for the baby's arrival).

TABLE 4. MOTHERING STYLES AND MATERNAL ISSUES

|  | Mothering Style | |
| --- | --- | --- |
| Phases and Issues | Type I | Type II |
| Phase I | | |
| Issue 1. Relation to staff | 31% | 27% |
| Issue 2. Relation to family | 16 | 19 |
| Issue 3. Dealing with conflicts | 22 | 33 |
| Issue 4. Dealing with treatment | 31 | 21 |
|  | 100% | 100% |
| Phase II | | |
| Issue 1. Nurse | 40% | 43% |
| Issue 2. Baby | 35 | 44 |
| Issue 3. Equipment | 25 | 13 |
|  | 100% | 100% |
| Phase III | | |
| Issue 1. Nurse | 22% | 17% |
| Issue 2. Baby care | 25 | .23 |
| Issue 3. Patients | 8 | 9 |
| Issue 4. Motherhood | 12 | 23 |
| Issue 5. Self-control | 21 | 19 |
| Issue 6. Home | 12 | 9 |
|  | 100% | 100% |
| Number of coded incidents per phase | | |
| Phase I | 245 | 194 |
| Phase II | 192 | 241 |
| Phase III | 1,007 | 985 |
| Totals for all phases | 1,444 | 1,420 |

During phase III, type II mothers had the higher percentage of incidents coded as issue 4 (working through commitment to baby and motherhood).

TABLE 5. MOTHERING STYLES AND RATED APPROACHES TO MATERNAL ISSUES

| Phases and Issues | Type I | | Type II | |
|---|---|---|---|---|
| | Unw (%) | W (%) | Unw (%) | W (%) |
| Phase I | | | | |
| Issue 1. Relation to staff | 41 | 59 | 29 | 71 |
| Issue 2. Relation to family | 73 | 27 | 49 | 51 |
| Issue 3. Dealing with conflicts | 82 | 18 | 74 | 26 |
| Issue 4. Dealing with treatment | 59 | 41 | 41 | 59 |
| All issues, phase I | 62 | 28 | 49 | 51 |
| Phase II | | | | |
| Issue 1. Nurse | 47 | 53 | 37 | 53 |
| Issue 2. Baby | 71 | 29 | 52 | 48 |
| Issue 3. Equipment | 38 | 62 | 40 | 60 |
| All issues, phase II | 54 | 46 | 48 | 52 |
| Phase III | | | | |
| Issue 1. Nurse | 50 | 50 | 30 | 70 |
| Issue 2. Baby care | 52 | 48 | 43 | 57 |
| Issue 3. Patients | 59 | 41 | 40 | 60 |
| Issue 4. Motherhood | 53 | 47 | 41 | 59 |
| Issue 5. Self-control | 62 | 38 | 51 | 49 |
| Issue 6. Home | 57 | 43 | 47 | 53 |
| All issues, phase III | 55 | 45 | 42 | 58 |

*Mothering Styles and Rating of Solutions to Maternal Issues.* Table 5 compares the mothers, grouped by styles of mothering, with reference to their solutions of the maternal issues. For each type, the proportion of total responses (to an issue) attributed to each rating is computed as a percentage. A difference of ten percentage points will be considered as meaningful.

Type II mothers scored the higher percentage of "workable approach" ratings on maternal issues 1, 2, and 4 in phase I, on issue 2 in phase II, and on issues 1, 3, 4, 5, and 6 in phase III.

*Discussion of Mothering Styles and Maternal Issues.* Type II mothers scored a higher percentage of "workable approach" ratings on maternal issues which we found to be critical prior to phase III in our analysis of maternal issues against outcome of hospitalization. These are issues 2 and 3 of phase I. In phase II, type II mothers more frequently addressed themselves to problems dealing with motherhood. Consequently, we have concluded that the patterns of mothering do not simply characterize mothers during a particular period of hospitalization but are, in fact, a manifestation of long-standing behavioral patterns.

*Mothering Styles and Outcome.* Of the six type I mothers, four were judged unsuccessful and two moderately successful. Of the five type II mothers, three were judged successful, one moderately successful, and one unsuccessful. All three S mothers were type II; four of the five U mothers were type I.

Although we found that type I mothers and U mothers responded similarly to the maternal issues, we have not concluded that type I mothers can be "expected" to have a poor outcome. A more prudent interpretation is that type I mothers tend to have a manner of relating to their babies and of avoiding particular issues which very frequently provokes the staff into behavior which is not therapeutic. The data suggest that it is possible to have a degree of success with women who do not relate in a close manner to their babies, and that it is also possible to fail with a mother who involves herself with her baby.

Important, then, is not the style of mothering after the baby arrives in joint admission, but rather the behavioral under-pinnings to the styles and how they emerge in relation to the treatment staff in the process of resolving the maternal issues before the baby arrives. Treatment failures may represent a misunderstanding of the person being treated and not, as is often prematurely concluded, a principle that people with certain characteristics are not amenable to treatment.

It seems to us that the interrelationship of the maternal issues, mothering styles, and family data of the mother should direct our attention much more to the ongoing experiences of the mother—and that recognition of these experiences and our reaction to them may be the most productive means at our disposal for helping the mother. It is quite clear that when a mother, despite her style of mothering, strikes a familiar and positive chord in us, she tends to profit from our work with her.

# part 3

## children of
## mentally ill mothers

*David H. Gallant*

. . . A little girl aged 5, living alone with her widowed mother, one day saw a scarecrow in a field adjacent to her home. It waved to her and whistled. She heard it say that it would come and get her. She told her mother, who was perturbed by what she heard and said that when she was small scarecrows sometimes got free and came into the house, and that when they did you could usually expect a death to take place. . . . The next morning the mother told her neighbor that "they" were not going to get her or her child and that she knew what they were up to. She and the child now slept in the basement, both in a state of great apprehension, and the mother began to have nightmares. She explained to the child that the "scarecrow people" were now devising all sorts of tricks such as dreams to get into the house and kill the occupants. According to the mother, it was the child that they were after and according to the child, it was the mother.

E. J. Anthony, "The influence of maternal psychosis on children—*Folie à deux*," in E. J. Anthony and T. Benedek, eds., *Parenthood* (Boston: Little, Brown, 1970), pp. 574–75.

My father ... is a man of painstaking and critical mind, who dislikes hastily improvised generalizations, and is not afraid of starting a fight when he finds historic truth twisted to fit respectable traditions. Among many other things he taught me the value of systematic work, even in small matters. My mother was very intelligent, energetic, and fundamentally a very kind person; her rather neurotic temperament, however, made our family life somewhat troublesome. One of the direct consequences of this situation was that I started to forego playing for serious work very early; this I obviously did as much to imitate my father as to take refuge in both a private and a non-fictitious world. Indeed, I have always detested any departure from reality, an attitude which I relate to the second important influential factor of my early life, *viz.*, my mother's poor mental health; it was this disturbing factor which at the beginning of my studies in psychology made me intensely interested in questions of psychoanalysis and pathological psychology. Though this interest helped me to achieve independence and to widen my cultural background, I have never since felt any desire to involve myself deeper in that particular direction, always much preferring the study of normalcy and of the workings of the intellect to that of the tricks of the unconscious.

Jean Piaget. In E. G. Boring, H. Werner, R. M. Yerkes, and H. S. Langfeld, eds., *A history of psychology in autobiography* vol. 4 (New York: Appleton, 1952), pp. 237–38.

# Introduction to Part 3

We have seen that joint admission provides a mother with an opportunity to resume care of her child in a protected and therapeutic setting. It further gives the staff of the hospital an opportunity both to observe and to intervene in the ongoing mother-child relationship. Clearly one of the major aims of this intervention is to influence favorably the development of the child, although increasing the mother's effectiveness and pleasure in her role and her sense of self-esteem are also objectives.

In chapter I we described our primary concerns at the time of our first joint admission. High on the list was the question of the influence of mentally ill mothers on their children. We were also interested in the impact upon a child which might be attributed to living in a psychiatric ward. Part 3 deals with the first matter in some detail through a survey of the literature on the children of psychotic mothers. Following this is an empirical study of a small number of children, some of whom lived on the ward, some of whom had care elsewhere, and some of whom had normal mothers. The study bears upon both sets of influences— the psychopathology of the mother and the effects of joint admission—and it explores mediating factors which might help to account for observed differences in the children. At present there are few alternatives for children of psychotic mothers other than to be cared for by their mothers. The potentially favorable impact of a setting such as joint admission which offers the child supplementary caretakers is important if we take seriously the deficits in personality and in mothering capacity to be reported in the fourth part of this book.

# 6

# Background, Aims, and Design of the Study

The systematic study of the children of mentally ill mothers was undertaken to fulfill three separate but interrelated research aims. The first was to determine whether the joint admission program had beneficial, indifferent, or negative effects upon the children. The possibility of physical harm to the children was a concern frequently expressed at the beginning, but at particular issue was whether the mental hospital was an appropriate environment for the care of an infant and for the development of a child during his early formative years. A number of theoretical and research studies have attributed to a distorted family environment a significant role in the development of psychopathology (Wynne, 1968). The distorted environment, characterized by contradictory, inconsistent, or vague communications, deviant or inconsistent roles, and aberrant behavior, is thought to influence behavior adversely at all stages of development. Does not a psychiatric hospital ward contain such noxious influences in abundance, besides presenting the child with a bewildering multiplicity of caretakers?

The second aim was to describe the characteristics of young children of psychotic mothers with particular reference to the significance of these characteristics for the later development of mental illness. Chidren of schizophrenic mothers are ten times as likely to develop schizophrenia as are children in the general population (Reisby, 1967). Knowledge of the development of such characteristics prior to the age of risk may help to delineate the pathogenic process and to formulate programs of primary prevention.

The third aim of this study was to explore the factors, forces, and processes which contribute (a) to the characteristics of young children of psychotic mothers and (b) to the effect that the joint admission program has upon the children. The child of a mentally ill mother experiences the mental illness as a change or disruption in his care; this care may or may not have been deviant before the onset of the illness. The child is also subjected to a number of secondary influences as a consequence of the illness. Because of her hospitalization he is separated from his mother and experiences the care of one or more surrogate caretakers in either a familiar or an unfamiliar environment. These separations, occurring at different ages, more or less frequently, take their toll (Yarrow, 1961, 1964). Perinatal complications, occurring with an increased incidence in mentally ill mothers, are known also to influence development adversely (Paffenberger, 1961; Sobel, 1961; Pasamanick et al., 1956). We shall explore, as far as the data permit, the probable contribution of these factors to the development of the children.

## REVIEW OF THE LITERATURE

To realize our aims we required more than the developmental test data and the qualitative summaries of the children's behavior which we had been gathering at the beginning of the study. To guide us in selecting for our investigation specific aspects of the children's behavior, we turned to a review of the literature. Reports of research on children of psychotic parents were our primary resource; we also found clues to possible early signs of later behavioral dysfunction in studies of the early developmental history of psychopathological adults and children, and in studies of sequelae of maternal illness and hospitalization, such as separation.

*Children of Psychotic Parents as a High-Risk Group.* Offspring of psychotic parents are a focus of research because they constitute a high-risk group for the later development of psychosis and other mental and emotional disorders. While the incidence of schizophrenia in the general population is slightly less than 1 percent, approximately 14 percent of children with one schizophrenic parent and 34 percent of children with two schizophrenic parents will themselves develop a schizophrenic disorder (Reisby, 1967; Rosenthal, 1966). As Mednick and McNeil (1968) and Garmezy (1971) have pointed out, the study of high-risk, vulnerable children offers several advantages over the study of pathological adults for the investigation of precursors of later pathology. These children, in most cases, have not been identified as deviant, and the differences existing between them and low-risk children are not confounded with the effects of institutionalization, drugs, or other therapies. Nor is their behavior attributable to the consequences of severe psychopathology, such as attempts at compensation for psychotic symptoms. Furthermore, distortions inherent in the process of retrospective reconstruction are avoided by limiting the study to current childhood behaviors.

*Characteristics of Children of Psychotic Parents.* A number of noteworthy studies have investigated the general adjustment and the incidence of emotional disorder in preadolescent and adolescent children of psychotic parents (Canavan and Clark, 1923; Cowie, 1961; Fanning et al., 1938; Preston and Antin, 1932; Sussex et al., 1963; Mass, 1957; Iwascki, 1957; Sunier and Meijers, 1951; Gardner, 1949; Lampron, 1933; Ekdahl et al., 1962). In general, their findings have been contradictory, and many of the studies are limited by small sample size, absence of control groups, and lack of standarized procedures and measures. They do suggest that children of psychotic mothers may be poorer in overall adjustment (Canavan, Ekdahl, Iwascki, Mass, Sussex) and that the impact of the parental illness on the child is related to the length of hospitalization, the type of overt symptomatology, and the length of time since the mother's illness (Cowie, Mass, Fanning, Iwascki). It is important to note, however, that a number of studies reported no increase in symptomatology or maladjustment in these children (Fanning, Preston, Sunier). ✓ See note.

Some later and more adequately controlled studies have examined more specific measures of adjustment and behavior.

McClellan and Pugh (1962) reported that eleven- to thirteen-year-old children of psychotic mothers lagged in grade placement and IQ as compared to classroom controls. This trend was strengthened when the comparison involved only the children of schizophrenic mothers.

Beisser, Glasser, and Grant (1967), using parental interviews and teacher ratings of children of hospitalized schizophrenic, hospitalized neurotic, and "normally adjusted" mothers, found more behavioral deviation in children of schizophrenic mothers than in children of normal control mothers. However, the differences were found only in codings of child behavior derived from maternal interviews and teacher ratings; indices of deviation obtained from paternal interviews did not differentiate among the groups, and the children of schizophrenic mothers were generally indistinguishable from the children of neurotic mothers. Beisser suggests that this was due to the presence of severe pathology in the hospitalized neurotic mothers. Four of the five individual behavior deviation items, derived from maternal interviews, which distinguished the two pathological groups from the "normal" families, represented aggressive or acting-out types of behavior. Beisser believes that this may have reflected a special sensitivity to these kinds of behaviors in the deviant homes, so that they were overreported and did not reflect real differences in the behavior of the children.

Anthony (1968, 1969), in an intensive clinical study of six- to twelve-year-old children of psychotic parents, reported a number of clinical disturbances in these children: the recurrence of "characteristic episodes of withdrawal, mistrustfulness, or extreme regression" (1968, p. 181). A small number of children exhibited "micropsychotic" episodes characterized as paranoid, or hebephrenic; some exhibited delusions, hallucinations, and other psychotic symptoms, usually, but not always, paralleling the parents' symptoms. Ten to twenty percent of the children exhibited a "brittle normality" (1969).

A number of genetically oriented studies of the incidence of schizophrenia in the offspring of schizophrenic parents have formed the basis of the risk figure reported above (Kallman, 1938; Rosenthal, 1966; Heston, 1966; Heston and Denney, 1968; Rosenthal et al., 1968). These studies emphasize that the offspring and other biological relatives of schizophrenics not only are predisposed to a schizophrenic disorder, but are also prone to develop some other form of psychopathology (Heston, 1966, 1968; Kety et al., 1968). Kety and his associates (1968, p. 359) have therefore proposed that it is more appropriate in high-risk groups to refer to a "spectrum of disorders having some features in common with schizophrenia but varying considerably in intensity."

These genetically oriented studies have focused mainly on the development of psychiatric symptoms during the period of risk. Mednick and Schulsinger (1968) have studied behavioral and physiological reaction patterns which might serve as precursors of psychopathology in adolescent children of schizophrenic mothers. They found that, in comparing the school reports of such children with those of a matched group of children of nonpsychiatric mothers, the high-risk group were seen as passive, nervous, upset, and withdrawn. Teachers observed that they had few friends and were shy, reserved, and silent. Their IQ (Wechsler Intelligence Scale for Children) was slightly though significantly lower; the differences were most manifest on the arithmetic and coding subtests. On a continuous word association test, the high-risk children gave more clang responses, chain associations, and repetitions of the response words. In comparing the two groups as to galvanic skin response to stress stimuli, that of the high-risk group was more rapid, greater in amplitude, generalized more and recovered more quickly.

Mednick and Schulsinger (1968) also compared twenty high-risk children who developed severely abnormal behavior subsequent to the initial behavior assessments ("sick group") with a matched group of high-risk children who had not succumbed to psychopathology ("well group") and a matched group of low-risk children ("low-risk group"). They were compared on measures taken prior to the onset of deviant behavior in the sick group.

The differences between the sick group and the well and low-risk groups on the initial measures were similar to the previously cited differences between the high-risk and the low-risk groups. When upset or excited, the reaction of the children in the sick group persisted longer than the reaction in the well or low-risk groups, and the children in the sick group were rated as more disturbing to the class. The IQ differences did not reach significance; however, on the continuous association test, the sick group "distinguished itself by frequently rattling off a whole series of words which were interrelated but contextually relatively irrelevant" (1968, p. 282). The sick group also tended, in its associations, to slide away from the original stimulus word, tending to associate more to the last response than to the original stimulus. The GSR of the sick group was more rapid, greater in amplitude, more generalized, recovered more quickly, and habituated less than the GSR of the well or low-risk groups.

The studies reviewed thus far indicate that a number of characteristics may differentiate preadolescent and adolescent high-risk children from their low-risk peers. A composite picture suggests that the high-risk child has a slightly lower IQ (McClellan and Pugh, 1962; Mednick and Schulsinger, 1968), may be socially withdrawn and unresponsive or aggressive and disruptive (Anthony, 1969; Beisser et al., 1967; Mednick and Schulsinger, 1968), may manifest poor school and social adjustment (Canavan and Clark, 1923; Ekdahl et al., 1962; Fanning et al., 1938; Beisser et al., 1967; Mass, 1957; Iwascki, 1957), may exhibit periodic psychotic symptoms (Anthony, 1968, 1969), and may present a picture of autonomic over-reactivity (Mednick and Schulsinger, 1968). Though these behavioral variables may not be directly transferred to the study of early infancy, one may investigate in young children behaviors either phenotypically similar or developmentally related to those features characteristic of older children of psychotic mothers (Garmezy, 1971).

Direct observations of the early development of children of psychotic mothers have been carried out by Sobel (1961), Fish (1963, 1971) and Fish and Alpert (1962, 1963). Though the findings are limited by the small number of subjects studied and the absence of normal control groups, the richness of observational detail gathered on these children over a period of time makes them a valuable source of potentially significant precursors of later pathology. Sobel followed eight children born to parents both of whom were schizophrenic. Half the children were reared by their biological parents and half were placed in foster homes. By eighteen months, three of the children (all reared by biological mothers) were hyperactive, appeared sad, showed little spontaneous play, and were irritable. Two of these three children evidenced motor retardation, one losing the ability to sit up after she had been sitting for a month.

Fish followed the early development of alertness, reactivity, motor development, social responsiveness, and vestibular function in sixteen infants of hospitalized, chronic schizophrenic mothers (Fish, 1963, 1971; Fish and Alpert, 1962, 1963). Four infants manifested marked early developmental deviations in the direction of excessive apathy or irritability. These deviations declined in time and by age two; only the most irritable child was still grossly deviant (Fish, 1963; Fish and Alpert, 1962, 1963). During the neonatal period, however, half of the infants showed an unusual pattern of arousal characterized by a dissociation between different components of arousal. A typical dissociated pattern was the presence of unusually alert visual following accompanied by abnormally reduced motor reactivity and absent crying (Fish, 1963). Disorders "of the timing and integration of neurological maturation" (Fish, 1971, p. 475) were observed in these infants, similar in kind to asynchronies previously observed in the early development of children who later were diagnosed as having childhood schizophrenia.

This [asynchrony] may affect any of the functions controlled by the central nervous system, but it can be measured most readily in the first year of life, when it affects postural and locomotor development, and in the next few years in visual-motor and language development.

There may be unusual fluctuations in the rates of various aspects of development, with periods of marked acceleration and retardation succeeding one another, sometimes with the transient loss of a previously acquired ability . . . . A child may be able to stand . . . precociously but be unable to roll over, or be able to roll over but be unable to sit [Fish, 1971, pp. 475–76].

These studies of young infants complement those discussed relative to older children. They suggest that young children of psychotic mothers may differ from low-risk children in demonstrating deviations of activity and reactivity, affect expression, attention maintenance, locomotor and visual-motor development, social responsiveness, and language development. They further suggest that there may be irregularities in the rate of development in such children. Previously acquired developmental achievements may momentarily regress. Some abilities may develop precociously while at the same time in the same child others may lag. "This may produce discrepancies between different functions (locomotion, visual-motor, language, and so on) or among several aspects of any one of them" (Fish, 1971, p. 476). The studies also suggest that deviations and maladaptations apparent early in the first year of life may not be readily detected after eighteen months of age.

*Early Adaptation of Psychopathological Adults and Children.* Studies utilizing fundamentally different designs have also provided clues to precursors of later pathology. Some studies utilized school records of pathological adults (Lane and Albee, 1963, 1964; Kasanin and Veo, 1932; Barthell and Holmes, 1968; Watt et al., 1970). Others followed into adult life the outcome of deviant child development, usually initially identified at a child guidance clinic, by using the clinic and other available records (Bowman, 1934; Birren, 1944; Wittman and Steinberg, 1944; Frazer, 1953; Nameche et al., 1964; Gardner, 1967; Morris et al., 1956; O'Neal and Robins, 1958; Robins, 1966). Another approach has been the longitudinal follow-up of unselected or normal populations of children, some of whom will develop subsequent behavioral deviations (Thomas et al., 1968).

The early adaptation of children with deviant behavioral outcome was characterized by lower tested intelligence than that of their classmates; they were poorer utilizers of their intellectual ability, and their achievement patterns tended to decline as they grew older (Birren, 1944; Lane and Albee, 1963, 1964). These intellectual and achievement deficits were accompanied by interpersonal and social maladaptive patterns. Some children exhibited a shy, withdrawn, anxious, depressed, "shut-in" personal and social orientation. Others showed antisocial, impulsive, "externalizing" social orientation involving interpersonal and classroom disruptiveness, inattentiveness, and, quite often, abuse and damage to people and property. Watt et al. (1970) reported that boys and girls manifest substantially different patterns of preschizophrenic school maladaptation. The boys were primarily disruptive, uncooperative, dysphoric, and antisocial, while the girls were primarily overinhibited, shy, and introverted. ✷

The hypothesis that later psychopathology may be preceded by early extremes of behavior, such as overactivity or under-activity, is supported by investigations using the longitudinal follow-up of an unselected population. Young children who developed developmental disorders, in the course of a longitudinal study of individual differences in temperament, were characterized as showing either active symptoms or passive symptoms (Thomas et al., 1968). These groups differed from each other and from the body of asymptomatic children on a number of prepathological temperamental characteristics: "The clinical cases were characterized by an excessive frequency of either high or low activity, irregularity, withdrawal responses to novel stimuli, nonadaptability" (p. 182). They were also under- or overintense in their responses, were more distractable, and tended to be either over- or underpersistent.

*Maternal Separation.* The voluminous literature on the effect of maternal separation has been ably summarized by a number of workers (Ainsworth, 1962; Casler, 1961; Yarrow, 1961). Few of the studies deal with situations directly comparable to the type of separation and age of children in our sample—a brief, reversible separation during the first two years of life. However, these studies do suggest that separation reactions are observed in children from the age of seven months (Schaffer and Callender, 1959; Spitz, 1946). Initial reactions are generally those of sadness, weeping, and apprehension (Heineke and Westheimer, 1965; Schaffer and Callender, 1959; Spitz, 1946). This may be followed by apathy and withdrawal, retardation of development, and possible loss of recently acquired developmental achievement (Spitz, 1946), a drop in development quotient (Spitz, 1946; Schaffer, 1965), disturbances of appetite and either refusal to eat (Spitz, 1946; Schaffer and Callender, 1959) or overeating (Heineke and Westheimer, 1965), and disturbances in interpersonal relations characterized by either fearful clinging and demandingness, or apprehensive, apathetic withdrawal, or the succession of one pattern by the other (Spitz, 1946; Schaffer and Callender, 1959).

The behavioral disturbances may persist for varying periods

following reunion with the family, although Schaffer (1965) reported that DQ returned to preseparation levels immediately following reunion. Factors such as the level of social stimulation during separation may influence the intensity and duration of some of these separation reactions. Schaffer found that young children receiving high levels of social stimulation during maternal separation manifested no DQ decrement; Rheingold (1956) reported that systematic social stimulation raised the level of social responsiveness in institutionalized infants.

## DATA COLLECTION

*Infant Behavior Scales.* Our survey of the reports of the three groups of studies—the development of children of psychotic mothers, the early adaptation of psychopathological children and adults, and the sequelae of short-term maternal separation— suggested that young children of psychotic mothers tend to develop deviations in domains of behavior broadly characterized as cognitive, interpersonal, and affective. These children tend to exhibit unevenness in the acquisition of locomotor skills and discrepancies in the level and rate of development of different behavior domains. They may evidence an increase in such behaviors as irritability, rocking, and head banging—behaviors symptomatic of developmental problems.

Accordingly, we developed a set of rating scales to assess aspects of cognitive, interpersonal, affective, and symptomatic behavior which could be observed and rated during the administration of a developmental test to young children. We also derived measures of developmental level and variability from the developmental test. Table 1 lists and briefly describes the infant behavior scales.

The domain of cognitive development was subdivided into separate groups of scales: language development, sensory-motor behavior, object manipulation, and attention deployment. Active language development, analogous to language production, and passive language development, analogous to language comprehension (Fraser et al., 1963), are separately rated on scales 1 and 2. Sensory-motor behavior contains four scales (3–6) for rating the child's success in cognitive attainment on developmental test items which tap theoretically different

## TABLE 1. DESCRIPTION OF INFANT BEHAVIOR SCALES

I. Cognitive development

A. Language development

1. *Active language development*. Spontaneously naming objects, pictures, people, asking for specific things, naming objects and pictures pointed to.
   1 = Very immature    4 = At age norm    7 = Very advanced

2. *Passive language development*. Pointing to named pictures and objects, following instructions.
   1 = Very immature    4 = At age norm    7 = Very advanced

B. Sensory-motor behavior

3. *Immediate memory*. The child's ability to respond appropriately to stimuli that were perceptually present earlier. Evaluated in situations where objects are hidden, beads secretly removed from a container, or hiding and finding games are played. Piaget's permanence tests are used here.
   1 = Very immature    4 = At age norm    7 = Very advanced

4. *Perceptual-motor behavior*. Responding to the particular perceptual characteristics of objects. Fitting forms into formboards. Putting pegs in holes. Thought to be analogous to perceptual analysis.
   1 = Very immature    4 = At age norm    7 = Very advanced

5. *Constructive behavior*. Emphasized here, rather than the fitting of objects with complementary contours into one another as in scale 4, is the placing of one object upon another, or putting together into new combinations or possibilities objects not usually associated. Thought to be analogous to divergent thinking.
   1 = Very immature    4 = At age norm    7 = Very advanced

6. *Effectual behavior*. Means-end behavior, causal behavior, using objects to achieve effects. Evaluated in tests such as getting the pellet out of the bottle, using a stick to extend reach, ringing bell.
   1 = Very immature    4 = At age norm    7 = Very advanced

C. Object manipulation

7. *Variety of object manipulation*. Rated from stereotypy at one end to great variety and originality at the other.
   1 = Very stereotyped; all objects manipulated in same way
   4 = Objects responded to in terms of their individual characteristics
   7 = Very varied: many objects handled in many different ways, some new and original

8. *Investment in objects*. At the low end, as well as the child who manipulates little, is the child who, though manipulating appropriately and sustainedly, does so with little affect. At the high end is the child who plays with gusto, looks forward to getting new objects.
   1 = Manipulates little or with little interest and animation
   4 = Manipulates appropriately with some affect
   7 = Much manipulation accompanied by animation

9. *Relative involvement in observation versus manipulation*. Whether the child is more of an observer than a doer is assessed.
   1 = Engages exclusively or predominantly in observation
   4 = Combines evenly or shifts easily from observation to manipulation
   7 = Engages exclusively or predominantly in manipulation

D. Attention deployment

10. *Duration of attention.* The length of time the child attends to what he is doing, whether looking or manipulating.
   1 = None or fleeting
   4 = Somewhat sustained (fifteen to thirty seconds)
   7 = Extended (more than ninety seconds)

11. *Distractibility.* The degree to which ongoing behavior is interrupted and interfered with by the occurrence of other stimulation, external or internal.
   1 = Completely absorbed in activity; impervious to interruption
   4 = Generally absorbed, but sometimes distracted
   7 = Extremely distractible; ongoing behavior constantly interfered with

12. *Persistence.* The child's ability to pursue directed activity, both when unimpeded and in the face of obstacles.
   1 = Extremely unpersistent; no directed effort
   4 = Moderately persistent; pursues things on four to five occasions
   7 = Extremely persistent; makes repeated and very vigorous efforts

13. *Impulsivity.* The degree to which desire results directly in action, rather than in reflection and consideration.
   1 = Extremely unimpulsive; always moves slowly and thoughtfully
   4 = Somewhat impulsive; responds fairly quickly and occasionally without observing or reflecting adequately
   7 = Extremely impulsive; responds immediately and quickly

II. Interpersonal behavior

14. *Reaction to strangers.* The extent and duration of the child's negative response to the tester and other strangers.
   1 = No reaction; no change in behavior or affect upon approach of a stranger
   4 = Definite inhibition, avoidance or crying, quickly clearing up
   7 = Extreme inhibition, avoidance or crying, sustained throughout testing session.

15. *Specificity of interpersonal relations.* The degree to which the child's relations with different people are different; the degree to which the interaction is colored by the person with whom the child is interacting.
   1 = Completely unspecific; reacts alike to all
   4 = Moderately specific; some activities modified by the person with whom the child is interacting
   7 = Completely specific; all activities modified by the person with whom the child is interacting

16. *Depth of interpersonal relations.* This refers to the intensity with which the child relates to people, the degree to which interaction matters, the energy that is bound up in it
   1 = Extremely shallow     4 = Somewhat deep     7 = Very deep

17. *Instrumental versus intrinsic relations.* The degree to which inter-actions are entered into for ulterior aims, with the person and the interaction serving as means to other ends, versus the degree to which interactions are entered into for their own sake, with the interaction an end in itself
   1 = Highly instrumental; all interactions serving instrumental aims
   4 = Interactions evenly divided between instrumental and intrinsic
   7 = All interactions intrinsic

18. *Relative involvement with objects and people.* The degree to which the child is invested in and interacts with and prefers things or people
1 = Exclusively or preponderantly involved with objects
4 = Divides attention and activity evenly between things and people
7 = Exclusively involved with people

III. Mood and affect

19. *Depression.* The degree to which depressive affect is manifested in crying or apathy or "sad" expression.
1 = Not at all.
4 = Moderately depressed—sadness expressed three to four times
7 = Extremely depressed—either crying sadly all the time or withdrawn and apathetic all the time

20. *Positive affect.* The degree to which positive affect is manifested in smiling, laughing, vocalizing.
1 = Not at all
4 = Moderately happy—positive affect expressed four to five times
7 = Extremely happy—positive affect manifest practically all the time

IV. Symptomatic behavior

21. *Symptomatic behaviors.* The frequency and duration of each of the following behaviors: finger sucking, mouthing objects, banging objects, throwing and dropping objects, rocking, head banging and crying.
1 = Not at all
2 = Slight, the behavior occurs once or twice
3 = Moderate—the behavior occurs three to four times
4 = Marked—the behavior occurs five or more times.

cognitive capacities (Meyers et al., 1964). The object manipulation scales center on the number and variety of schemas displayed in handling objects (7), the energy with which the child manipulates (8), and the balance between action and observation (9). Four scales (10–13) focus upon attention deployment; they probe attention duration (10), distractibility (11), persistence (12), and impulsivity (13).

The domain of interpersonal behavior samples the child's reaction to strangers (14), the specificity and depth of his observed relations (15 and 16), the degree to which interpersonal interaction by itself is rewarding (17), and the balance between interaction with inanimate objects and people (18). Scales 15 and 16 are global scales, with highly subjective rating criteria.

The domain of mood and affect rates expressions of depression or apathy (19), and positive affect (20)

Symptomatic behavior is studied by summing a rating of the frequency and duration of occurrence for a number of possibly pathognomonic behaviors displayed by children in the age groups studied (scale 21).

*Reliability of the Scales.* After the scales had been defined and experience obtained in their utilization, ambiguities of definition and criteria of scale point placement were clarified. Reliability was then estimated for two aspects : (1) inter-observer reliability, i.e., the degree of agreement between two independent raters rating the same child at the same time; and (2) test-retest reliability, i.e., the stability of a particular behavior over time.

To evaluate inter-observer reliability, two observers made independent ratings immediately after developmental test sessions on nine different children. The reliability is reported as percent inter-observer agreement. For each scale, the possible range is from 0, if the observers rated differently in all nine cases, to 100%, if they agreed in all nine. For the seven-point scales, the inter-observer agreement ranged from 22% to 88%, with the average agreement, 52.8%. If, instead of comparing complete inter-observer agreement, we compare the number of times the observers rated within one scale point of each other, the reliabilities are considerably higher. Agreement within one scale point ranged from 67% to 100% for the seven-point scales, averaging 87.6%. On the four- and five-point scales, the average complete inter-observer agreement was 70%, and the average of agreement within one point was 98%.

For an estimate of the test-retest reliability of the scales, five children between the ages of one and two were retested and rated three months after their initial ratings. The test-retest reliability proved to be almost exactly as stable as the interobserver reliability. For the seven-point scales the average complete agreement was 49.7%; the average agreement within one scale point was 86.9%. For the four-point scales the average complete agreement was 65% and the average agreement within one scale point was 90%.

The least reliable scales and those scales on which all children received identical ratings were dropped from subsequent use, leaving the scales as described in table 1. We concluded from the reliabilities that the scales measured characteristics of the children rather than characteristics of the examiners, that they measured facets of behavior relatively stable over a short period of time, and that they did not reflect more momentary or fleeting influences.

*Developmental Test Measures.* To supplement the information provided by the rating scales, measures of developmental level and variability were derived from the Bayley and Cattell developmental tests. The measure of developmental level used was the DQ, an index analogous to IQ. It places the child's development in relation to other children his age. A DQ of 100 is average; a higher DQ indicates relative advancement, and a lower DQ relative retardation.

The measure of developmental variability used was an index of intra-test scatter. A child's performance on the Bayley or Cattell scale is represented by a range of items, some of which are passed and some of which are failed, bounded by a block of items all of which are passed (basal level) and a block of items all of which are failed (ceiling level). A child who passes all items at a given age level and fails all items above that level shows no irregularity or "scatter" in his performance. The larger the zone of passes and fails, the greater the scatter. Harris and Shakow (1937, 1938) reviewed a number of studies utilizing different measures of scatter. The measure of scatter we have devised is simple and straightforward. It is the difference in days between the age placement of the first ceiling item and the age placement of the last basal item.

Such scatter may be indicative of two sets of developmental problems. First, it may reflect momentary distractions or absences, deficient ability to maintain a task set, or a variety of other phenomena generally categorized as attentional problems (Rapaport et al., 1968). Second, high intra-test scatter may be due to unevenness of development. At any age, the items in a developmental scale are sampled from different behavioral areas: locomotor development, prehension development, perceptual discrimination, language development, and so forth. High variability can indicate either underdevelopment in one or more areas or precocious development in one or more areas, or a combination of retardation and precocity. Hence it may serve as an index of the developmental asynchronies which Fish (1971) described.

*Study Procedure*. Seven children of joint admission mothers are the central subjects of the study. Three comparison groups (to be described more fully below) were selected: (1) a group of seven children whose psychotic mothers had not participated in the joint admission program (non-joint admission children); (2) a group of fourteen children of nonhospitalized normal mothers; (3) a group of six children of normal mothers for comparison with the joint admission children at an age younger than that at which the first two groups were compared with the joint admission group.

The joint admission children were tested bi-weekly during their mothers' hospitalization. After discharge, they were tested every six weeks until their first birthday, and every three months during their second year.

These testing sessions and observation periods took place on the ward, in an observation room at the hospital, or at the patient's home. Each session consisted of a brief interview and observation period, followed by the administration of a developmental test. The sequence of items administered and the pace of the test were adapted to the child's tempo and the setting. At the end of the session the test was scored, and a brief summary of the highlights of the child's development was dictated and subsequently transcribed. When the rating scales of infant behavior had been developed and introduced into the data collection program, the children were rated after the developmental test had been scored and before the developmental summary was dictated.

The Bayley Scales of Mental and Motor Development (Bayley, 1965) were used during the first year of the child's life. Since the form available at the time was standardized only to the age of fifteen months, the Cattell Infant Intelligence Scale (Cattell, 1946) was used during the second year of the child's life. This procedure was followed for the children in the comparison groups.

*Criteria for Group Differences*. Because of the small number of children in the present study and the great number of variables influencing their development, we view this research as an exploratory study. To explore patterns of similarities and differences between groups, we have adopted an arbitrary criterion for group differences. For the rating scale data, the criterion is an average difference of six-tenths of a scale point, with the further requirement that this difference not be contributed by one deviant case. Differences in DQ and scatter are accompanied by a $p$ value for a $t$-test. In this study, however, the $p$ value is not intended as an estimate of the likelihood that such a difference occurred by chance, but rather as a descriptive indication of the relative magnitude of the difference.

# 7

# Development of Joint Admission Children

## TWO CASE HISTORIES

*Joe.* Joe was seen at eight months of age in a foster home where he had been living for four months following an unsuccessful period of joint admission; his mother had been hospitalized two weeks after his birth. He was receiving very adequate care in a comfortable suburban home from a competent, warm mother with a five-year-old son of her own.

Although Joe was developing well normatively (DQ 113), there were marked unevennesses in his development. His mental scale DQ was twenty points higher than his motor scale DQ, and there was even more marked unevenness in his motor development. Although he was walking very well with a little support and cruising adroitly around the house in a walker, he was singularly helpless when left to his own devices. He neither crawled nor raised himself to a sitting position; although, reportedly, he occasionally turned from his back to his abdomen, he did not do so during the visit, crying when placed on his back.

He was very interested in exploring the properties of things· turning, fingering, and ringing a little handbell; examining a toy car closely, fingering the parts separately and rotating the wheels; looking attentively at colored pictures in a baby book. However, he seemed quite *unspecific* in his social behavior. He was not bothered by the investigator's presence, and did not protest being separated from his foster mother and placed in a highchair by the investigator; nor did he need to keep her in view or otherwise reassure himself of her presence while so separated. Once, after presenting some objects to him on the tray of the highchair, I thought it would be better to remove the tray and push the chair against the table. As I removed the tray, Joe, apparently attempting to follow his reflection in the tray, toppled out of the chair. I caught him halfway down with his head below his feet. He was distressed and cried, but was consoled by me, did not reach for his foster mother, and could soon be placed back in his chair, manipulating toys. He was, however, socially responsive and initiated social interaction, but primarily on the basis of proximity and immediate need.

The unevenness of his development was reflected in his test scatter, which was higher at this time than at nineteen months. Although the cognitive-motor discrepancy diminished gradually, disappearing by fifteen months, his lack of preference for his natural mother clearly persisted even after being reunited with her for some time, with Joe occasionally turning toward the stranger for reassurance rather than to his mother, and manifesting indifference to the arrival and departure of strangers. However, by nineteen months of age, nine months after reunion with his mother, Joe was occasionally seen to turn to her for comforting during our home visits.

*Becky.* Becky, eight months old, was observed ten weeks after her mother's discharge. Although her DQ was 103, age-appropriate, she too was uneven in her development. She was friendly, curious, and responsive, as was Joe, but motor development lagged behind mental development: 23.5 points separated the motor DQ of 90.2 from the mental DQ of 113.7.

In contrast to her excellent perceptual, manipulatory, and linguistic development, her motor development was markedly retarded. She was unable to sit alone longer than momentarily, and did not crawl or support her weight on her feet when held erect. She tended to sit with her arms held stiffly extended, the fingers extended and fanned, and, while sitting, she would move suddenly to the right or the left thrashing her arms and legs. Either prone or supine, she periodically stiffened her trunk and arched her back.

Her motor retardation, awkwardness, and mannerisms gradually disappeared. By twelve months, the arm posturing and other motor mannerisms had disappeared and failed to reappear for the duration of our contact. At eighteen months, when she had been walking independently for three or four weeks, she was still moving around awkwardly. This motor development was accompanied by a decrease in intra-test scatter.

Becky's reaction to her mother's arrival and departure varied from time to time. At the visits at twelve and fifteen months, she manifested indifference; at eighteen months, mild distress; at twenty-one months, indifference; and at twenty-four months, prolonged and severe distress. By twenty-one months, a tendency toward compulsive behavior and defenses was noted: she appeared concerned with order, with keeping things in their places, and with cleanliness. She spent a good deal of time playing with the formboard, arranging the Stanford-Binet clock sequence, and wiping and cleaning the doll's face, hands, and feet.

The other children whom we came to know displayed varied though similar lines of development, showing early unevennesses and symptoms that diminished in time, though there were usually some residual problems.

## SPECULATIONS AND PREDICTIONS

How are we to understand why this improvement took place? It seems reasonable to suppose that a mother who experiences a serious emotional disturbance early in the life of her child may adversely influence the child's development through a number of avenues: by providing inadequate physical care; by providing erratic, contradictory, insufficient, or overwhelming stimulation; and by being either withdrawn emotionally or inappropriately angry at her child. Further, the mother's hospitalization interrupts the developing mother-child bonds and creates discontinuity in caretaking. These factors, we reasoned, would adversely affect the child's intellectual development, leading to developmental asynchronies and consequently more variable development. They would also result in affective and interpersonal disturbances such as depression, anxiety, excessive clinging or dependency or apathetic withdrawal.

Time, we speculated, would contribute in part to the improvement in the children. As the period of acute upset receded, there would be increased opportunity to marshal defensive and adaptive resources to deal with the multiple disturbances occasioned by the mother's illness. This process would take place with both joint admission and non-joint admission children.

The joint admission procedure may facilitate this process through a number of routes: reducing the period of maternal separation; taking some pressure off the mother by permitting her to care for the child in a context where resources such as baby-sitters are available; helping the mother to acknowledge, confront, and work through—in the child's presence—issues in her illness which relate to the child; and educating the mother to provide positive support for the child's development. These factors, we hoped, would diminish to some degree the adverse consequences of maternal mental illness for the child.

*Prediction of Results of Testing.* We therefore predicted that joint admission children, although developing less adequately than normal children, would develop more satisfactorily than non-joint admission children and would be more even in their development as reflected in less test scatter; they would be more advanced in cognitive development as reflected in a higher DQ and in higher ratings on language development and other scales assessing cognitive development; they would do better than non-joint admission children on a number of scales designed to measure adaptive aspects of cognitive processes: measures of object manipulation and attention; and they would interact more and in a more differentiated manner with people, express more affect, and behave less symptomatically.

## POST-DISCHARGE TESTING

In order to explore the effects of the joint admission program upon the development of the children, we felt it desirable to evaluate the children at a time several months after their mothers' discharge. This time lapse was to allow for the subsidence of the immediate effects of the mother's illness on the family—the stresses attendant upon separation and the strain of the mother's negotiating her return to the community and her family.

It seemed essential to compare the children at ages as nearly uniform as possible to reduce to a minimum the variability within our small group. From the group of joint admission children whom we had followed with periodic testing, we selected the test nearest to the child's eighteen-month birthday, provided that this test occurred six or more months after the mother's discharge. The application of these criteria yielded a group of seven children, eighteen months old, tested ten months (on average) after maternal hospitalization. Their development was then compared with that of a group of children of mentally ill mothers who had *not* experienced joint admission. Effort was made to match the groups on the following characteristics: age at time of testing, sex of child, birth order, number of children in the family, age of child at admission, length of hospitalization, and time since discharge. Table 2 shows that the matching procedure was successful on all but two variables: joint admission children were nearly three months younger at the time of their mothers' admission, and their mothers were hospitalized longer than the non-joint admission mothers.

TABLE 2. COMPARISON OF JOINT ADMISSION AND NON-JOINT ADMISSION GROUPS ON MATCHING VARIABLES

|  | Joint Admission N = 7 | Non-Joint Admission N = 7 |
|---|---|---|
| Child's age at admission | 2 mos., 18 days | 5 mos., 9 days |
| Child's age at discharge | 8 mos., 3 days | 9 mos., 12 days |
| Length of hospitalization | 165.1 days | 123.3 days |
| Age at testing | 18 mos., 9 days | 18 mos., 3 days |
| Time since discharge | 10 mos., 6 days | 8 mos., 25 days |
| Number of boys | 3 | 3 |
| Number of girls | 4 | 4 |
| Number of first-born | 3 | 3 |
| Number of later-born | 4 | 4 |

*Findings.* As table 3 shows, our expectations were largely confirmed. The joint admission children have a DQ ten points higher than that of the non-joint admission children, and have a considerably lower test scatter, 93 compared to 142 (p = .08 two-tailed).

On scales 1–6, language development and sensory-motor behavior, the joint admission children rate higher on five of the

TABLE 3. DQ, SCATTER, AND BEHAVIOR SCALE RATINGS FOR JOINT AD-
MISSION CHILDREN AND NON-JOINT ADMISSION CHILDREN AT EIGHTEEN
MONTHS

|  | Joint Admission N = 7 | Non-Joint Admission N = 7 |
|---|---|---|
| DQ | 107.6 | 97.6* |
| Scatter | 93.0 | 142.0** |
| Language development scales |  |  |
| 1. Active language development | 4,8 | 3.0 |
| 2. Passive language development | 5.0 | 4.5 |
| Sensory-motor behavior scales |  |  |
| 3. Immediate memory | 4.0 | 4.5 |
| 4. Perceptual-motor behavior | 5.0 | 4.3 |
| 5. Constructive behavior | 4.2 | 3.8 |
| 6. Effectual behavior | 3.7 | 3.5 |
| Object manipulation scales |  |  |
| 7. Variety of object manipulation | 5.0 | 4.0 |
| 8. Investment in objects | 5.6 | 4.2 |
| 9. Observation versus manipulation | 5.0 | 4.8 |
| Attention deployment scales |  |  |
| 10. Duration of attention | 5.8 | 5.0 |
| 11. Distractibility | 2.3 | 2.8 |
| 12. Persistence | 5.5 | 4.8 |
| 13. Impulsivity | 3.0 | 2.3 |
| Interpersonal behavior scales |  |  |
| 14. Reaction to strangers | 3.0 | 2.2 |
| 15. Specificity of interpersonal relations | 3.3 | 3.0 |
| 16. Depth of interpersonal relations | 3.7 | 3.2 |
| 17. Instrumental versus intrinsic relations | 2.8 | 2.8 |
| 18. Relative involvement with objects and people | 3.2 | 3.2 |
| Mood and affect scales |  |  |
| 19. Depression | 1.7 | 1.3 |
| 20. Positive affect | 5.2 | 4.5 |
| Symptomatic behavior |  |  |
| 21. Sum symptomatic behaviors | 8.5 | 8.7 |

*$p = .12$ (two-tailed)
**$p = .08$ (two-tailed)

six; on only two of the scales does the difference reach the
criterion of 0.6 of a scale point. The non-joint admission
children are much poorer than the joint admission children in
active language development (scale 1)—the ability to use words
to label or command. This difference, 1.8 points, is the largest
difference obtained, and is due to the fact that the non-joint
admission children did very poorly on this scale, considerably
more poorly than on any other cognitive scale. The groups did

not differ on passive language development (scale 2), performing appropriate acts such as pointing to stimuli upon request. The joint admission children rated higher on perceptual-motor behavior (scale 4), responding to formal properties of objects.

In measures of object manipulation and attention (scales 7–13), the joint admission children were noted to manipulate objects with greater variety (7) and with greater investment (8) than did non-joint admission children. They also attended longer (10), were more persistent (12), and more impulsive (13). All differences were in the expected direction except for the greater impulsivity of the joint admission children. This may reflect the more passive orientation of the non-joint admission children.

Of all the behavior domains rated, there were fewer differences between the two groups in the area of interpersonal behavior (scales 14–18). Of the five scales making up this domain, the groups differed on only one: joint admission children showed more stranger anxiety than did the non-joint admission children (14).

The joint admission children also expressed more positive affect (scale 20). However, they were not simply a happier group of children; they also tended to show more negative affect (19) (not reaching 0.6 of a scale point difference), indicating that they expressed emotion more than the non-joint admission children, who tended to react with inhibition of emotion.

There were no differences in the groups in manifestation of symptomatic behavior such as rocking, crying, and head banging, as measured at the time of testing (scale 21).

In summary, while the groups differed in all behavior domains—cognitive, interpersonal, and affective—the major differences emerged in cognitive development, in which the joint admission children had a higher DQ, less scatter, more advanced active language and perceptual motor development; they manipulated objects with greater variety and investment; they were more attentive, persistent, and impulsive, and tended more to express affect, particularly positive affect. Differences between the groups were least in the domain of interpersonal behavior, where joint admission children reacted more to strangers.

## ALTERNATIVE INTERPRETATION OF THE FINDINGS

Before concluding that these differences are attributable to the joint admission process, we must examine a number of possible alternatives stemming from the fact that mothers were not randomly assigned to the two groups.

The joint admission decision was based on a number of considerations, among which were the acceptability of the program to the patients and their families, the judgment of risk to the child, and the estimate by the hospital and research project staff of the likelihood of benefit to the mother from the program. It is possible, then, that a mother who was invited to participate in the program and who accepted might have differed from the non-joint admission mother on a number of attributes which, in turn, might have influenced the child's development in a manner similar to the pattern we found. Consider intelligence: Was not a more verbal, intelligent woman, one more able to formulate issues, to express affect in words, and to communicate these to the staff, more likely to have been judged a good risk for joint admission than a relatively unintelligent, nonverbal woman; and was she not, in turn, more likely to have had a child who was more attentive, verbal-persistent, etc.? And might not the same have been true for social class, education, and severity of illness? Was not a woman of higher social status and better education, who was more acutely ill, more likely to have been invited to participate in the joint admission program, and to have accepted? And was she not more likely to have had a child who conforms to the patterns we have described for the functioning of the joint admission children?

In order to evaluate the contribution of these additional factors to the obtained difference among the children, we compared the joint admission and non-joint admission women on IQ, years of education, socioeconomic status, and number of hospital admissions. The mothers did not differ on IQ, education, or SES, but the non-joint admission mothers were sicker. Whereas all but two of the joint admission mothers were hospitalized for the first time with the current admission, all but one of the non-joint admission mothers had been hospitalized at least once before. Sicker, more chronic mothers were thus overrepresented in the non-joint admission group, and it might be for this reason that the joint admission children did better than the non-joint admission children. The plausibility of this interpretation is strengthened by the data presented in table 4, column A, which shows that the children of first admission mothers (acute) were developing quite similarly to the joint admission children, when compared to the children of mothers with one or more previous hospitalizations (chronic). Like the joint admission children when compared to the non-joint admission children, children of acutely ill mothers had a slightly higher DQ than did children of chronically ill mothers. Whereas the groups did not differ on intra-test scatter, on seven (scales 1, 4, 8, 10, 12, 14, 20) of the nine rating scales which distinguished joint from non-joint admission children, the children of the acutes differed in the same direction from the children of chronically ill mothers. On the other two scales (7, 13) they differed in the same direction as did the joint admission children, but with not enough magnitude to reach the criterion of 0.6 of a scale point.

The question of whether the differences between the joint admission and non-joint admission children were due to the greater number of severely ill mothers in the non-joint admission group can be clarified by comparing joint admission children with non-joint admission children, holding severity of illness constant; that is, by comparing the children separately for acutely ill mothers and for chronically ill mothers. The presence of only one acutely ill mother in the non-joint admission group makes the comparison for children of acutes impossible; we can, however, compare joint admission with non-joint admission children for chronically ill mothers, thus obtaining an estimate of the independent contribution of joint admission to the development of the children in our group, over and above severity of the mother's illness.

As table 4, column B, shows, the same pattern of differences between joint admission and non-joint admission children was maintained with severity of illness held constant: the DQ of the joint admission children was higher, they had considerably less scatter, and differed in the same direction on seven (scales 1, 4, 7, 8, 10, 12, 14) of the nine scales which previously distinguished joint admission from non-joint admission children.

TABLE 4. CHILDREN'S MEASURES RELATED TO CHRONICITY OF MOTHER'S ILLNESS

| | A DQ, Scatter, and Behavior Scale Ratings for Children of Acutely and Chronically Ill Mothers at 18 Months | | B DQ, Scatter, and Behavior Scale Ratings for Children of Joint and Non-Joint Admission Chronically Ill Mothers | |
|---|---|---|---|---|
| | Acute N=6 | Chronic N=8 | Joint-Admission N=2 | Non-Joint Admission N=6 |
| DQ | 106.6 | 99.7 | 112.6 | 94.5 |
| Scatter | 119.6 | 113.1 | 84.0 | 124.8 |
| Language development scales | | | | |
| 1. Active language development | 4.6 | 3.4 | 4.5 | 3.0 |
| 2. Passive language development | 5.2 | 4.4 | 5.0 | 4.4 |
| Sensory-motor behavior scales | | | | |
| 3. Immediate memory | 4.0 | 4.3 | 4.0 | 4.4 |
| 4. Perceptual-motor behavior | 5.2 | 4.3 | 5.0 | 4.0 |
| 5. Constructive behavior | 3.6 | 4.3 | 5.0 | 4.0 |
| 6. Effectual behavior | 3.8 | 3.4 | 3.5 | 3.4 |
| Object manipulation scales | | | | |
| 7. Variety of object manipulation | 4.6 | 4.4 | 5.6 | 4.0 |
| 8. Investment in objects | 5.2 | 4.6 | 6.0 | 4.0 |
| 9. Observation versus manipulation | 4.8 | 5.0 | 5.0 | 5.0 |
| Attention deployment scales | | | | |
| 10. Duration of attention | 6.0 | 5.0 | 6.0 | 4.6 |
| 11. Distractibility | 2.4 | 2.7 | 2.5 | 2.8 |
| 12. Persistence | 5.6 | 4.9 | 6.0 | 4.4 |
| 13. Impulsivity | 2.8 | 2.6 | 2.5 | 2.6 |
| Interpersonal behavior scales | | | | |
| 14. Reaction to strangers | 3.4 | 2.0 | 3.5 | 1.4 |
| 15. Specificity of interpersonal relations | 3.4 | 3.0 | 3.5 | 2.8 |
| 16. Depth of interpersonal relations | 3.8 | 3.1 | 3.5 | 3.0 |
| 17. Instrumental versus intrinsic relations | 3.0 | 2.7 | 2.5 | 2.8 |
| 18. Relative involvement with objects and people | 3.4 | 3.0 | 2.5 | 3.2 |
| Mood and Affect Scales | | | | |
| 19. Depression | 1.4 | 1.6 | 1.6 | 1.6 |
| 20. Positive affect | 5.2 | 4.6 | 4.5 | 4.6 |
| Symptomatic behavior | | | | |
| 21. Sum symptomatic behavior | 9.2 | 8.2 | 8.0 | 8.2 |

*Summary and Conclusion.* It is unlikely that the overrepresentation of more severly ill mothers in the nonintervention group accounts *by itself* for the differences in the children's development; in all likelihood, participation in the program made a significant contribution to the children's development. We think it worthy of note that differences were not equally distributed among the different behavioral domains of cognitive development, interpersonal behavior, and affect. The major impact of the program as evidenced by the major differences among the children was upon the evenness and level of cognitive development, with intra-test scatter and seven out of thirteen cognitive scales discriminating between the groups; the program had least impact on interpersonal relations, where only one of five scales discriminated between the groups.

The data, then, supported the conclusion that the program had a beneficial though differential effect upon the children's development. There was no support for the fear that the program was harmful to the children.

## CHILDREN OF PSYCHOTIC MOTHERS COMPARED TO CHILDREN OF NORMAL MOTHERS

Our original hypothesis held that children of psychotic mothers as a group (joint admission and non-joint admission children considered together) would differ from children of normal controls in the same direction that non-joint admission children differed from joint admission children. We expected that the joint admission program would serve to counter the cognitive, interpersonal, and affective deficits in children of psychotic mothers, placing the joint admission children intermediate between the non-joint admission children and the children of normal controls. To test these expectations, a comparison group of children of normal, nonhospitalized mothers was matched with the pooled group of children of psychotic mothers on age of the child at testing, family size and composition, maternal education, and social class.

Table 5 presents the matching characteristics for the pooled group of children of psychotic mothers and the normal control group.

Both groups were administered the Cattell scale (all were over

TABLE 5. COMPARISON OF CHILDREN OF PSYCHOTIC MOTHERS AND CHILDREN OF NONHOSPITALIZED NORMAL MOTHERS ON MATCHING VARIABLES

|  | Children of Psychotic Mothers N = 14 | Children of Nonhospitalized Normal Mothers N = 14 |
|---|---|---|
| Age at testing | 18 mos., 6 days | 18 mos., 13 days |
| Maternal education | 13.3 years | 13.7 years |
| Social class | 3.4 | 3.5 |
| Number of boys | 6 | 6 |
| Number of girls | 8 | 8 |
| Number of first-born | 6 | 6 |
| Number of later-born | 8 | 8 |

twelve months) and their test-taking behavior was rated by means of the infant behavior scale.

*Results.* Table 6 compares the children of joint admission, non-joint admission, and normal control mothers. Surprisingly, in comparison to the control group, the joint admission and non-joint admission children diverge in a number of measures of cognitive development. Joint admission children were found to be doing *better* than the normal controls in both active and passive language development, and perceptual-motor behavior. The joint admission children manipulated objects more variably, and were more attentive and persistent than the children of nonhospitalized mothers. In contrast, the non-joint admission children were poorer in cognitive development than the normal controls. They tended to have more test scatter ($p = .22$ two-tailed), were poorer in active language development, were less interested in objects, and were more distractible than normal controls.

In interpersonal behavior, in contrast to cognitive behavior, both the joint admission and non-joint admission children consistently earned poorer ratings than the normal control group. Both groups of children of psychotic mothers were judged to have less specific interpersonal relationships, more instrumental (as opposed to intrinsic) interpersonal relationships, and to be more involved with things than with people. In addition, the non-joint admission children (but *not* the joint admission children) reacted to a lesser degree to strangers, and were

TABLE 6. DQ, SCATTER, AND BEHAVIOR SCALE RATINGS FOR JOINT AD-
MISSION CHILDREN, NON-JOINT ADMISSION CHILDREN, AND NORMAL
CONTROL CHILDREN AT EIGHTEEN MONTHS OF AGE

|  | Joint Admission N = 7 | Non-Joint Admission N = 7 | Normal N = 14 |
|---|---|---|---|
| DQ | 107.6 | 97.6 | 101.2 |
| Scatter | 93.0 | 142.0 | 110.6* |
| Language scales | | | |
| 1. Active language development | 4.8 | 3.0 | 4.1 |
| 2. Passive language development | 5.0 | 4.5 | 4.1 |
| Sensory-motor scales | | | |
| 3. Immediate memory | 4.0 | 4.5 | 4.2 |
| 4. Perceptual-motor behavior | 5.0 | 4.3 | 4.3 |
| 5. Constructive behavior | 4.2 | 3.8 | 3.8 |
| 6. Effectual behavior | 3.7 | 3.5 | 3.5 |
| Object manipulation scales | | | |
| 7. Variety of object manipulation | 5.0 | 4.0 | 4.1 |
| 8. Investment in objects | 5.6 | 4.2 | 5.2 |
| 9. Observation versus manipulation | 5.0 | 4.8 | 4.6 |
| Attention deployment scales | | | |
| 10. Duration of attention | 5.8 | 5.0 | 5.2 |
| 11. Distractibility | 2.3 | 2.8 | 2.2 |
| 12. Persistence | 5.5 | 4.8 | 4.8 |
| 13. Impulsivity | 3.0 | 2.3 | 2.1 |
| Interpersonal relations scales | | | |
| 14. Reaction to strangers | 3.0 | 2.2 | 3.3 |
| 15. Specificity of interpersonal relations | 3.3 | 3.0 | 4.3 |
| 16. Depth of interpersonal relations | 3.7 | 3.2 | 4.0 |
| 17. Instrumental versus intrinsic relations | 2.8 | 2.8 | 3.9 |
| 18. Relative involvement with objects versus people | 3.2 | 3.2 | 3.9 |
| Affect scales | | | |
| 19. Depressive affect | 1.7 | 1.3 | 1.4 |
| 20. Positive affect | 5.2 | 4.5 | 5.6 |
| Symptomatic behavior | | | |
| 21. Sum symptomatic behaviors | 8.5 | 8.7 | 8.3 |

*$p = .22$ two-tailed for difference between non-joint admission and normal
control groups

judged to have more shallow interpersonal relations than the
normal controls. Furthermore, non-joint admission children
were judged to manifest less positive affect than were the
normal controls.

*Hypotheses to Account for Differences.* In summary, children of
psychotic mothers generally were judged to have poorer

interpersonal relations than children of normal controls; they tended to express less positive affect but did not suffer general cognitive impairment. Non-joint admission children did more poorly in some aspects of cognitive development, but joint admission children consistently did better than the normal controls. How may we explain this unanticipated and puzzling result? Two hypotheses may be considered to account for the cognitive superiority of the joint admission children over the normals.

1. One or more aspects of the joint admission program may constitute an enriched cognitive environment, more growth-enhancing than the average home environment. Which components of the joint admission program may be considered as sources of an enriching, stimulating influence? The prime candidate must be the period of residence in the mental institution when the plentiful supply of surrogate caretakers on the hospital ward provides a high level of stimulation and environmental responsiveness. The joint admission child, in his playpen in the dayroom, or crawling, or cruising about in his walker, has a continually interesting spectacle to observe; he has numerous adults who play with, talk to, and cuddle him. Contrast this with the level and patterning of stimulation available in many domestic environments during this period of early development: solitary play, or play with somewhat older siblings, with only intermittent adult stimulation provided by members of the nuclear family when they are available. That variation in maternal play and responsiveness can positively influence infant cognitive development within the normal range has been shown by Rubenstein (1967). She demonstrated that five-month-old infants with attentive mothers were more curious and explored more at six months than infants with inattentive mothers. It was during this age period that six out of seven of the joint admission children were in the hospital.

But if mental hospital residence, with its provision of a high level of stimulation and multiple surrogate caretakers, can offset early cognitive correlates of maternal psychosis, why did not residence in this environment compensate for the early interpersonal deficits! One possible answer is that multiple mothering does not counter the interpersonal correlates of psychotic mothering (deviant or sub-optimal care, separation, or surrogate mothering) but has effects similar to psychotic mothering. Rabin (1965), for example, found that kibbutz children, who were exposed to multiple mothering from birth and to a change of *metapelet* (caretaker) at nine months of age, were, in the second year of life, in comparison to home-reared Israeli children, retarded on the personal-social subscale of the Griffiths Mental Development Scale (Griffiths, 1954). Deficient performance on this subtest, according to Griffiths, "suggests that the child is not learning at the expected rate for his general ability level, those items of behavior that depend on his relations with his milieu" (1954, p. 36). Rabin's work with kibbutz children suggested to him that the experience of multiple mothering and early separation from significant caretakers resulted in "diffuse early object relations which are frustrating and anxiety provoking to the budding ego and cause a degree of withdrawal from interpersonal relations" (Rabin, 1965, p. 110). Children of mentally ill mothers, those cared for in foster homes or by available relatives, as well as those cared for by their own mothers in a joint admission program, experienced both maternal separation and multiple mothering. We may hypothesize that these experiences exerted an influence on their early interpersonal relationships comparable to that exerted by the similar experiences of kibbutz children. If, however, the hospital milieu constituted an enriched cognitive environment, then the cognitive development of the joint admission children may have thereby been enhanced.

2. The joint admission children were followed longitudinally; they were tested several times prior to the testing at eighteen months which is the basis of the present comparison.

It is possible that familiarity with the tester, the testing situation, and the test items contributed to the superior cognitive development of this group. If true, why was not greater familiarity with the tester reflected in the rating scales of interpersonal behavior and affect?

Familiarity is also a possible source of the comparative cognitive superiority of the joint admission children over the non-joint admission children. It is not, however, relevant to the differences between the non-joint admission children and the children of normal controls, since these groups were tested only once.

*Summary.* The early development of children of psychotic mothers did not deviate uniformly from that of children of normal control mothers. The interpersonal relations of children of both joint admission and non-joint admission mothers were judged to be impaired in comparison with children of normal controls. Joint admission children, however, were clearly superior to children of normal controls in a number of measures of cognitive development, while children of non-joint admission mothers were inferior to children of normal controls in this developmental domain. Two hypotheses, cognitive-enrichment and test-familiarity, were considered to account for the cognitive superiority of joint admission children; we advance the former as probable cause. Children of psychotic mothers manifest early deficits in cognitive, interpersonal, and affective development. The joint admission program, probably through providing an environment stimulating to cognitive development, offsets the cognitive deficits and seems to provide an environment more favorable for early language and cognitive development than that expected in the average home. The interpersonal deficits tend to be most refractory to intervention, and probably require continued intervention efforts.

# 8

# Maternal Psychoses and the Development of Joint Admission Children: Mediating Factors

What features of the joint admission program facilitated the superior cognitive growth of the children? Residence on the ward, a likely choice, is but one aspect of a multidimensional intervention process. Our clinical conviction is that at numerous points in the development of the children we could detect a relation between clinical improvement in the mother, the change in her handling of the child, and subsequent improvement in the child's development. Some of these clinical hypotheses have been described and illustrated by Hartman (in part 2 of this book). However, since our research was not designed to examine these relations, their systematic evaluation must await appropriately designed future research.

In scrutinizing the common interpersonal deficit of both joint admission and non-joint admission children, we have assigned significance to certain situational or environmental correlates of maternal hospitalization: maternal separation, multiple mothering, and altered patterns of maternal care prefiguring the psychotic episode and continuing through subsequent phases of the illness. Recent research and theory in the intergenerational "transmission" of psychosis have resulted in the consideration of genetic and perinatal contributions, in addition to environmental influences, as predisposing factors to mental illness.

212

## GENETIC CONTRIBUTIONS

Buttressed by studies of family concordance, genetic factors have been inferred as causal factors in mental illness. However, the design of the studies which provide the empirical basis of the hypothesized genetic factors is subject to methodological criticism; symptomatic and deviant modes of behavior found to "run" in families can be transmitted and maintained by social heredity as well as by biological heredity (Wender, 1969). These two sources are confounded in the design of most previous studies.

The recent reports of the study of adoptees by Heston (1966) and by Rosenthal et al. (1968), and of the study of the biological and adoptive families of adoptees by Kety et al. (1968), offer a methodological advance which permits the separation and evaluation of the independent contributions of genetic and environmental factors to the development of psychosis. By studying children of schizophrenic mothers separated early in life and adopted and reared by "normal" parents, and by using variations of this design such as comparing the adoptive and biological parents of adult hospitalized schizophrenics who were adopted early in life, these investigators have demonstrated beyond question that there is a genetic contribution to the development of some schizophrenias.

Recent estimates of the relative contribution of genetic influences (the amount of variance accounted for by genetic as compared to environmental influences) derived from studies of the concordance rate for schizophrenia in identical and fraternal twins (Hoffer and Pollin, 1970) are considerably lower than earlier estimates. Current research efforts are directed at the nature of the inherited vulnerability or vulnerabilities (Garmezy, 1972; Erlenmeyer-Kimling, 1968; Wynne, 1969) and their modes of interaction with environmental influences which may act to suppress, enhance, or otherwise shape their eventual adaptive consequences.

Our research design does not enable us to evaluate genetic contributions per se, since the development of the children by the time we are studying them is the resultant of a complex interplay of genetic, perinatal, and environmental influences

Our design does permit us to utilize the available data in order to explore hypotheses about the influence of such variables as length of hospitalization and age of child at hospitalization on the development of the high-risk group of children of psychotic mothers—a group with a presumed high genetic loading for vulnerability to psychosis. Our data also permit us to explore the interaction of perinatal complications and psychosis in the mother upon the children's development.

## PERINATAL COMPLICATIONS

Paffenbarger (1961) and Sobel (1961b) reported an increased incidence of perinatal complications in women who had had a psychotic episode prior to, during, or shortly after their pregnancies. Perinatal complications have been implicated in a wide variety of physical, neurological, and psychiatric disorders (Pasamanick et al., 1956). Of particular relevance for us is the implication of perinatal complications in the later development of serious emotional and behavioral disorders such as childhood schizophrenia (Pollack and Woerner, 1966) and adult schizophrenia (Stabeneau and Pollin, 1967). Mednick (1970) has reported that perinatal complications are associated with the later development of psychosis within a high-risk group of children of chronic schizophrenic mothers. Among such children he found that those who had themselves succumbed to serious emotional disturbance in early adult life had had more numerous and severe perinatal complications than did both children who had not succumbed and children of normal mothers.

We found, when we studied the birth records of the six joint admission children for whom they were available, that three of these children were born with serious complications of delivery. Two had cord complications with delayed respiration, one requiring the administration of oxygen; the third child was delivered by caesarian section because of fetal distress after a labor of thirty-two hours. This is, of course, an extremely high incidence, considerably exceeding that reported by Sobel (1961b), Paffenbarger (1961), and Mednick (1970), and is probably due to chance in our small sample. However, it provided an opportunity to explore the relation between birth complications and development.

To do so we selected a group of children of non-hospitalized mothers and matched them individually with each of our joint admission children on the following variables: sex, birth weight, complications of pregnancy and delivery, length of labor, birth order, condition of the newborn child, and age at time of testing. Of the six children of nonpsychotic mothers selected as controls, three had had birth complications. One was delivered by caesarian section after a prolonged labor; cephalopelvic disproportion was present, and the umbilical cord was wound twice around the neck. The other two had cord complications, were slow to breathe, and required oxygen administration. We were able to select these controls through the cooperation of the National Institute of Neurological Diseases and Stroke Collaborative Study at Boston Lying-In Hospital. This group, among others, had been conducting a prospective study of perinatal complications, keeping careful pregnancy and delivery records and evaluating, by means of the Bayley scale, the behavioral development of the children at thirty-one to thirty-nine weeks of age. This enabled us to compare, at thirty-one to thirty-nine weeks—an age for which we had similar testing on all children—the DQ and scatter as functions of mental illness in the mother and perinatal complications. Table 7 shows that the children of psychotic mothers (in this discussion the joint admission children are treated as a sample of children of

TABLE 7. DQ AND SCATTER OF EIGHT-MONTH-OLD CHILDREN OF PSYCHOTIC MOTHERS AND NORMAL CONTROLS WITH AND WITHOUT BIRTH COMPLICATIONS

|  | Mental Scale | | Motor Scale | | Total Scale | |
|---|---|---|---|---|---|---|
|  | DQ | Scatter | DQ | Scatter | DQ | Scatter |
| Children of psychotic mothers | | | | | | |
| Complications (N = 3) | 111.3 | 107.2 | 103.3 | 75.8 | 107.0 | 134.5 |
| No complications (N = 3) | 97.0 | 66.2 | 92.7 | 41.9 | 95.0 | 100.5 |
| Total group (N = 6) | 104.2 | 86.7 | 98.0 | 58.9 | 101.0 | 117.5* |
| Children of normal mothers | | | | | | |
| Complications (N = 3) | 105.7 | 81.1 | 107.3 | 40.6 | 105.7 | 93.8 |
| No complications (N = 3) | 116.0 | 51.2 | 101.0 | 39.4 | 108.7 | 76.2 |
| Total group (N = 6) | 110.8 | 65.9 | 104.2 | 40.0 | 107.2 | 85.2* |

*$p = .06$ (two-tailed)

psychotic mothers, without regard to the program of intervention) had greater intra-test scatter: they passed and failed items over a larger range of age norms than did the normal controls. This difference is so consistent that it approaches statistical significance for the total scale scatter ($p = .06$ two-tailed test).

However, the relation between perinatal complications and scatter is our focus here, and this finding is most interesting. In both groups, the children with complications had greater scatter than did children without complications; however, for children of psychotic mothers the difference between children with and without complications is twice as great as for children of normal mothers with and without complications (34 compared with 17.6).

These data suggest that having both a psychotic mother and perinatal complication results in unevenness in development and, inferentially, greater vulnerability to developmental maladaptation. They further suggest that perinatal complications have greater potential for developmental deviation in children of psychotic mothers than in children of normal controls. The data are compatible with Mednick's results in this regard, though the age of his population and his dependent variable are very different from ours.

The increased incidence of perinatal complications in psychotic mothers (Paffenberger, 1961; Sobel, 1961), in addition to the increased maladaptive potential of perinatal complications for children of psychotic mothers, should be considered probable antecedents of the known high risk of this vulnerable group. The process through which these conditions contribute to future maladaptive behavior remains to be elucidated. Mednick (1970) has conjectured that these effects are mediated through minimal damage to the hippocampus. Others (Kornetsky and Mirsky, 1966) have suggested the midbrain and brainstem reticular activating system as the locus of disordered function. Whatever future research determines the proximal physiological trace of perinatal stress to be in high-risk children, it is reasonable to suppose that this residue will interact with a variety of later developmental contingencies, and it is to a consideration of these that we shall turn in the following section.

It should be noted that the scatter of the joint admission children was considerably greater than that of the normal control group, verging on statistical significance, while essentially the same group of children ten months later have slightly less scatter than has a different control group (see table 6). It is possible that the joint admission children were actually more disturbed at the earlier age, which was closer to the psychotic episode of the mother and the attendant separation. When seen at eighteen months of age, ten months after their mothers' discharge, they had been cared for consistently by their mothers for a period of at least eleven months, and the mothers had had the benefit of continued psychotherapy and nursing aftercare. This decline, from the first to the second year of life, of developmental disturbance in the children of psychotic mothers is consistent with the developmental course in such children as reported by Sobel (1961a) and Fish (1963).

## LENGTH OF HOSPITALIZATION, SURROGATE CARETAKERS, AND SEX OF CHILD

The children in the joint admission and non-joint admission groups varied among themselves on a number of factors which are potential contributors to their development. In order to evaluate their influence upon the children's development, we related these variables to DQ and rating scale measures at eighteen months, and adopted the following procedure to study the contribution of the variables. The relation of each variable to DQ, scatter, and behavior ratings was examined separately for the joint admission and non-joint admission group. If the relation was different for each group, or hovered around zero, there was assumed to be no relation to the development of the children in this sample. If the relation was the same in both groups, they were pooled and the contribution of the variable to the children's development was evaluated for the entire group of children of psychotic mothers.

When this criterion was used, the following variables had no influence on the development of the children as we measured it: length of mother's hospitalization, number of interim caretakers, and sex of child.

One would have expected that length of hospitalization

would relate to the children's development in a manner similar to severity of maternal illness, for which it is often used as an indicator. However, the study hospital was a teaching hospital. Patients were selected for their teaching value, and the typical chronically ill patient was transferred to a larger, nonteaching, state hospital. Patients with a better prognosis were generally the recipients of intense and prolonged psychotherapeutic effort. Consequently length of hospitalization in this setting was probably weakly associated with favorability of prognosis. The joint admission group, more acutely ill than the more chronic non-joint admission group, was hospitalized longer, by a period of forty-five days (see table 2).

The absence of a relation between surrogate care and the development of the children was surprising and warrants a closer inspection. Child care during the mother's hospitalization was rated on a three-point scale: 1 = continuous surrogate figure, throughout, usually a grandmother or other relative; 2 = one continuous caretaker maintained, usually the father who sees the child every night, with a housekeeper taking care of the child during the day; 3 = shifting caretakers, usually in a number of relatives' homes or foster homes. We found, unexpectedly, that the non-joint admission group had more continuous care than the joint admission children. Six of the seven non-joint admission children were rated 1. In contrast, only two of the seven joint admission children were rated 1. Two were rated 2, that is, kept in their own homes, seeing the fathers at night and having housekeepers or friends help out during the day; and three were shifted around, spending part of the time in foster homes.

In retrospect, this difference is less surprising: the greater instability of surrogate care in the joint admission group may very well have been a significant consideration in the decision to try joint admission, and the adequacy of surrogate care in the non-joint admission group may have been a factor in not interrupting the caretaking arrangement. It must also be remembered that we evaluated the effect of surrogate care several months after the event. It may be that the range of variations in care that we encountered did affect the child at the time of the care, but that the effect was transient and disappeared after a period of reunion with the mother. Since inadequacy of surrogate care is partially confounded with joint admission, the deleterious effect of discontinuous surrogate care may have been offset by the beneficial effects of the joint admission program.

## AGE AT SEPARATION

It is clear that young children of psychotic mothers share, among many characteristics, one that is of overriding importance —the fact of separation from their mothers. This separation and its attendant correlate, surrogate care and multiple mothering, we consider a significant contributing factor to the course of the children's development.

Although we have emphasized similarities between the maternal separation of the children we have studied and that experienced by other groups as reported in the literature, it is useful to delineate some of the differences. Most of the reported studies of developmental consequences of separation fall into two categories: they deal either with the concurrent effects of brief separtion or with the long-term effects of chronic separation, which is often accompanied by severe deprivation. The separation experienced by the children in the present study is in a sense intermediate between these two. The separation period was brief, four months or under in most cases, and the children were reunited with their mothers at the end of the period. In many cases they had had intermittent contact with the mothers during the period of separation, and in almost all cases they were in continuous contact with their fathers and were cared for by other familiar relatives. However, the consequences of the separation were studied at a time period somewhat removed from the experienced separation—an average of ten months. Furthermore, the separation in our group occurred against a background of deviant or altered maternal behavior accompanying either or both the early state of the psychosis and the mother's pre-illness character structure.

Since the separation experienced by the children of psychotic mothers is in some ways unique, it is probable that information about the impact of age of separation upon children's development obtained with other populations is not directly transferable to this group. Such information did prove useful in helping to frame our expectations. In general, brief separations followed by reunion with the mother are most disruptive if they occur after the age of six months (Schaffer and Callender, 1959).

We anticipated, therefore, that the child whose mother's hospitalization took place in the early months of his life would have less scatter, and would be rated better on the infant behavior scales, than would the child of a mother who was hospitalized later in his life.

*Grouping Procedure for Early and Late Separation.* The age of the children at their mothers' hospitalization ranged from four days to fourteen months and five days. We divided our group of fourteen children into two equal groups, an early admission group and a late admission group. Eight weeks of age provided a natural cutting point which yielded four early admissions and three late admissions in the joint admission group, and three early and four late admissions in the non-joint admission group. The ages of the children at hospitalization in the early group ranged from four days to one month and eleven days, averaging twenty-four days; the ages of the children in the late group ranged from two months and twenty-two days to fourteen months and five days, averaging seven months and five days. Acutely ill and chronically ill mothers were equally represented in both early and late groups, and their periods of hospitalization were approximately equal, 145 days for the early group and 132 days for the late group.

*Results.* Table 8 presents the DQ, scatter, and behavior ratings at age eighteen months for early and late groups. As expected, the children separated before eight weeks have a considerably lower scatter ($p = .04$, two tailed). However, contrary to expectation, the children separated early are rated much lower in all scales of interpersonal behavior. These differences are larger and more consistent than those obtained from any other comparison. Those children whose mothers were hospitalized shortly after the birth are both more even in their cognitive development and less adequate in their interpersonal development than children separated from their ill mothers at a later age. How are we to account for this?

TABLE 8. DQ, SCATTER, AND BEHAVIOR RATINGS AT EIGHTEEN MONTHS
FOR EARLY AND LATE SEPARATION GROUPS

| | Early Separation N = 7 | Late Separation N = 7 |
|---|---|---|
| DQ | 105.3 | 100.0 |
| Scatter | 85.0 | 150.0* |
| Language development scales | | |
| 1. Active language development | 4.3 | 3.5 |
| 2. Passive language development | 4.2 | 5.3 |
| Sensory-motor behavior scales | | |
| 3. Immediate memory | 4.0 | 4.3 |
| 4. Perceptual-motor behavior | 4.7 | 4.7 |
| 5. Constructive behavior | 4.2 | 3.8 |
| 6. Effectual behavior | 3.3 | 3.8 |
| Object manipulation scales | | |
| 7. Variety of object manipulation | 4.5 | 4.5 |
| 8. Investment in objects | 5.0 | 4.0 |
| 9. Observation versus manipulation | 5.3 | 4.5 |
| Attention deployment scales | | |
| 10. Duration of attention | 5.3 | 5.5 |
| 11. Distractibility | 2.8 | 2.3 |
| 12. Persistence | 5.2 | 5.2 |
| 13. Impulsivity | 3.0 | 2.3 |
| Interpersonal behavior scales | | |
| 14. Reaction to strangers | 2.2 | 3.0 |
| 15. Specificity of interpersonal relations | 2.7 | 3.7 |
| 16. Depth of interpersonal relations | 2.7 | 4.2 |
| 17. Instrumental versus intrinsic relations | 2.3 | 3.3 |
| 18. Relative involvement with objects versus people | 2.3 | 3.5 |
| Mood and affective scales | | |
| 19. Depression | 1.3 | 1.7 |
| 20. Positive affect | 4.7 | 5.0 |
| Symptomatic behavior | | |
| 21. Sum symptomatic behaviors | 8.8 | 8.7 |

*$p = .04$ (two-tailed)

*Hypothesis and Discussion.* A clue is provided by the other
behavior scales which are related to age at separation. Children
separated early, in addition to showing less scatter and poorer
interpersonal relations, are doing better in active language
development, are more invested in objects, more invested in
manipulation rather than observation, and are more impulsive

than children separated from their mothers at a later age. Is it not plausible that the early separated children (those children separated before two months and for an average period of four and one-half months before being reunited for a continuous period with their mothers), in the absence of a continuous interpersonal "object" early in their development, do not have the opportunity to form a firm attachment to a person, and therefore put their energies into perceptual and manipulatory activity? In contrast, those children separated later (after eight weeks of age and up to fourteen months of age) have had an opportunity to form a primary attachment, rudimentary though it is. Separation taking place after this attachment, involving expectancies and dependencies, may result in affective disturbance, and in deployment of resources to deal with this disturbance and to restore the disrupted relationship. Hence, less "energy" for perceptual and manipulatory exploration, more "investment" in people.

We hypothesize, then, that the children separated early will develop more evenly, but at a price of diminished involvement with people. There is some evidence from other studies to provide general support for this hypothesis, though one must remember that such evidence is derived from studies using different populations and different situations. Schaffer and Callender (1959) found that children (younger than six months) entering a hospital for brief hospitalization did not manifest the prolonged disruptive aftereffects that older children did. However, in addition to separation (for a shorter period than our subjects) these infants were subjected to distressing medical procedures. Yarrow (cited in Caldwell, 1962) found that infants placed in adoptive homes at three months of age showed little sign of disturbance during the post-placement period, whereas 86 percent of children placed at six months manifested upset during that period. Furthermore, increasing disturbance was found at one-month intervals from three months to one year. If this age-related disturbance was due to disruption of a deepening relationship with the preadoption caretakers, it is supportive of our hypothesis. Again, one must be reminded that for children of psychotic mothers, maternal separation occurs against a background of disturbed mother-child relationships that may color the separation in a manner different from other situations. However, until studies comparing separation in children of normal and disturbed mothers enable us to refine the proposed hypothesis, it may be useful to apply what we have learned of separation in other situations to this almost invariable concomitant of maternal psychosis. The results suggest that the age of the child at his mother's hospitalization affects the variability and patterning of his development.

## SUMMARY AND CONCLUSION

In order to evaluate the effect upon the development of young children of a program of joint admission of mentally ill mothers and children, joint admission children were compared to non-joint admission children and children of nonhospitalized normal mothers on a number of rating scale measures of cognitive development, interpersonal behavior, affect expression, and symptomatic behavior, and on measures of cognitive level and variability derived from developmental test data.

It was found that the children of mothers who participated in the program of joint admission, in comparison to non-joint admission children, showed less intra-test scatter and were rated more favorably on a number of scales of cognitive development, interpersonal behavior, and affect expression. A number of alternatives to the joint admission program were considered and rejected as bases for the findings, and it was concluded that the joint admission program exerted a favorable influence upon the children's development. However, its effect was not uniform; it was greatest upon cognitive development and it exerted least impact upon the development of interpersonal relationships. There was no indication that the program was harmful to the children in any way.

In comparison to children of nonhospitalized normal mothers, children of psychotic mothers were judged to have poorer interpersonal relations; they tended to express less positive affect, but did not suffer general cognitive impairment. Non-joint admission children did more poorly in some aspects of cognitive development, and joint admission children consistently did better, than children of normal controls. One hypothesis advanced to account for these results was that a mental hospital ward may provide a superior, enriching, growth-enhancing environment for the cognitive development of young children.

The contribution of several variables to the development of the children was considered. Length of hospitalization, the number and continuity of surrogate caretakers, and the sex of the child made no difference, in contrast to the occurrence of perinatal complications, and the age of the child when the mother was hospitalized.

Perinatal complications were associated with more uneven development at eight months in children both of psychotic mothers and of nonhospitalized, normal mothers; however, perinatal complications were associated with twice as great an increase in scatter in children of psychotic mothers as in children of normal mothers. These data suggest that perinatal complications may have an increased maladaptive potential for children of psychotic mothers.

Children who were eight weeks of age or less when their mothers were hospitalized were more even in development, superior in some aspects of cognitive development, but less adequate in interpersonal development than were children who were older. The hypothesis advanced to account for this was that children separated from their mothers at an early age do not have an opportunity to form a social attachment, and so invest their energy early in the nonanimate object world. Children separated later, after a rudimentary attachment has been found, probably react to separation with disturbance, attempt to restore the disrupted relationship, and are less interested in inanimate objects.

We concluded that young children of psychotic mothers suffer cognitive, interpersonal, and affective deficits which may be significant antecedents of later psychopathology. It is probable that the joint admission program offsets these deficits to some degree. The cognitive deficits appeared most responsive to intervention; however, the interpersonal deficits proved more refractory to intervention, and may require more intensive intervention effort in the future. Factors such as perinatal complications and age of the child at mother's hospitalization can affect the variability and patterning of the child's development.

# References to Part 3

Ainsworth, M. D. 1962. The effects of maternal deprivation: A review of findings and controversy in the context of research strategy. In *Deprivation of maternal care: A re-assessment of its effects.* Geneva: W.H.O. Public Health Papers, no. 14.

Anthony, E. J. 1968. The developmental precursors of adult schizophrenia. In D. Rosenthal and S. Kety, eds., *The transmission of schizophrenia,* pp. 293–316. Oxford: Pergamon.

———. 1969. A clinical evaluation of children with psychotic parents. *American Journal of Psychiatry* 126: 177–84.

Barthell, C. N., and Holmes, D. S. 1968. High school yearbooks: A nonreactive measure of social isolation in graduates who later became schizophrenic. *Journal of Abnormal Psychology* 73: 313–16.

Bayley, N. 1965. Comparisons of mental and motor test scores for ages 1–15 months by sex, birth order, race, geographic location and education of parents. *Child Development* 36: 379–411.

Beisser, A. R.; Glasser, N.; and Grant, M. 1967. Psychosocial adjustment in children of schizophrenic mothers. *Journal of Nervous and Mental Diseases* 145: 429–40.

Birren, J. E. 1944. Psychological examination of children who later became psychotic. *Journal of Abnormal and Social Psychology* 39: 84–95.

Bowman, K. M. 1934. A study of the pre-psychotic personality in certain psychoses. *American Journal of Orthopsychiatry* 4: 473–98.

Caldwell, B. M. 1962. The usefulness of the critical period hypothesis in the study of filiative behavior. *Merrill-Palmer Quarterly* 8: 219–42.

Canavan, M., and Clark, R. 1923. The mental health of 463 children from dementia-praecox stock. *Mental Hygiene* 7: 137–48.

———. 1936. The mental health of children of dementia-praecox stock: Second report. *Mental Hygiene* 20: 463–71.

225

Casler, L. 1961. Maternal deprivation: A critical review of the literature. *Monographs of the Society for Research in Child Development* 26, no. 2 (serial no. 80).

Cattell, P. 1940. *The measurement of intelligence of infants and young children.* New York: The Psychological Corporation.

Cowie, V. 1961. The incidence of neurosis in the children of psychotics. *Acta Psychiatrica Scandinavica* 37: 37–71.

Ekdahl, M.; Rice, E.; and Schmidt, W. 1962. Children of parents hospitalized for mental illness. *American Journal of Public Health* 52: 428–35.

Erlenmeyer-Kimling, L. 1968. Studies of the children of schizophrenic parents: Pointers for the analysis of gene-environment interaction. Paper presented at the 124th Annual Meetings of the American Psychiatric Association, Boston, Mass.

Fanning, A.; Lehr, S.; Sherwin, R.; and Wilson, M. 1938. The mental health of children of psychotic mothers. *Smith College Studies in Social Work* 8: 291–343.

Fish, B. 1963. The maturation of arousal and attention in the first months of life: A study of variations in ego development. *Journal of the American Academy of Child Psychiatry* 2: 253–70.

———. 1971. Contributions of developmental research to a theory of schizophrenia, In J. Hellmuth, ed., *Exceptional infant*, pp. 473–82. New York: Brunner/Mazel.

Fish, B., and Alpert, M. 1962. Abnormal states of consciousness and muscle tone in infants born to schizophrenic mothers. *American Journal of Psychiatry* 119: 439–45.

———. 1963. Patterns of neurological development in infants born to schizophrenic mothers. In J. Wortis, ed., *Recent advances in biological psychiatry* vol. 5 pp. 24–37. New York: Plenum Press.

Fish, B.; Shapiro, T.; Halpern, F.; and Wile, R. 1965. The prediction of schizophrenia in infancy: III A ten year follow-up report of neurological and psychological development. *American Journal of Psychiatry* 121: 768–75.

Fraser, C.; Bellugi, U.; and Brown, R. 1963. Control of grammar in imitation, comprehension, and production. *Journal of Verbal Learning and Verbal Behavior* 2: 121–35.

Frazer, H. E. 1953. Children who later became schizophrenic. *Smith College Studies in Social Work* 23: 125–249.

Gardner, G. 1967. The relationship between childhood neurotic symptomatology and later schizophrenia in males and females. *Journal of Nervous and Mental Diseases* 144: 97–100.

Gardner, N. H. 1949. The later adjustment of children born in mental hospitals to psychotic mothers. *Smith College Studies in Social Work* 19: 137–48.

Garmezy, N. 1970. Vulnerable adolescents: Implications derived from studies of an internalizing-externalizing symptom dimension. In J. Zubin and A. M. Freedman, eds., *Psychopathology of adolescence*, pp. 212–39. New York: Grune and Stratton.

———. 1971. Vulnerability research and the issue of primary prevention. *American Journal of Orthopsychiatry* 41: 101–16.

————. 1972. Models of etiology for the study of children who are at risk for schizophrenia. In M. Roff, L. Robins, and M. Pollack, eds., *Life history research in psychopathology*, vol. 2.

Griffiths, R. 1954. *The abilities of babies*. New York: McGraw-Hill.

Harris, A. J., and Shakow, D. 1937. The clinical significance of numerical measures of scatter on the Stanford-Binet. *Psychological Bulletin* 34: 134–50.

————. 1938. Scatter on the Stanford-Binet in schizophrenics, normal and delinquent adults. *Journal of Abnormal and Social Psychology* 33: 100–11.

Heinicke, C. M., and Westheimer, I. 1965. *Brief separations*. New York: International Universities Press.

Heston, L. 1966. Psychiatric disorders in foster home reared children of schizophrenic mothers. *British Journal of Psychiatry* 112: 810–25.

Heston, L., and Denney, D. 1968. Interactions between early life experience and biological factors in schizophrenia. In D. Rosenthal and S. S. Kety, eds., *The transmission of schizophrenia*, pp. 363–76. Oxford: Pergamon.

Hoffer, A., and Pollin, W. 1970. Schizophrenia in the NAS-NRC panel of 15,909 veteran twin pairs. *Archives of General Psychiatry* 23: 469–77.

Iwascki, A. 1957. Some impacts of schizophrenic mothers upon the psycho-social adjustment of elementary school age children. Unpublished masters thesis. School of Social Work, University of Southern California.

Kallman, F. J. 1938. *The genetics of schizophrenia*. New York: Augustin.

Kasanin, J. A., and Veo, L. 1932. A study of school adjustments of children who later in life became psychotic. *American Journal of Orthopsychiatry* 2: 212–27.

Kety, S. S.; Rosenthal, D.; Wender, P. H.; and Schulsinger, F. 1968. The types and prevalence of mental illness in the biological and adoptive families of adopted schizophrenics. In D. Rosenthal and S. S. Kety, eds, *The transmission of schizophrenia*, pp. 345–62. Oxford: Pergamon.

Kornetsky, C., and Mirsky, A. 1966. On certain psychopharmacological and physiological differences between schizophrenics and normal persons. *Psychopharmacologia* (Berl.) 8: 309–15.

Lampron, E. 1933. Children of schizophrenic parents: Present mental and social status of one hundred eighty-six cases. *Mental Hygiene* 17: 82–91.

Lane, E. A., and Albee, G. W. 1963. Childhood intellectual performance of adult schizophrenics. *Journal of Abnormal and Social Psychology* 67: 186–89.

————. 1964. Early childhood intellectual differences between schizophrenic adults and their siblings. *Journal of Abnormal and Social Psychology* 68: 193–95.

McClellan, S. G., and Pugh, T. F. 1962. Childhood development following maternal mental illness. Paper presented at 90th annual meeting of American Public Health Association, Miami, Florida.

Mass, A. L. 1957. Children with mentally ill mothers. Unpublished masters thesis, School of Social Work, University of Southern California.

Mednick, S. A. 1970. Breakdown in individuals at high risk for schizophrenia: Possible predispositional perinatal factors. *Mental Hygiene* 54: 50–63.

Mednick, S. A., and McNeil, T. F.. 1968. Current methodology in research on the etiology of schizophrenia. *Psychological Bulletin* 70: 681–93.

Mednick, S. A. and Schulsinger, F. 1968. Some premorbid characteristics related to breakdown in children with schizophrenic mothers. In D. Rosenthal and S. S. Kety, eds., *The transmission of schizophrenia*, pp. 267–91. Oxford: Pergamon.

Meyers, C. E.; Dingman, H. F.; and Orpit, R. E. 1964. Four ability-factor hypotheses at three preliterate levels in normal and retarded children. *Monographs of the Society for Research in Child Development* 29 (serial no. 96).

Morris, H. H.; Escoll, P. J; and Wexler, R. 1956. Aggressive behavior disorders of childhood: A follow-up study. *American Journal of Psychiatry* 112: 991–97.

Nameche, G.; Waring, M.; and Ricks, D. F. 1964. Early indicators of outcome in schizophrenia. *Journal of Nervous and Mental Disease* 139: 232–40.

O'Neal, P. and Robins, L. N. 1958. Childhood patterns predictive of schizophrenia: A 30-year follow-up study. *American Journal of Psychiatry* 115: 385–91.

Paffenbarger, R., Jr. 1961. The picture puzzle of the postpartum psychoses. *Journal of Chronic Diseases* 13: 161–73.

Pasamanick, B.; Rogers, M.; and Lilienfeld, A. M. 1956. Pregnancy experience and the development of childhood behavior disorder. *American Journal of Psychiatry* 112: 614–18.

Pollack, M., and Woerner, M. G. 1966. Pre- and peri-natal complications and "childhood schizophrenia": A comparison of five controlled studies. *Journal of Child Psychology and Psychiatry* 7: 235–42.

Preston, G., and Antin, R. 1932. A study of children of psychotic parents. *American Journal of Orthopsychiatry* 2: 231–41.

Rabin, I. A. 1965. *Growing up in the Kibbutz*, New York: Springer.

Rapaport, D.; Gill, M. M.; and Schafer, R. (R. R. Holt, ed.). 1968. *Diagnostic psychological testing*. New York: International Universities Press.

Reisby, N. 1967. Psychoses in children of schizophrenic mothers. *Acta Psychiatrica Scandinavica* 43: 8–20.

Rheingold, H. L. 1956. The modification of social responsiveness in institutional babies. *Monographs of the Society for Research in Child Development* 21, no. 2 (serial no. 63)

Robins, L. N. 1966. *Deviant children grown up*. Baltimore: Williams and Wilkins.

Rosenthal, D. 1966. The offspring of schizophrenic couples. *Journal of Psychiatric Research* 4: 169–88.

———. 1970. *Genetic theory and abnormal behavior*. New York: McGraw-Hill.

Rosenthal, D.; Wender, P. H.; Kety, S. S.; Schulsinger, F.; Welner, J.; and Ostergaard, L. 1968. Schizophrenics' offspring reared in adoptive homes. In D. Rosenthal and S. S. Kety, eds., *The transmission of schizophrenia*, pp. 377–92. Oxford: Pergamon.

Rubenstein, J. 1967 Maternal attentiveness and subsequent exploratory behavior in the infant. *Child Development* 38: 1089–1100.

Schaffer, H. R. 1965. Changes in developmental quotient under two conditions of maternal separation. *British Journal of Social and Clinical Psychology* 4: 39–46.

Schaffer, H. R., and Callender, W. M. 1959. Psychologic effects of hospitalization in infancy. *Pediatrics* 24: 528–39.

Sobel, D. E. 1961a. Children of schizophrenic patients: Preliminary observations on early development. *American Journal of Psychiatry* 118: 512–17.

— — —. 1961b. Infant mortality and malformations in children of schizophrenic women. *Psychiatric Quarterly* 35: 60.

Spitz, R. A. 1946. Hospitalism: A follow up report on investigation described in vol. 1. *Psychoanalytic Study of the Child* 2: 113–17.

Stabeneau, J. R., and Pollin, W. 1967. Early characteristics of monozygotic twins discordant for schizophrenia. *Archives of General Psychiatry* 17: 723–34.

Sunier, A., and Meijers, N. A. 1951. The influence of a chronic psychosis in one of the parents upon the development of the child. *Folia Psychiatrica* 54: 151–55.

Sussex, J. N.; Gassman, F.; and Raffel, S. C. 1963. Adjustment of children with psychotic mothers in the home. *American Journal of Orthopsychiatry* 33: 849–54.

Thomas, A.; Chess, S.; and Birch, H. G. 1968. *Temperament and behavior disorders in children.* New York: New York University Press.

Watt, N. F.; Stolorow, R. D.; Lubensky, A. W.; and McClelland, D. C. 1970. School adjustment and behavior of children hospitalized for schizophrenia as adults. *American Journal of Orthopsychiatry* 40: 637–57.

Wender, P. 1969. The role of genetics in the etiology of the schizophrenias. *American Journal of Orthopsychiatry* 39: 447–58.

Wittman, M. P., and Steinberg, D. L. 1944. A study of prodromal factors in mental illness with special reference to schizophrenia. *American Journal of Psychiatry* 100: 811–16.

Wynne, L. C. 1968. Methodological and conceptual issues in the study of schizophrenics and their families. In D. Rosenthal and S. S. Kety, eds., *The transmission of schizophrenia*, pp. 185–99. Oxford: Pergamon.

— — —. 1969. Strategies for sampling groups at high risk for the development of schizophrenia. Workshop Position Paper. NIMH-sponsored conference on high-risk for schizophrenia. June.

Yarrow, L. J. 1961. Maternal deprivation. Toward an empirical and conceptual re-evaluation. *Psychological Bulletin* 58: 459–90.

— — —. 1964. Separation from parents during early childhood. In M. L. Hoffman and L. W. Hoffman, eds., *Review of Child Development Research*, pp. 89–130. New York: Russell Sage Foundation.

# part 4

## character, mental illness, and mothering

*Bertram J. Cohler*

Psychoanalytic investigations have revealed that parents anticipate the child's failure in the area of their own developmental conflicts. Unaware, as parents mostly are, of the repressed conflicts of their childhood, the transactional processes evolve relatively smoothly until the child reaches the developmental level at which the parent, because of [her] own developmental conflict, unconsciously anticipates the child's conflict and therefore becomes insecure in her responses to the child's behavior. It is the task of the "psychopathology of parenthood" to study the manifestations and the intrapsychic and interpersonal dynamics of the regressive spirals that evolve in such critical phases of parenthood which leave transient or permanent scars in the parent and her child.

Therese Benedek, "The Family as a Psychologic Field," in E. J. Anthony and T. Benedek, eds., *Parenthood: Its Psychology and Psychopathology* (Boston: Little, Brown, 1970), pp. 130–31.

# Introduction to Part 4

Glancing backward at the first three parts of this book, we may pause briefly to delineate two themes which have been evolving.

The first is the commitment to empirical investigation. In part 1, clinical predictions, irrational fears, and common sense expectations were studied through interview responses from a sampling of ward staff and patients. In part 2, quantification of the nurse-mother interactions and statistical analyses, where appropriate, gave added weight to the central concepts underlying the therapeutic approach. In the third part, both formal testing and quantified behavioral observations again provided a basis for some confidence in the findings, even though the number of children studied was small. Quantification and empiricism reach their fullest evolution in part 4, where new investigatory techniques specifically developed for this project are presented and where sophisticated psychometric analytic and research design considerations are in the forefront.

The second theme is easy to trace but difficult to label precisely. It begins with a therapeutic application to a simple case and weaves its way farther and farther from this therapeutic context and closer to meaningful generalizations about mental illness and mothering. Part 1 started with a report of the first joint admission case; from there it went on to practical administrative and clinical matters in joint admission. This was followed by three chapters dealing with a conceptual framework for therapeutic work with the patient qua mother and a study of such work. Though generalizing from multiple cases, the presentation nevertheless featured the richness of individual case vignettes, the observations were confined essentially to the joint admission sample, and the orientation was therapeutic. In part 3, joint admission cases were compared with others in the course of examining the developmental status of the children in our study. Focusing upon possible specific effects of the joint admission experience and attempting to separate these from the more general relations between maternal psychopathology and child development, the orientation became evaluative rather than therapeutic.

In part 4 we have moved from the interface of the mother's emotional disturbance and the treatment program to consideration of a stable and enduring aspect of her psychological being—her character and how it is expressed through the medium of projective techniques. Within an epigenetic framework, character is investigated in terms of interpersonal issues or stages, and the level of conflict resolution which may be inferred with regard to these issues. The data are used to derive three empirical factors which have relevance to mothering in a specific interpersonal context, and these are related to various measures of psychopathology and child-rearing attitudes. This study considers both joint admission mothers and others whose hospitalization was more traditional, and compares this group with carefully matched nonpsychiatric mothers.

The results of these investigations have rather clear implications for the planning of treatment programs for psychotic mothers of young children. Such programs must look beyond the symptomatic relief of the patient and seek to modify her more enduring limitations in interpersonal relatedness and the maladaptive attitudes and feelings about mothering if the risk to emotional disorder in her offspring is to be reduced.

# 9

# Psychosocial Development and the Antecedents of Conflict Regarding Child Care

The development of mental illness during the first years after childbirth is a function both of a woman's present life situation and of her character—her capacity for establishing mature and appropriate interpersonal relationships. To the extent that a woman reacts to her husband, her baby, and her own parental family in ways which are not congruent with her roles as wife, mother, and adult, she is unable to respond to others in terms of realistic demands and expectations. Comparing a group of mothers hospitalized for mental illness during the first years following childbirth with a group of nonhospitalized women in the community, this study examines the hypothesis that hospitalized mothers show greater conflict than nonhospitalized women regarding the resolution of prior issues in psychosocial development, and are less able than nonhospitalized women to respond in an adaptive manner to the developmental conflict created by the assumption of the maternal role.

## AN EPIGENETIC PERSPECTIVE

Beginning with Freud, psychoanalytic theory has recognized the importance for an individual's subsequent adaptation of his perceptions of prior interpersonal experiences, and the inner reality which develops as a result of more or less satisfying

236

experiences with important figures in early childhood socialization (Isaacs, 1952; Guntrip, 1961). Indeed, this view is clearly
stated by Freud in *The Ego and the Id*, where he observes that
"the character of the ego is a precipitate of abandoned object-
cathexis" and that it contains a "record of past object choices"
(1923, p. 36). This record of past object choices or mental
representations in large part determines an individual's subsequent capacity to derive satisfaction from interpersonal
relationships.

The totality of present and past object choices, or object
relations, provides the basis of that ego function which we have
termed character, which may be defined as that stable function
of the ego which comprises habitual modes of perceiving and
structuring mental representations of relationships with significant figures in psychosocial development. Character develops,
over the life cycle, as a result of the reconciliation of conflicts
between the demands of maturational and socialization processes, and determines the individual's subsequent capacity for
achieving mature and satisfying interpersonal relationships. As
Erikson (1963), Balint (1947, 1951), and Fairbairn (1952) all have
observed, character continues to evolve, even through adulthood.

Psychosocial development refers to the process as a result of
which character is initially formed and subsequently modified,
and is marked by a number of preadult and adult phases. Each
of these phases is represented by a unique "core" conflict
between the self and some significant others which, in the
words of Bibring (1959), represents "developmental phenomena
at points of no return between one phase and the next, when
decisive changes deprive former central needs of their significance, forcing the acceptance of highly charged new goals and
functions" (1959, p. 116). Depending upon the resolution of the
core conflict associated with each of these phases, the founda-
tions are laid for a more or less successful future adaptation.

Psychoanalytic theorists have frequently observed that conflict in forming mature object relations may well be the most
sensitive index of psychopathology, as well as the most exact
index of developmental asynchronicity (Hartmann, 1953; Spitz,
1959; Ritvo, 1962; Rangell, 1965; Hurvich and Bellak, 1968). The
sphere of object relations appears to be particularly sensitive to
such developmental imbalances as may exist in an individual's

present mode of adaptation and may provide evidence of psychological conflict, even when other aspects of ego functioning, such as cognition and perception, do not reflect such conflict.

The manner in which an individual resolves the core of nuclear conflicts associated with each of the several phases of preadult and adult psychosocial development results in more or less adaptive, appropriate, and mature modes of relating to others. Appropriate resolution of nuclear conflicts associated with preadult and adult phases of psychosocial development renders one more immune to regression during periods of stress. However, to the extent that there has been unresolved conflict, particularly regarding earlier phases of psychosocial development, it will be more difficult to deal appropriately and realistically with adult phases of psychosocial development. When stress is experienced regarding the demand for more differentiated and complex modes of relating to others, such as is represented by marriage, parenthood, or work, regression is initiated in the direction of those preadult phases regarding which there is the greatest unresolved conflict. This position is consistent with Freud's observations (1911, 1913b, 1917b) on the meaning of fixation and regression for the psychic organization and functioning, as well as with the subsequent formulations of Nunberg (1932), Fenichel (1945), and Nagera (1964).

## PREADULT AND ADULT CHARACTER DEVELOPMENT

Since the publication of Freud's *Three Essays on Sexuality* (1905), considerable attention has been paid by physicians, educators, and personality theorists to the delineation of the phases of preadult and adult psychosocial development which contribute to the development of character (Ribble, 1943; Fenichel, 1945; Sullivan, 1953; Erikson, 1963). Caldwell's (1964) review provides a good summary of the empirical literature regarding the socialization process, based on developmental studies and observation of both children and parent-child interaction. While they may place greater or lesser emphasis upon ego-psychological or libidinal formulations, clinical reports by psychoanalytic investigators have arrived at good consensus regarding the content of the core or nuclear conflicts associated with these several phases of preadult and adult psychosocial development.

The first, or "oral incorporative," phase of psychosocial development concerns the development of feelings of contentment and satisfaction obtained from interpersonal relationships (Abraham, 1924a, 1924b, 1925; Glover, 1924; Klein, 1932; Balint, 1932; Edgcumbe and Burgner, 1973). The nuclear conflict associated with this first phase, *sufficiency versus dependency*, when resolved in an adaptive manner, leads to the feeling that one can ask for and receive help and support from others and that one's demands will not be overwhelming either to self or to others. The failure to resolve the developmental conflict associated with this issue leads to the feeling either that one's needs are so great that it is impossible for them to be satisfied, or that one will never be cared for to the extent that one desires to be, or even that, since such care is impossible, interpersonal relationships have little to offer that cannot be provided with greater satisfaction by autistic withdrawal.

The second, or "oral expulsive," phase concerns the development of feelings of trust, understanding, and empathy (Abraham, 1916, 1924a; Klein, 1932; Fairbairn, 1952; Parsons and Bales, 1955; Erikson, 1963, 1964). When the nuclear conflict associated with this phase of *trust versus mistrust* is resolved in an adaptive manner, there is a feeling that the world is basically a safe place, that others can be trusted, and that one can empathize with them. The failure to resolve the nuclear conflict associated with this phase leads to a pervasive sense of suspicion and rage, often described as a paranoid mistrust of others. In commenting upon the trust/mistrust dimension, Prelinger and Zimet observe:

Trust may be defined as a deeply ingrained conviction that one's needs, material and emotional, will be satisfied; that the world and the people in it are basically good, abundant in their supplies, and well meaning. . . . Mistrust may be defined as a sense of always living precariously, that good things never last . . . that the world contains many hidden dangers, that people are out to exploit or even "get" you [1964, pp. 64–65].

In general, psychoanalytic theorists believe that unresolved conflict regarding these two earliest phases of psychosocial development is associated with a qualitatively greater impairment in the subsequent capacity for sustained or meaningful relationships than is true for any subsequent phase (Jacobson, 1964, 1967; Modell, 1968).

The common theme running through various accounts of the core conflict associated with the third or "anal expulsive" phase of development is that of control—especially control over destructive wishes toward others (Freud, 1916; Jones, 1918; Abraham, 1921, 1925; Reich, 1933; Bibring, 1953; Erikson, 1963, 1964). Resolution of the nuclear conflict associated with this phase of *anger versus destructiveness* involves the capacity for the modulated expression of anger felt toward others. It is assumed that anger is a basic human feeling. The developmental task is not that of learning to experience anger but rather of learning to express this anger in an appropriate and modulated manner. Where there is concern that these feelings will "get out of hand" unless carefully controlled, or where there is a feeling that one is not in control of one's feelings, then it may be assumed that the nuclear conflict associated with this phase has not been resolved.

A number of theorists do not distinguish between what are often described as the two "anal" phases of psychosocial development (Bibring, 1953; Parsons and Bales, 1955; Frikson, 1963). However, some differentiation between these two phases seems to be of theoretical importance. Whereas the issue in the first, or "anal expulsive," phase is that of appropriate control of angry feelings, the issue in the later, or "anal retentive," phase is that of concern with the establishment of a sense of will or purpose (Freud, 1908, 1913b; Jones, 1918; Abraham, 1921, 1925; Reich, 1933; Parsons and Bales, 1955; Erikson, 1963, 1964). Where the nuclear conflict associated with this phase of *autonomy versus control* has been resolved, interpersonal relationships are marked by flexible exercise of autonomy and purpose. Feelings of doubt, shame, and cautious conformity, concern with possible domination by others, feelings of having to compromise one's own interests for the sake of others, or even rebelliousness and counterconformity mark the failure to resolve the nuclear conflict regarding this phase of psychosocial development.

The nuclear conflict associated with the fifth phase of

preadult psychosocial development, the so-called "oedipal" phase, concerns the development of feelings of competence and positive self-regard (Reich, 1933; Bibring, 1953; Erikson, 1963, 1964). Resolution, in an adaptive manner, of the nuclear conflict associated with this phase, *self-esteem versus inferiority*, leads to feelings of initiative, worth, and purpose, and of adequacy as a man or woman, particularly when viewed from the perspective of the internalized opposite-sex parent. Conflict regarding the resolution of this phase is characterized by feelings of worthlessness and the inability to achieve one's own goals, together with feelings of incompleteness or of being defective. These feelings of inadequacy may be warded off by concern with competition and with winning out over others, or else by manipulation of others, or attempts to show off to others or to show them up (Shapiro, 1965).

Less attention has been paid to adult than to preadult psychosocial development, and there has been less general agreement that this developmental process continues throughout the life cycle. Freud suggested, in *Mourning and Melancholia* (1917a), that the psychological management of grief involved in mourning the death of a loved one constituted a major developmental task of adulthood. Caplan and Grunebaum (1967) and others have suggested that throughout adulthood there are a variety of developmental tasks, each of which presents the individual with a unique crisis or conflict to be resolved. For example, there is considerable agreement among psychodynamic theorists that the successful attainment of mature dependence, intimacy, or mutuality depends upon the manner in which these adult developmental tasks are resolved (Fairbairn, 1946, 1949; Sullivan, 1953; Erikson, 1959, 1963, 1964). This formulation is also consistent with the clinical studies of Rapoport (1967), Rapoport and Rapoport (1965), and Goodrich (1968) concerning courtship, engagement, and marriage, and with the studies of Benedek (1959), Bibring (1959, 1961), Pavenstedt (1961), and the studies reported in Anthony and Benedek (1970) concerning parenthood.

Two phases of adult psychosocial development can be delineated that are of particular significance in the study of adaptation to the maternal role. The first of these phases, *mutuality versus isolation*, concerns the ability to sustain a commitment to another person, and to derive satisfaction from sharing of oneself with another. Evidence that the nuclear conflict associated with this phase has not been resolved in an adaptive manner may be observed in instances where one feels isolated, alone, and alienated. While this phase of psychosocial development is resolved to a greater or lesser extent, depending upon both the manner and the degree to which earlier issues— particularly the first two issues in psychosocial development— were resolved, the relevant conflict for this phase is that of the ability to attain a mature closeness within the context of a mutual relationship.

The second of the two adult phases, *nurturance versus self-absorption*, regards the feelings evoked by caring for another, above and beyond feelings of obligation and responsibility. One who has resolved the nuclear conflict associated with this phase feels a sense of generativity which transcends concerns with suffering, sacrifice, and allocation of scarce financial and emotional resources. Failure to resolve the conflict associated with the phase leads to feelings of self-preoccupation, self-indulgence, and self-absorption. As Prelinger and Zimet observe, in discussing this phase: "There is a deeply sensed interest or involvement in establishing and guiding the next generation . . . . Stagnation represents an absence of such generative involvement; it may result in self-indulgence and may be represented in a subjective sense of impoverishment and lack of genuine purpose" (1964, p. 71).

## HOSPITALIZATION FOLLOWING CHILDBIRTH

We have suggested that character, as an ego-adaptive function, refers to an individual's capacity for a variety of more or less appropriate relationships with others. Adult character is largely determined by the manner in which nuclear conflicts associated with the several phases of preadult and adult psychosocial development are resolved. Nowhere is this process more clearly observed than in the study of women hospitalized for a severe emotional disturbance in the first years following childbirth. A number of authors have attempted to isolate and describe what they term a "postpartum" syndrome (Hamilton, 1962), although this is not a recognized term in psychiatric nomenclature. It is not surprising that there is such little agreement in the literature regarding the duration of this postpartum period, which is said to apply to any period from the first few days following childbirth (Saunders, 1929) to the first six weeks following childbirth (Anderson, 1933), to one year or more (Ryle, 1961), to any time following delivery (Piker, 1938).

Some authors have maintained that the risk of onset of such severe disturbances is greatest in the first three months following childbirth, a finding which leads these investigators to infer a biochemical explanation (Hamilton, 1962). However, recent work reported by Melges (1965) suggests that there may be little validity in such an explanation. In spite of his own theoretical predilection for the biochemical view, Melges concludes that:

although certain hormonal changes may alter the clinical picture, there is little evidence for a classical delirium resulting from metabolic changes during the puerperium, for cognitive tests and EEGs were not abnormal. . . . Thus, the assertion that the postpartum syndrome presents a delirium, reflecting cerebral insufficiency secondary to puerperal metabolic abnormalities, is seriously challenged as a major etiology for these disorders [1965, pp. 12–13].

The psychological study of mental illness in women following childbirth focuses on the role of the mother's personality, and, in particular, on conflict in maternal psychosocial development, as an important factor in the development of this disturbance. The guiding hypothesis has been stated most clearly by Helene Deutsch.

Every woman brings into [motherhood] certain emotional factors and conflicts, that is, a certain psychodynamic background partly determined by her life situation, partly by her inner disposition due to her whole psychological development. From this, we can understand that while the beginning of motherhood poses the most mature task of femininity it will also tend to revive all the infantile conceptions of pregnancy and motherhood and childhood emotional reactions [1948, p. 14].

Deutsch's observation is well illustrated by one of the patients in

Melges's (1965) study, who observed that child care was difficult for her because "I am going so far into the past that I cannot hold on to the present" (1965, p. 8).

The earliest work in this area tended to focus on the symbolic meaning of the baby for the mother herself. Reports by Zilboorg (1928), Linn and Polatin (1950), and Rosberg and Karon (1959) suggest that mothers who are hospitalized for an emotional disturbance following childbirth show fewer physical symptoms during pregnancy than nonhospitalized women. These authors all agree that the baby has a special meaning for the mother who will have postpartum difficulty; such a woman feels filled up and content during pregnancy and experiences childbirth as a loss of basic supplies.

Just exactly what the mother feels filled up with is not an easy matter to determine. Rosberg and Karon (1959) believed that the baby had an "oral" meaning for the mother. Their observations led them to conclude that the woman liable to a postpartum disturbance is always unconsciously searching for the lost breast. These authors suggested that one possible replacement for the breast might be her husband's penis, since his semen is somewhat the same color as milk. The mother may then come to view the fetus as an oral replenishment; childbirth represents a traumatic loss of these badly needed supplies. Other authors have maintained that the special meaning of the baby for the mother lies more in being filled up with feces or with a penis (Freud, 1908, 1916) or, as Zilboorg (1928) and Deutsch (1945) have maintained, a combination of both feces and a penis.

It is clear that the baby may come to mean many different things to the mother. As both Milrod (1954) and Markham (1958) have pointed out, the loss through childbirth may mean not just one loss, but rather many, depending upon the nature of the conflicts experienced in the mother's own psychosocial development. Formulations such as those of Zilboorg and Rosberg and Karon rely solely on the observer's interpretation of the meaning of the childbirth experience for a particular mother and assume that the postpartum syndrome represents a particular kind of disturbance with a unique set of dynamics. Furthermore, this view assumes that the postpartum syndrome can be understood without reference to the mother's feelings about the child-rearing experience itself.

Many of these problems are highlighted in Ginsparg's (1956) empirical study of Zilboorg's hypothesis. Comparing a group of mothers hospitalized within the first year following childbirth, a group of mothers hospitalized sometime after the youngest child's first birthday, and a group of nonhospitalized control mothers, Ginsparg reports that results obtained with the Blacky Test (Blum, 1949) showed greater oedipal conflict among both groups of hospitalized women than among nonhospitalized mothers.

Ginsparg also found that, compared with mothers hospitalized early after childbirth, mothers hospitalized later showed greater "oral" conflict and greater impairment in the capacity to form relationships. Contrary to Zilboorg's hypothesis, mothers hospitalized earlier after childbirth demonstrated less deviant scores on the Minnesota Multiphasic Personality Inventory (MMPI) Female Masochism scale than the mothers hospitalized later. Using a thematic apperceptive measure of character (John, 1953; Grummon and Jones, 1954), Ginsparg found that most women in both the early and later hospitalized groups clustered near the lowest (most disturbed) point on a developmental scale. It is our conclusion, however, that this technique measures primarily a general factor of the degree of psychopathology and expresses distress rather than degree of conflict pertaining to the several phases of psychosocial development.

Depending upon the manner and the degree to which a woman has resolved prior nuclear conflicts in her own psychosocial development, she reacts to the developmental tasks of motherhood in quite different ways—a factor not considered by Ginsparg in her study. Markham (1958, 1961) has reported on a clinical study which suggests that a woman's perception of the childbirth situation itself depends not upon any a priori symbolic significance but upon the mother's own character development. Among a group of women hospitalized within the first weeks following childbirth, Markham does find certain similarities across cases. Based on her clinical interpretation of her material, she concludes that: "The psychological data of all eleven cases revealed the presence of severe oral deprivation or frustration in childhood which seemed to produce an early depressive reaction. . . . The striking feature In these cases was that every woman manifested a parasitic and/or symbiotic attachment to a maternal figure, combined with hostility of murderous dimensions" (1958, p. 182).

In her next study, Markham compares these eleven psychotic mothers with twelve postpartum women who had never sought psychiatric assistance, and reports that evidence of depression, oral dependency, hostility toward the mother figure, and castration feelings was found in almost every record of the *control* subjects. This leads her to suggest that the childbirth experience leads either to the reawakening of earlier separation anxiety, to a sense of the loss of a love object, or to a reawakening of unsatisfied oral-dependency cravings. However, the normal mothers in her study showed a greater variety of defensive techniques to ward off the depression and did not display the uncontrolled and regressive affect manifested by the hospitalized mothers.

Normal mothers less frequently viewed their children as rivals for oral supplies and as a drain on their own emotional resources, and seemed to resolve their feelings of depression and desire for a dependent and childlike relationship by giving to the baby and by providing companionship for the baby. Furthermore, not one of the twelve normal mothers was judged to have a symbiotic attachment to her own mother, while every one of the eleven hospitalized mothers was viewed as being unable to separate her own identity from that of her mother. Finally, it should be noted that these nonhospitalized mothers did not evidence the "emptiness" which was so characteristic of the hospitalized mothers.

Studies by Hilgard (1953), Hilgard and Newman (1959), Hilgard and Fisk (1960), and especially Sampson, Messinger, and Towne (1964) have also focused on the mother's perception of her relationship with her own mother as a factor in the development of emotional disturbances following childbirth. On the basis of a study of seventeen schizophrenic mothers who were hospitalized during the first years following childbirth, Sampson and his associates distinguish between what they term a "crisis of separation" and a "crisis of identification." One group of six women showed a pattern of moving back to their parental home at times of stress during marriage. Finally, after childbirth, when they were no longer able to go back and seek care from their own mothers, they were unable to function on their own. The authors describe this crisis of separation from the mother as follows:

These women encountered a critical struggle in early adult life when their own strivings, defenses against infantile object ties, and the requirements of reality pressed by the wider society led them to seek or to accept movement out of symbiotic bonds. This movement . . . initiated panic and an attempt to restore symbiotic relationships. This retreat, in turn, activated struggles against anxieties about fusion [1964, p. 31].

These women would appear to demonstrate fixation at a very early phase of psychosocial development. Sufficiency/dependency conflict seems to be central in their reaction to the child-rearing situation.

Mothers in the second group, characterized by what Sampson et al. refer to as the "crisis of identification," seemed to have experienced a crisis similar to the "anniversary reaction" described by Hilgard and her associates. These women view their own mothers as unacceptable identification figures. Acceptance of the maternal role evokes negative feelings regarding their own mothers, and as they begin to see a parallel between the way in which their own mothers cared for them and the way they are caring for their own babies, they begin to fear that they will turn out just like their own mothers. Sampson et al. comment, in discussing this crisis of identification:

[These] wives experienced difficulties . . . primarily in the establishment of an appropriate female identity which would promote and sustain intimate heterosexual relations and feminine role performances. These difficulties seemed to be associated not with *leaving* mother (as was the case with the separation crisis), but with *being* mother or at least being some aspect of their internalized mother image. . . . Childbearing and childrearing pressed for the synthesis of identifications with the young mother's own mother [1964, pp. 65–66].

Women suffering from a "crisis of identification" would appear to show greater conflict regarding somewhat later developmental phases. The core conflicts of anger versus destructiveness, autonomy versus control, and, especially, self-esteem versus inferiority seem particularly related to this crisis, although more primitive conflicts may also be associated with it.

Other reports have also discussed this "crisis of identification," notably Pavenstedt (1961), and especially Rheingold (1964) in his detailed study of maternal destructiveness. Rheingold singles out for intensive investigation a group of mothers, generally from his own psychiatric practice, who described a hostile relationship with their own mothers and who felt themselves to be the object of their mothers' destructive wishes. This hostile and destructive relationship then became the basis of the patient's attitudes toward her own daughter. Rheingold also pointed out that this identification provoked a good deal of anxiety in the patient herself, since she feared that she might act in the same destructive manner toward her own daughter as she believed her mother acted toward her.

There is some empirical support for the hypothesis that the crisis of identification is found more often in hospitalized than in nonhospitalized women. Gottheil, Paredes, and Exline (1968) report that, in their study, hospitalized women showed greater conflict than nonhospitalized mothers in their identification with their mothers. The two groups did not differ at all in the degree of conflict which they showed regarding their identification with their fathers. Furthermore, while greater perceived interpersonal distance between self and mother was associated with greater self-reported psychopathology, there was little relation between psychopathology and distance from father.

The studies of Hilgard and her associates, Sampson et al., Pavenstedt, Rheingold, and Gottheil et al. focus primarily on those aspects of maternal character which evoked conflicts related to the mother's perception of herself as a woman, although Sampson et al. do recognize another and more primitive conflict which evoked separation anxiety within the mother herself.

The nature and degree of conflict experienced in maternal psychosocial development is related not only to the issues precipitating hospitalization, but also to the mother's response to treatment, such as the joint admission of mother and child to the wards of a research-oriented state mental hospital (Weiss et al., 1964). Women who were judged to have made the best use of this treatment method showed, across a variety of projective materials, greater psychotic disturbance, increased conflicts regarding sexual identification, and perception of childbirth as a castration threat. Mothers rated as having made only satisfactory use of the program showed more conflict concerning oral dependency, as well as sexual conflict which had a decidedly oral quality. Patients rated as unsuccessful in their use of the program showed a strong fear of abandonment and a very limited ability to differentiate themselves from their babies.

It is probable that the mothers judged to have made the best use of the joint admission program were women who would be classified by Sampson et al. as indicating a "crisis of identification," while the mothers judged as less successful would be more likely to manifest a "crisis of separation." These findings also suggest that mothers manifesting greater conflicts regarding earlier phases of character formation are less able to utilize such specialized treatment programs.

## SUMMARY AND STATEMENT OF HYPOTHESES

Our review of the literature concerning both hospitalized and nonhospitalized mothers suggests a number of hypotheses which warrant systematic empirical study. Considering first the contrasting perceptions of significant relationships among hospitalized and nonhospitalized mothers, we have hypothesized that hospitalized mothers will show greater impairment in their capacity to form mature relationships. Markham's (1958, 1961) studies suggest that hospitalized mothers may be differentiated from nonhospitalized mothers particularly with regard to conflict regarding the first two phases of preadult character development, those regarding the nuclear conflicts of sufficiency/dependency, and trust/mistrust. In addition, since regression to preadult modes of perceiving and relating to others is said to result from an inability to relate in the differentiated manner required of an adult, these hospitalized mothers would also be expected to show greater conflict than nonhospitalized mothers regarding both of the adult phases of character development, during which resolution of conflicts involving mutuality versus isolation and nurturance versus self-absorption takes place.

The results of the studies by Markham and by Weiss et al.

(1964) also suggest that hospitalized mothers show more maladaptive attitudes than nonhospitalized mothers regarding their feelings of competence in perceiving and meeting the baby's needs, learning to separate one's own needs from those of one's baby, and, in particular, establishing reciprocity with the baby. The impairment that hospitalized mothers manifest in their capacity to form relationships may also be manifested in their feeling less able to establish a mutual relationship with the baby.

Within the group of hospitalized mothers, findings from Ginsparg's (1956) study suggest that mothers hospitalized during the first year following childbirth (a so-called early hospitalization group) will evidence *less* impairment in their capacity to form relationships than mothers hospitalized at some point after the first postpartum year. In addition, these early-breakdown mothers would be expected to show a *less* chronic premorbid social history and *greater turmoil* in the six months preceding hospitalization than the later-breakdown mothers, as well as a greater feeling of social competence as measured by a self-report inventory. In the early hospitalization group, hospitalization would typically be expected to occur as a result of situational stress, while among women in the later hospitalization group, hospitalization would more typically be associated with the exacerbation of a chronic disturbance.

# 10

# Method of Study

Two groups of subjects were used in this study: a sample of thirty-five mothers admitted to the Massachusetts Mental Health Center over an eighteen-month period, and a matched sample of thirty-five nonhospitalized women who had never sought psychiatric help.[1]

The sample of hospitalized mothers represents primarily a group of acutely disturbed patients. While the average length of hospitalization was fairly brief (ninety-two days), the range was from four to sixty weeks. A majority of the mothers (58 percent) had never been hospitalized before. Tabulation of the established diagnoses of the thirty-five patients indicated that 40 percent were diagnosed as psychotic (either a schizophrenic or an affective disorder). Of the 60 percent of the patients who were "without psychosis," most manifested either a situational (depressive) reaction, usually accompanied by some suicidal wishes, a personality trait disorder, or an emotionally unstable personality. Ratings of interviews conducted by the social

---

1. While the original sample contained 35 hospitalized mothers individually matched with 35 nonhospitalized mothers on the relevant background characteristics, two hospitalized mothers were transferred to another hospital before picture-thematic materials could be administered. For all analyses reporting data based on the IAT, the sample consisted of 33 hospitalized mothers and 35 nonhospitalized mothers. The loss of the two hospitalized women did not lead to any greater group differences between hospitalized and nonhospitalized mothers on the relevant demographic variables.

worker assigned to each patient indicated that 51 percent of the mothers had shown definite changes in their behavior toward their families in the six months preceding hospitalization, suggesting that, for the majority of cases, the mother's disturbance was of recent origin.

Comparison with data reported by Dreeben (1962) suggests that, with the exception of the relatively shorter stay in the hospital of the patients in the present sample, they were fairly typical of the female admissions over the course of any given year. It is probable that since these women had family responsibilities, greater effort was made to return them to the community than is true for the patient population as a whole. Table 1 indicates that 55 percent of the mothers were admitted during the first eight months following childbirth.

It should be noted that only ten of the thirty-five mothers were primiparae. This compares closely with nine primiparae for the nonpatient sample, as well as with data obtained during

TABLE 1. AGE OF YOUNGEST CHILD AT MOTHER'S HOSPITALIZATION (to the nearest month)

| Child's Age | N | Percentage | Cumulative Percentage |
|---|---|---|---|
| One month and below | 4 | 12 | 12 |
| Two months | 1 | 3 | 15 |
| Three months | 1 | 3 | 18 |
| Four months | 6 | 18 | 36 |
| Five months | 0 | 0 | 36 |
| Six months | 1 | 3 | 39 |
| Seven months | 2 | 6 | 45 |
| Eight months | 3 | 9 | 54 |
| Nine months | 0 | 0 | 54 |
| Ten months | 1 | 3 | 57 |
| Eleven months | 0 | 0 | 57 |
| Twelve months | 1 | 3 | 60 |
| Thirteen through eighteen months | 2 | 6 | 66 |
| Nineteen through twenty-four months | 3 | 9 | 75 |
| Twenty-five through thirty months | 3 | 9 | 84 |
| Thirty-one through thirty-six months | 5 | 16 | 100 |
|  | 33 | 100 | 100 |

Mean = 13.08 months   Median = 8 months   Standard deviation = 11.42 months
The data do not include two women who were transferred from the hospital before all data could be collected.

repeated administrations of the maternal attitude scale to a much larger normative sample (Cohler et al., 1970). The age of the youngest child at the time of the mother's admission varied from nine days to thirty-six months, which was the upper age limit of the study.

The sample of nonhospitalized mothers was recruited via newspaper advertisements. Data from a study by Cohler et al. (1968) indicated that mothers recruited in such a manner do not display notable psychopathology and seem, at least in terms of their MMPI profiles, to be similar to other "normal" samples such as that described by Gloye and Zimmerman (1967) or Lanyon (1968). Hospitalized mothers were matched with non-hospitalized mothers on the basis of the age and sex of the child and the mother's education and religion (Catholic versus non-Catholic). These matching variables were selected as a result of earlier work (Cohler et al., 1970), which had indicated that a variety of psychological factors related to the onset of emotional disturbances in mothers were also related to these background variables.

As shown in table 2, the sample of hospitalized and nonhospitalized mothers was well matched on the relevant demographic variables. The value of Student's t for each of the

TABLE 2. COMPARISON OF HOSPITALIZED AND NONHOSPITALIZED MOTHERS ON MATCHING VARIABLES ($N = 35$ for each group)

| Matching Variables | Patients | | Controls | | | |
|---|---|---|---|---|---|---|
| | Mean | Std. Dev. | Mean | Std. Dev. | t-test | p |
| Husband occupation[a] | 3.89 | 1.92 | 3.66 | 1.66 | 0.53 | n. s. |
| Husband education | 3.20 | 1.56 | 3.17 | 1.32 | 0.08 | n. s. |
| Wife education | 3.83 | 1.08 | 3.77 | 0.93 | 0.24 | n. s. |
| Wife age[b] | 3.20 | 1.09 | 3.14 | 1.02 | 0.22 | n. s. |
| Age (in months) of youngest child | 13.23 | 11.21 | 15.31 | 11.76 | 0.75 | n. s. |
| Number of children | 2.29 | 1.30 | 2.60 | 1.48 | 0.93 | n. s. |
| Wife SES | 42.51 | 16.61 | 40.69 | 13.73 | 0.50 | n. s. |

[a]Mother's own education and husband's education and occupation were coded according to a seven point scale; a higher score indicates fewer years of education (the obtained means are equivalent to about 11¼ years for both groups) and a lower-ranked occupation.

[b]Wives' ages range from 20 to 45 and were coded according to a nine-point scale. The obtained means are equivalent to an age of approximately 26 years in both groups.

matching variables is quite small, permitting us to accept the hypothesis that the groups of hospitalized and nonhospitalized mothers do not differ in any significant manner on these matching variables.

## BACKGROUND VARIABLES

Information was collected from all hospitalized and nonhospitalized subjects regarding their own educational attainment, husband's occupation, religious preference, and age, as a part of a more extensive family information questionnaire. A brief screening measure of the subjects' current level of intellectual functioning was also obtained, using the Shipley-Hartford Retreat scale of intelligence (Western Psychological Services, 1963). This self-administered and objectively scored test measures two aspects of intellectual functioning, vocabulary level, and verbal and numerical abstraction. Several investigators have found high correlations (in the .80's and .90's) with more complete and individually administered measures of intelligence (Monroe, 1966).

## THE ASSESSMENT OF MATERNAL CHARACTER

The measure used in the assessment of conflict in maternal psychosocial development, the Interpersonal Apperception Technique (IAT), consists of seven scales for rating stories told in response to a series of pictures portraying interpersonal relationships.[2]   The IAT was developed after a review of previous measures (Cohler, 1973) suggested that a variety of methodological problems would be involved in using either paper-and-pencil measures or previously developed picture-thematic measures such as Blum's (1950, 1962) Blacky Test, John's rating scales for use with the standard TAT series (John, 1953; Grummon and Jones, 1954), Gruen's (1964) scales for measuring psychosocial development in older persons, or Prelinger and Zimet's (1964) scales for rating personality functions.

___

2. Copies of the manual for the Interpersonal Apperception Technique are available free of cost from the authors.

## DESCRIPTION OF THE IAT

Scales have been developed to rate the extent to which the nuclear conflict has been resolved which is associated with each of the seven phases of preadult and adult psychosocial development: sufficiency/dependency, trust/mistrust, anger/destructiveness, autonomy/control, self-esteem/inferiority, mutuality/isolation, and nurturance/self-absorption. Each of these phases is scored on the following five-point scale:

1 = Complete comfort in dealing with the phase. While the subject may not have completely resolved all conflict associated with the phase, the phase has been resolved in an adaptive and appropriate manner.

2 = Generally an appropriate resolution of the phase, although there is some evidence of discomfort or lack of satisfaction in resolving the nuclear conflict associated with the phase.

3 = Some ability to resolve the nuclear conflict associated with that phase, at least to the extent that some positive resolution is possible. However, there is considerable discomfort and some reliance upon defensive strategies as a way of dealing with the conflict which the phase evokes in the subject.

4 = Generally an inappropriate or inadequate resolution of the nuclear conflict associated with the phase. A great deal of conflict is evidenced, and there is little evidence that the subject feels satisfaction or comfort in dealing with this phase.

5 = Evidence of impairment in resolving the nuclear conflict associated with the phase, to such an extent that the subject may not even be able to deal with the phase, except at the level of fantasy.

In scoring a particular story for a particular phase, the rater's first task is to determine if a story is salient, or thematically relevant to the phase being considered. If the story is judged to be salient, the rater then decides upon the weight, on this five-point scale, to assign to the story. In general, a score of 1 means that a subject has resolved with definite ease the nuclear conflict associated with the particular phase being coded; her perception of the situation being described is both mature and appropriate. Relatively few subjects will receive such a rating for any picture. A score of 5 indicates absolutely no attempt to resolve the nuclear conflict associated with the particular phase, except via withdrawal into a fantasy world. Scores of 2, 3, and 4 are somewhat more difficult to differentiate. Levels 2 and 3 differ generally in terms of the intensity of the conflict, while levels 3 and 4 differ in terms of the person's ability to resolve the nuclear conflict associated with a particular phase and the degree of discomfort which is felt regarding interactions said to be prototypic of that particular phase. In most cases, the subject is likely to receive a 3 if she is able to provide some spontaneous solution to the conflict described in the story, while a 4 is given if the subject is not able to see any way in which the conflict may be resolved.

The scoring procedure which we have developed yields three separate scores for each phase or dimension of psychosocial development: (1) an index of the salience or concern to the subject of that particular phase or dimension (number of scorable pictures); (2) a combined index of the extent to which the core conflict associated with a particular phase has been resolved (the mean of standard scores across all salient pictures); (3) the rank of a particular conflict score compared to the other six scores (ipsative rank for each phase). This scoring procedure enables us to make maximal use of the data and provides for separate measures of salience and intensity as suggested by Prelinger and Zimet (1964). The use of standard scores permits correction for the differential "pull" of pictures regarding the presence and intensity of conflict relevant to each of the seven phases.

The relation between the separate salience and conflict scores is represented by the summary conflict score, which is calculated on the basis of the sum of the standardized scores divided by the number of salient stories out of the possible set of seventeen which are scorable for that dimension. The higher this summary score, the less the subject has been able to resolve the core conflict associated with a particular developmental phase. The rank ordering of these summary conflict scores suggest the relative importance for the subject of each of these seven phases, independent of the amount of conflict regarding each of the phases. The summary conflict scores are ranked in order of decreasing magnitude, the rank of 1 being assigned to the score which shows the greatest amount of conflict.

## PICTURES USED WITH THE IAT

The present form of the Interpersonal Apperception Technique employs nine of the pictures (1, 2, 6GF, 7GF, 10, 12, 13MF, 15, 18GF) from the second published version of the Murray (1943) Thematic Apperception Test, together with eight pictures developed especially for the present study, in accordance with the guidelines established through the work of Henry (1956), Kagan (1959), Kenny (1964), Lesser (1961), and Murstein (1961, 1963). These newly developed pictures, which are shown in figure 1, were created in order to elicit responses relevant to a woman's concept of herself and to each of the significant relationships in her life.[3]   The set of seventeen pictures includes fourteen which are relevant to a woman's relationships, respectively, with her mother (five), with her father (three), with her husband (three), and with her children (three). One picture concerns the woman's relationship with a sister or other female peer, and three pertain to her own aspirations and self-image.

## EVALUATION OF INTER-RATER RELIABILITY

As is characteristic of projective techniques in general, determination of the reliability of scoring is somewhat complex. It should be emphasized that picture-thematic methods are not tests in the psychometric definition of this term. As Atkinson (1950), McClelland (1958), Murstein (1963), and Zubin, Eron, and Schumer (1965) all note, it is difficult to apply traditional concepts of internal consistency or test-retest reliability to this approach. In the present study, the two raters coded pretest materials for a given phase, after which they met to discuss their ratings and to resolve possible differences. They then independently rated all 68 protocols on that particular phase; reliability figures were calculated on the basis of these independent ratings. Following the suggestions of Murray (1938) and Taft (1959), the two raters then met to resolve differences and to arrive at a final pooled rating for each subject. Several weeks after these ratings had been completed, the two raters repeated

---

3. Copies of the individual pictures drawn especially for the Interpersonal Apperception Technique are available from the authors.

Figure 1: Eight pictures designed especially for the Interpersonal Apperception Technique.

the process of arriving at pooled judgments in order to determine the reliability of the method.[4]

TABLE 3. INDEPENDENT INTER-JUDGE AGREEMENT: INTERPERSONAL APPERCEPTION TECHNIQUE

| Dimension | Conflict | | Salience | | Final Score | |
|---|---|---|---|---|---|---|
| | "A" | Range | Percentage | Range | Percentage | Range |
| Sufficiency/dependency | .889 | .711–.989 | .932 | 83.1–100 | .875 | 79.4–92.6 |
| Trust/mistrust | .851 | .351–1.00 | .958 | 89.0–100 | .935 | 87.9–97.0 |
| Anger/destructiveness | .850 | .400–1.00 | .970 | 90.6–100 | .959 | 85.3–100 |
| Autonomy/control | .860 | .400–1.00 | .919 | 75.8–100 | .894 | 73.5–98.5 |
| Self-Esteem/inferiority | .873 | .333–1.00 | .949 | 80.6–100 | .933 | 79.4–100 |
| Mutuality/isolation | .910 | .836–1.00 | .902 | 63.1–100 | .883 | 66.2–100 |
| Nurturance/self-absorption | .911 | .711–1.00 | .844 | 43.7–100 | .807 | 41.2–98.5 |

Table 3 indicates the reliability of the two separate raters' scores across the seventeen pictures, for each dimension, using Robinson's (1957) coefficient of agreement. The mean coefficient of agreement ("A") across all seventeen pictures is presented, together with the range of coefficients of agreement

4. Two of the pictures from the standard Murray (1943) TAT series presented such difficulty in scoring that they are worthy of special note. TAT picture 18GF was extremely difficult to score on the dimension of Anger vs. destructiveness. This picture is described by Murray (1943) as follows: "A woman has her hands squeezed around the throat of another woman whom she appears to be pushing backwards across the banister of a stairway." This is one of the few pictures in the original Murray series which presents a conflict situation to such an extent as to evoke strong defensive reactions. Indeed, only 23 per cent of the subjects in the present study told stories which acknowledged, either directly or indirectly, that the picture portrayed an aggressive act. While special ground rules were developed for coding this story on this dimension, it would seem best, in future work with the Interpersonal Apperception Technique, not to include 18GF in the series.

Problems also arose in coding TAT picture 7GF on the dimension of Nurturance vs. self-absorption. This picture is described by Murray (1943) as follows: "An older woman is sitting on a sofa close beside a girl, speaking or reading to her. The girl, who holds a doll in her lap, is looking away." Many subjects in the present study identified with the little girl holding the doll or baby rather than with the adult figure seated beside her. Rather than eliminate this picture, we coded it for the extent to which the maternal figure could recognize and fulfill the child's needs, regardless of whether the subject had identified with the adult or child figure.

for each picture. It should be noted that this figure does not include those cases where one or both raters decided that a picture was not salient for a particular phase. The next two columns of table 3 indicate the mean percentage of agreement between the raters, across the seventeen stories, regarding the classification of a picture as salient or not salient, and the range of these percentages of agreement figures across the seventeen pictures for each phase. The last two columns refer to the agreement between the two raters concerning the total score; since this figure includes instances in which both raters agreed that a picture was not salient for that phase (0 point disagreement).

Seven weeks after the protocols had been scored on all seven dimensions, the raters rescored the protocols of twelve subjects, selected at random, on all seven dimensions; seven of these records came from the group of hospitalized subjects while five of these records came from the group of control subjects.

It is possible that the original ratings of these seven subjects were remembered in making the repeat ratings. However, it was our impression that memory factors were of little significance in rescoring: the time lapse since the initial rating, in addition to the fact that the two raters had each coded a total of 780 stories on seven different dimensions, for a grand total of 5,460 separate ratings, helped minimize the role of memory factors in determining these subsequent ratings of seven subjects.

After pooled ratings had been determined for each subject, on each story, across all seven dimensions, the scores were summed across all stories, and the number of stories judged as salient was also tabulated. Both the sum scores across each picture over each dimension and the number of stories judged salient were compared for each of the subjects between the original testing session and the repeat session. Rank-order correlations for both the sum scores and the number of stories judged as salient were then computed. The results of this reliability study are reported in table 4. It can be seen that the correlations between the original and repeat pooled judgments are quite satisfactory for six of the seven dimensions. While the correlations on the nurturance/self-absorption dimension are moderate, they are not as high as those for the other dimensions and may be due to rater fatigue.

TABLE 4. RANK-ORDER CORRELATIONS BETWEEN ORIGINAL POOLED
RATINGS AND REPEAT POOLED RATINGS (N = 12)

| | | | |
|---|---|---|---|
| A. Sufficiency/dependency | 1. Total | .96 | .01 |
| | 2. Sum salient | .61 | .02 |
| B. Trust/mistrust | 1. Total | .89 | .01 |
| | 2. Sum salient | .79 | .01 |
| C. Anger/destructiveness | 1. Total | .89 | .01 |
| | 2. Sum salient | .93 | .01 |
| D. Autonomy/control | 1. Total | .96 | .01 |
| | 2. Sum salient | .93 | .01 |
| E. Self-esteem/inferiority | 1. Total | 1.00 | .01 |
| | 2. Sum salient | .93 | .01 |
| F. Mutuality/isolation | 1. Total | .86 | .01 |
| | 2. Sum salient | .93 | .01 |
| G. Nurturance/self-absorption | 1. Total | .54 | .05 |
| | 2. Sum salient | .68 | .01 |

## INTERNAL STRUCTURE OF THE IAT:
## NORMATIVE AND CORRELATIONAL DATA

*Basic Statistics for Each Dimension.* The manual for the Interpersonal Apperception Technique was originally developed through the use of protocols obtained from a sample of several hundred hospitalized and nonhospitalized mothers of young children. The means, medians, and standard deviations for each of the seven phases are indicated in table 5.

It should be noted that data are presented separately for each of the three types of scores used in scoring each phase of character development: (1) the number of salient stories which are scorable on a particular dimension; (2) the relative rank assigned to any given dimension, relative to all other dimensions across each subject; and (3) the final score for the dimension, which is comprised of the conflict score or mean score across all seventeen pictures, where the score for any one picture consists of the standard score value equivalent to the raw score.

Two standard score means (excluding and including zeroes) are presented for five of the seven phases; all women gave at least one scorable story for each of the two phases associated with adult psychosocial development. Additional study of subjects receiving a score of zero (no scorable stories on that phase) showed that these women demonstrated even less

TABLE 5. NORMATIVE DATA, INTERPERSONAL APPERCEPTION TECHNIQUE[a]

| Dimension and Score | Mean | Stand. Dev. | Median |
|---|---|---|---|
| A. *Sufficiency/dependency* (67/1)[b] | | | |
| Number salient pictures | 3.43 | 1.63 | 3.00 |
| Raw ranks | 3.66 | 1.88 | 3.50 |
| Mean score (excluding zeros) | 48.86 | 8.19 | 48.63 |
| Mean score (including zeros) | 48.14 | 10.04 | 48.44 |
| B. *Trust/mistrust* (57/11) | | | |
| Number salient pictures | 2.20 | 1.88 | 2.00 |
| Raw ranks | 4.56 | 1.91 | 5.00 |
| Mean score (excluding zeros) | 48.20 | 8.93 | 47.81 |
| Mean score (including zeros) | 40.40 | 19.54 | 45.50 |
| C. *Anger/destructiveness* (58/10) | | | |
| Number salient pictures | 2.14 | 1.74 | 2.00 |
| Raw ranks | 5.11 | 1.74 | 5.50 |
| Mean score (excluding zeros) | 49.01 | 8.58 | 47.75 |
| Mean score (including zeros) | 41.81 | 19.08 | 45.69 |
| D. *Autonomy/control* (66/2) | | | |
| Number salient pictures | 3.78 | 1.92 | 4.00 |
| Raw ranks | 3.71 | 1.85 | 3.75 |
| Mean score (excluding zeros) | 50.38 | 8.19 | 49.47 |
| Mean score (including zeros) | 48.90 | 11.93 | 49.31 |
| E. *Self-esteem/inferiority* (62/6) | | | |
| Number salient pictures | 2.70 | 2.00 | 2.00 |
| Raw ranks | 3.54 | 2.05 | 3.50 |
| Mean score (excluding zeros) | 49.04 | 8.25 | 50.00 |
| Mean score (including zeros) | 44.72 | 15.99 | 49.44 |
| F. *Mutuality/isolation* (68/0) | | | |
| Number salient pictures | 3.25 | 1.57 | 3.00 |
| Raw ranks | 3.56 | 1.72 | 3.50 |
| Mean score | 49.81 | 8.27 | 49.78 |
| G. *Nurturance/self-absorption* (68/0) | | | |
| Number salient pictures | 3.31 | 1.25 | 3.00 |
| Raw ranks | 3.76 | 2.00 | 3.50 |
| Mean score | 50.05 | 8.47 | 50.25 |

[a]Normative data based on 68 women: 33 hospitalized for an emotional disturbance, 35 nonhospitalized.

[b]Figures in parentheses represent the number of subjects with at least one scorable story on a particular dimension and the number of subjects with nonscorable stories.

conflict than subjects scored as 1, which led us to retain both means in the normative data.

The phases of trust/mistrust and anger/destructiveness provided the largest number of zero scores and also the most skewed means and ranks, showing that most subjects who do tell stories scorable on these two dimensions receive scores indicating relatively little conflict. The mean and median number of salient stories scorable for a particular dimension or phase does not seem to vary greatly across dimensions, with the exception of autonomy/control, a phase for which there are approximately twice as many scorable stories as for other phases or dimensions; most women in this study appear to be quite involved in the conflict which this phase represents.

*Inter-Dimensional Correlations.* In discussing the empirical relations which obtain among the seven phases of preadult and adult character development, we shall consider separately (a) the number of salient stories scorable on each phase, (b) the rank assigned to the score obtained by subjects on this phase, relative to other dimensions, and (c) the conflict or mean score, based on the standard score equivalents of the raw scores obtained on each of the seventeen pictures for any one dimension.

Turning first to the number of scorable or salient stories (table 6), it can be seen that sufficiency/dependency, trust/mistrust, and self-esteem/inferiority are related to each other. It can also be seen that nurturance/self-absorption, anger/destructiveness, and autonomy/control appear to be fairly independent of the other four dimensions.

TABLE 6. INTERDIMENSIONAL CORRELATIONS (A. NUMBER OF SALIENT STORIES): INTERPERSONAL APPERCEPTION TECHNIQUE[a]

|  | Number of Salient Stories | | | | | | |
|---|---|---|---|---|---|---|---|
| Dimension | S/D | T/MT | A/D | A/C | Se/I | M/I | NSa |
| Sufficiency/dependency | ---- | | | | | | |
| Trust/mistrust | .37** | ---- | | | | | |
| Anger/destructiveness | .02 | .12 | ---- | | | | |
| Autonomy/control | .05 | .04 | .23* | ---- | | | |
| Self-esteem/inferiority | .45** | .49** | -.03 | .16 | ---- | | |
| Mutuality/isolation | .00 | .29* | .14 | .05 | .20 | ---- | |
| Nurturance/self-absorption | .00 | .04 | .06 | .03 | .13 | .14 | ---- |

[a]$N = 68$: 33 hospitalized women, 35 nonhospitalized women
*$p < .05$  **$p < .01$

In table 7 we have indicated the intercorrelations among the raw conflict scores (lower left part of matrix), between the raw and standard score conflict scores (diagonals, underlined), and among the conflict scores (upper right part of matrix). Moderate

TABLE 7. INTERDIMENSIONAL CORRELATIONS (B. RAW AND STANDARD-IZED MEAN SCORES): INTERPERSONAL APPERCEPTION TECHNIQUE[a, b]

| Dimension | S/D | T/MT | A/D | A/C | Se/I | M/I | N/Sa |
|---|---|---|---|---|---|---|---|
| Sufficiency/dependency | .93 | .34** | .18 | .23* | .38** | .46** | .40** |
| Trust/mistrust | .29* | .91 | .16 | .18 | .29* | .42** | .18 |
| Anger/destructiveness | .25* | .22 | .93 | .22 | .15 | .20 | .43** |
| Autonomy/control | .18 | .25* | .25* | .81 | .51** | .38** | .37** |
| Self-esteem/inferiority | .39** | .31** | .23* | .58** | .87 | .52** | .37** |
| Mutuality/isolation | .57** | .40** | .29* | .39** | .45** | .96 | .44** |
| Nurturance/self-absorption | -.06 | .16 | .42** | .33** | .32** | .45** | .96 |

[a]Correlations between raw and standard score based means appear in the diagonals.
[b]$N = 68.33$ hospitalized women, 35 nonhospitalized women.
*$p < .05$  **$p < .01$

correlations still obtain between the scores on sufficiency/dependency, trust/mistrust, self-esteem/inferiority, and mutuality/isolation. However, we also find substantial correlations between autonomy/control and self-esteem/inferiority, and nurturance/self-absorption and all other dimensions except sufficiency/dependency and trust/mistrust. While the conflict score based on the raw means is related to the conflict score based on the mean of the sum of the standard scored pictures (as can be seen from the italicized correlations in the diagonals), the relations which obtain between these conflict scores, based on standard scores, differ to a large extent from the raw conflict score intercorrelations. In general, the inter-dimensional correlations based on those standard score means are of moderate magnitude and significantly different from the "expected" zero-order correlations.

In table 8 we have indicated the intercorrelations of the raw rank scores. These low negative correlations between ranks are not independent, since a subject's rank on one dimension influences the rank on all other dimensions. Mosteller, cited by Waxler (1959), has demonstrated that the expected "baseline" correlation between any $n$ rankings may be derived from the following formula: $r = 1/(n-1)$. Using this formula, with seven ranks, a correlation of $-.16$ would be expected. None of the

TABLE 8. INTERDIMENSIONAL CORRELATIONS (C. CORRELATIONS BETWEEN RANKS): INTERPERSONAL APPERCEPTION TECHNIQUE[a, b]

| Dimension | Ranks | | | | | | |
|---|---|---|---|---|---|---|---|
| | S/D | T/MT | A/D | A/C | Se/I | M/I | N/Sa |
| Sufficiency/dependency | ---- | | | | | | |
| Trust/mistrust | -.17 | ---- | | | | | |
| Anger/destructiveness | -.13 | -.05 | ---- | | | | |
| Autonomy/control | -.38 | -.22 | -.01 | ---- | | | |
| Self-esteem/inferiority | -.07 | -.25 | -.16 | -.07 | ---- | | |
| Mutuality/isolation | -.14 | -.09 | -.36 | -.17 | -.33 | ---- | |
| Nurturance/self-absorption | -.31 | -.18 | -.20 | -.07 | -.20 | -.16 | ---- |

[a]No correlation between ranks differs significantly from the baseline correlation of -.16.
[b]$N = 68$: 33 hospitalized women, 35 nonhospitalized women.

obtained correlations, based on ranks, differs significantly from this baseline correlation; we can conclude that the ranks are not related to each other. This relative independence is important to note, since the analysis of the relation between these ranks and other data to be discussed in the present study assumes the independence of these ranks.

*Factor Analysis of Conflict Scores.* The interdimensional correlations we have presented are somewhat difficult to interpret. Indeed, one may ask what correlations between dimensions of psychosocial development might have been predicted in advance. In order to explore further the meaning of these correlations, a factor-analytic study was carried out on the conflict scores. Using a principal-components analysis, three factors were extracted which accounted for 72 percent of the common variance. In order to facilitate the psychological interpretation of this principal components analysis, these three factors were rotated to simple structure, using a verimax solution (Armor and Couch, 1972). This rotated factor structure is shown in table 9.

The first rotated factor can be labeled *impairment in forming object relations.* Three dimensions load high on this factor: sufficiency/dependency, trust/mistrust, and mutuality/isolation. The loading of the first two dimensions is not surprising and is consistent with the genetic point of view in psycho-

TABLE 9. ORTHOGONAL FACTOR LOADINGS: CONFLICT SCORES[a]

| Dimension | Impairment in Forming Object Relations | Dissatisfaction with Mothering[b] | Feelings of Inadequacy | Communality |
|---|---|---|---|---|
| Sufficiency/dependency | .681 | .222 | .229 | .566 |
| Trust/mistrust | .840 | .055 | .004 | .708 |
| Anger/destructiveness | .095 | .911 | .024 | .839 |
| Autonomy/control | .001 | .222 | .833 | .742 |
| Self-esteem/inferiority | .323 | .040 | .791 | .732 |
| Mutuality/isolation | .624 | .132 | .518 | .675 |
| Nurturance/self-absorption | .232 | .673 | .399 | .666 |
| Sum Sq. | 1.726 | 1.403 | 1.800 | 4.929 |

[a]N = 68: 33 hospitalized women, 35 nonhospitalized women.
[b]This factor has been reflected so that the positive pole indicates greater conflict and the negative pole indicates less conflict.

analytic theory which hypothesizes a relation between these two "oral" phases. The loading of mutuality/isolation on this factor suggests that an individual who is either extremely dependent or else totally self-sufficient as a way of defending against strong dependency needs, and who is, in addition, mistrustful of others and their motives, will also be unable to form mature relationships with others, such as is represented by a satisfying marital relationship. In sum, impairment in forming object relations represents feelings of deprivation, mistrust, and isolation from others versus feelings of satisfaction, empathy, and closeness derived from relationships with others.

The relative independence of these three dimensions from anger/destructiveness, autonomy/control, and nurturance/self-absorption is to be expected, but the fact that nurturance/self-absorption is also underrepresented on this factor is interesting. It would appear that the woman who achieves a high score on this factor has such difficulties in forming relationships that she has not yet reached the point where she can begin to resolve the conflicts presented by this phase in order to deal with the developmental task of nurturance.

The psychological meaning of the object relations factor can be illustrated by examining stories written by subjects scoring high and low conflict on it. Mrs. G, the subject with the highest score on this factor, narrated the following story:

This reminds me of a husband and a wife. And the wife is trying to explain to her husband how she thinks of things. And he's pondering over it but doesn't understand. He wants to know how she feels about him. She's thinking how nobody cares about her and she doesn't know how to love anyone—she can't remember the feeling. And he can't understand it. (Examiner: Outcome?) Either she'll die or she'll get help, or maybe she'll do something to end the marriage and destroy herself, or go on living the way she is, or get help if she can. (E: What does she do?) She just lets it go the way it's going.

This subject described very clearly the intertwined feelings of emptiness, lonliness, helplessness, and lack of understanding which are portrayed within the context of her marriage. The essence of difficulties in forming object relations is strikingly illustrated in this subject's comment that "*she doesn't know how to love anyone—she can't remember the feeling.*"

At the other pole of this factor is the woman who can feel warmth and who manifests the ability to both love and be loved, to understand others and feel understood by them. A story by Mrs. N is indicative of the positive pole on this factor:

I'd say this was a middle-aged couple. Ah, it's after supper and they've just eaten supper and now they've come into the living room . . . he's talking about his work and she's sitting there listening to him. He's talking about the day he's had. And then they sit down and he'll read the newspaper and she'll read a book. They care about each other.

This subject's story well reflects the opposite end of this factor in her statement that "*they care about each other.*" Trust and an ability to allow herself some dependency on others lead her to be able to develop closeness with her husband and a feeling of congruence between them.

The second factor indicates simple structure and has high negative loadings on two dimensions, anger/destructiveness, and nurturance/self-absorption. This second factor can be described as *feelings of dissatisfaction with mothering* (versus feelings of satisfaction with the maternal role). The woman earning a high score on this factor is likely to express overt anger and resentment at being a mother and having to care for children. The woman earning a low score is likely to be very concerned with mothering and positively involved in fulfilling the maternal role, perhaps even to the extent that she is unable to recognize some latent hostility which she feels toward the maternal role. In sum, this factor represents feelings of contentment with the role of wife and mother, versus feelings of resentment over the demands which she feels the child makes upon her.

The psychological meaning of the dissatisfaction-with-mothering factor can also be illustrated by reference to some sample stories from subjects earning high positive and high negative scores on it. Thus, Mrs. B, a subject earning a high score, told the following story:

The little boy's been playing with his ball. His mother's been sitting there watching him, but now she's sitting down because she's tired. And she's thinking that if she has to get up one more time to play ball with him, she'll scream. But he doesn't ask her to play anymore because he likes his ball. And after a while, they go home.

From this woman's story, the nurturant role is clearly a burden to her, and the depth of her resentment is very obvious. While she doesn't actually scream, she feels at times as if she would like to. While it may also be true that most mothers would feel this way at times, it is unlikely they would tell a story such as this unless they were indeed quite burdened by the demands and responsibilities of the maternal role, and unless they resented the demands which mothering placed upon them.

The woman earning a low score on this factor expresses little resentment and indicates contentment with the maternal role. Thus, one mother told the following story:

Mother and child. Spring day—and they're out in the park. And the child is playing with the ball. The mother is contented watching the child play. And then they go home.

Another mother told the following story:

This looks like the mother and her young boy went out for a walk in the park—his usual afternoon walk in the park. She's sitting on the bench, thinking of him, wondering if she's doing

right by him . . . it's a peaceful scene. The child seems to be
playing quietly. It looks safe and secure.

Thus, the mother receiving a low score expresses satisfaction
with the maternal role, although, quite clearly, she may also
express some doubt about her ability to live up to her
conception of what it means to be a mother. If the woman
receiving a high score has problems controlling her feelings of
resentment toward child rearing, the woman receiving a low
score may concomitantly have difficulty expressing her feelings
of resentment to such an extent that she may even deny her
anger and, instead, express her concern with her performance in
the maternal role and her ability to live up to her goals.

The third factor is marked by high positive loadings on two
dimensions: autonomy/control and self-esteem/inferiority. A
third dimension, mutuality/isolation, has a considerably lower
loading on this factor. The woman earning a high positive score
is both self-deprecatory and guilt-ridden. She has a negative
self-image, such as would be expected from the high contribution of self-esteem/inferiority. This conflict may relate, at least
in part, to her ability to stand on her own two feet and assert her
own will. This factor may be titled *feelings of inadequacy as a
woman versus positive self-regard*. A rather extreme example of
a woman scoring high is contained in the following story told
by Mrs. G.

That's a husband and wife—and they love each other very
much. They're talking about how they have to leave each other
forever and ever because the wife has sinned so badly (*cries*).
The wife is killed by society (*long pause*) (E: Why?) For what she
has done. (E: What has she done?) She committed a murder
(*long pause*) . . . she killed Christ.

This story presents a rather extreme example of feelings of
lack of self-worth and self-recrimination such as is frequently
found in patients suffering from depressive disorders. Mrs. G was
portrayed as a guilt-ridden woman with a poor self-image.
Contrast this with a story by Mrs. M, a woman with a positive
self-image:

This is a young married couple. And they're sitting on a bench,
which might even be in a doctor's waiting room. And . . . the

woman thinks she might be pregnant. And so she and her husband have come to the doctor to find out. So she goes into the doctor's office and he examines her and tells her that she is pregnant . . . and she goes out and tells her husband. And they're very excited about the idea of having a child. A little worried about it, because they weren't expecting a child quite so soon, and he's worrying about it. But it works out fine; and she has the baby and it's a beautiful child and they're both very happy and it all works out.

This story by Mrs. M compares strikingly with that of Mrs. G. While Mrs. G felt totally worthless and appeared to have taken on her shoulders the collective guilt of the world, Mrs. M felt that she could really be a woman and have a baby. The genetic point of view suggests that a positive self-image develops out of the resolution of the "phallic" phase in women (Deutsch, 1925), one which is marked by a positive resolution of the oedipal phase.

   Conflicts surrounding this phase and the development of a poor feminine self-image are said to result from an inability to resolve the core conflicts associated with this phase. For this reason, the following story told by Mrs. M was of some significance:

This is a picture of an older man talking with a younger woman. The man could be her father. And maybe it's Sunday afternoon and the family has just finished dinner, and they're sitting in the living room, and he comes over to find out what she has been doing all week. He's been busy and she's been busy, and this is their time to catch up with each other. And, ah, she tells him what she has been doing. She tells him about her job—and about the new fellow she met at work, and he listens and then he goes off to read the paper and she goes off to wash her hair. (E: And what is the relationship between them?) Well, it's a very warm relationship. She loves her father and her father loves her very much, and they're very close to each other.

   This subject told quite clearly of her affection for her father—an affection which has led her to develop a positive image of herself as a woman and as one who can have a baby. The reasons that she received a low negative score on this factor are quite consistent with psychodynamic formulations of this developmental phase (Deutsch, 1945; Bonaparte, 1953). These psychodynamic formulations suggest that low self-esteem and feelings of lack of satisfaction with oneself as a woman result from an inability to resolve oedipal problems. The fact that this woman clearly felt tender and close to her father, and felt that her father was interested in her as a daughter, has made it possible for her to view herself as an attractive woman and a woman who can respond in a feminine manner.

## MEASUREMENT OF MATERNAL PSYCHOPATHOLOGY

All subjects were individually administered the Minnesota Multiphasic Personality Inventory (MMPI) (Dahlstrom and Welsh, 1960). Three scales of subjective internal distress were included which are frequently used in the clinical analysis of the MMPI: social introversion (Si) scale, ego-strength (Es) scale, and the anxiety (A) or ego-resiliency scale, which represents the first rotated factor emerging from the factorial study of the standard clinical scales. Although the MMPI profile is of utility in clinical work, the usual clinical scales were not used in this study, for they contain such heterogeneous items that it is difficult to determine the meaning of high and low scores on any scale. In addition, the clinical scales have considerable item overlap. Wiggins (1969) has resolved many of the problems inherent in the use of the clinical scales in his derivation of face-valid content scales which have satisfactory internal consistency across independent samples of both men and women (Cronbach's [1951] alpha coefficient ranges between .57 and .86), contain almost no item overlap, and appear to differentiate various kinds of psychiatric samples from nonpsychiatric samples. In addition, the factorial study of these scales suggests that response styles and sets play a less significant role than is true for the better-known scales which comprise the clinical profile. Consistent with Wiggins's discussion, these thirteen scales may be described as follows (high scores on a scale are in the direction of the scale title):

*Social maladjustment (SOC)*: Social introversion and withdrawal; self-conscious and very reserved.

*Depression (DEP)*: Feelings of guilt, worry, and unhappiness, together with feelings of low self-esteem; classical depression.

*Feminine interests (FEM)*: Preference for activities conceived of as feminine in our culture.

*Poor morale (MOR)*: Lack of self-confidence, feelings of despair and hypersensitivity to others' feelings.

*Religious fundamentalism (REL)*: Churchgoer's convictions that his views are the "true" views; rigid, moralistic attitudes toward social life.

*Authority conflict (AUT)*: Perception of others as exploitative and unscrupulous; cynical distrust of others.

*Psychoticism (PSY)*: Feelings of unreality, loss of inner control, and reports of strange experiences; classical psychotic symptoms.

*Organic symptoms (ORG)*: Symptoms generally believed associated with CNS impairment, but also often the content of somatic delusional systems.

*Family problems (FAM)*: Harsh criticism of one's own parental family as unsympathetic and not understanding or supportive; criticisms of the way one was raised.

*Manifest hostility (HOS)*: Reaction to others in an aggressive, retaliatory, and vindictive manner.

*Phobias (PHO)*: Classical fears such as of heights, closed spaces, and darkness.

*Hypomania (HYP)*: Feelings of restlessness and inner tension; need for excitement and for impulsive actions.

*Poor health (HEA)*: Concern with health, particularly regarding gastrointestinal symptoms.

In Wiggins's 1969 report, these content scales showed essentially the same factor structure as had previously been reported for the "clinical" scales and, based on multivariate analyses, also showed the ability to discriminate between a variety of psychiatric and non-psychiatric samples.

## THE MATERNAL ATTITUDE SCALE

The maternal attitude scale (MAS), a 233-item Likert-type

instrument, was constructed according to Sander's (1962, 1964, 1969) formulation of the developing mother-child relationship in the first years of life. Particular attention was paid to attitudes toward reciprocity and encouragement of the child's sense of competence, issues which typically are omitted from other such paper-and-pencil measures of attitudes which are concerned primarily with the assessment of authoritarian child-rearing attitudes.

Each of the dimensions measured by the MAS refers to a particular developmental issue or crisis in the early mother-child relationship. Clearly, both the child's own development and his mother's continued effectiveness and satisfaction in the maternal role are shaped by the extent to which these developmental issues are resolved. Consistent with ego-psychological formulations of attitude formation and change (Smith, Bruner, and White, 1956), these attitudes toward child rearing permit a mother to appraise and interpret transactions involving herself and her child. To the extent that her appraisal and her interpretation are congruent with the child's needs or intentions, her attitudes are adaptive for the resolution of the particular issue or issues being negotiated at that time. In sum, a mother's attitudes regarding each of the child care issues may be viewed as adaptive or maladaptive to the extent that these attitudes facilitate or impair the resolution of a particular issue.

The construction of the MAS is described in greater detail by Cohler, Weiss, and Grunebaum (1970). Developed as a result of extensive pretest studies, this instrument yields standardized scores on five second-order orthogonal or independent factors (high scores on a factor are in the direction of the scale title):

1 = *Inappropriate versus appropriate control of the child's aggressive impulses*: Appropriate control reflects the attitude that children's impulses can be channeled into socially appropriate behaviors, rather than completely inhibited.

2 = *Discouragement versus encouragement of reciprocity*: Reciprocity reflects the attitude that infants can communicate and seek social interaction with their mothers and that mothers can understand and respond.

3 = *Appropriate versus inappropriate closeness*: Attitudes involving appropriate closeness suggest that a mother does not

view her baby as a narcissistic extension of the self, and does not seek to attain gratifications through the baby which have been missing in her own life.

4 = *Acceptance versus denial of emotional complexity in child rearing*: Acceptance involves a mother's recognition that motherhood is sometimes more work than pleasure and that mothers do not always know what is best for their children.

5 = *Comfort versus discomfort in perceiving and meeting the baby's (physical) needs*: Comfort implies that mothers feel that they can understand what babies want and provide for their babies' needs.

Two measures of a mother's characteristic mode of responding to the instrument were also obtained, an index of the willingness to agree with an item, regardless of the item content, and an index of the mother's tendency to express an attitude which differed from that of most mothers responding to that item.

## PREMORBID ADJUSTMENT

Data concerning premorbid adjustment among hospitalized mothers were obtained from hospital records completed by the patient's physician and by the social worker assigned to the family. Zigler and Phillips (1962) have indicated that degree of investment in the social environment is a good predictor both of the chronicity of a patient's disturbance and also of her prognosis. Vaillant (1962, 1964) has found that evidence of a rapid onset of the disturbance and a change in psychological functioning in the six months prior to hospitalization, of such magnitude as to be noticeable by the patient's family and relatives, serves as a good index of positive prognosis for rehabilitation.

Two independent raters obtained information regarding premorbid adjustment and prognosis, that is, the degree of investment in the social environment in the years preceding hospitalization and the amount of change evidenced in the patient's psychological functioning during the six months immediately preceding hospitalization. The inter-rater reliability for these indices is presented in tables 10 and 11. Inspection of

TABLE 10. MATERNAL PREMORBID SOCIAL ADJUSTMENT

| Score | Category[a] | N | Percentage | Cumulative Percentage |
|-------|-------------|---|------------|----------------------|
| 1. | Many friends, active social life, outgoing and gregarious | 7 | 22 | 22 |
| 2. | Some friends, fairly active social life, definite interests | 11 | 33 | 55 |
| 3. | A few close friends; somewhat quiet and shy, albeit with a few noticeable interests or involvements outside the home | 9 | 27 | 82 |
| 4. | Asocial: Withdrawn from others and apparently aloof from them; few friends or interests | 6 | 18 | 100 |
| | | 100 | 100 | 100 |

Mean = 2.42  Median = 2.00  Inter-rater agreement = 82 percent
[a] A higher score indicates a less satisfactory premorbid social adjustment.

TABLE 11. CHANGES IN PSYCHOLOGICAL FUNCTIONING PRIOR TO ADMISSION

| Category | N | Percentage | Cumulative Percentage |
|----------|---|------------|----------------------|
| 1. Abrupt changes of behavior within the past six months with odd behavior, mood swings, evidence of unwillingness to assume responsibility for household tasks or peculiar thoughts. | 11 | 33 | 33 |
| 2. Some noticeable change, although not marked, in the patient's behavior within the six months prior to admission. | 6 | 18 | 51 |
| 3. Some mild change, although not at all marked, in the patient's behavior within past six months. There is little evidence that the present disturbance represents any abrupt change in the patient's functioning. | 3 | 9 | 60 |
| 4. Little or no change in the patient's behavior within the past six months. Rather, there is evidence of continuation of a marginal or unsatisfactory mode of adjustment. | 13 | 40 | 100 |
| | 100 | 100 | 100 |

Mean = 2.55  Median = 2.00  Inter-rater agreement = 86 percent
A higher score indicates less change in the six months prior to admission.

table 10 suggests that the majority of the subjects in this study had a good premorbid social adjustment. Satisfactory inter-rater reliability was obtained in coding this variable. Data concerning the degree of change noticeable in the patient's functioning in the six months prior to hospitalization are shown in table 11. The subjects in this study, as a group, demonstrated a notable shift in their functioning in the months preceding hospitalization. Satisfactory inter-rater reliability was also obtained coding this variable.

## COLLECTION OF DATA

The sample of hospitalized mothers was gathered over an eighteen-month period. Each patient was tested within two weeks of admission or as soon thereafter as her physician said she was testable. After a physician had given permission for his patient to be included in the study, the patient was approached and asked if she would be willing to cooperate; we explained that we were interested in the manner in which children were raised and that we were studying mothers from all different walks of life, including mothers who had sought psychiatric assistance. Cooperation was strictly voluntary, and women were permitted to leave the study if they found the tests upsetting. Three hospitalized mothers refused at the outset to participate in the study, and two mothers relapsed into acute psychotic distress during the course of the testing so that it was impossible to collect the projective test from them; no mother who had volunteered to participate dropped out of her own accord after the testing had begun.

It should be noted that a number of steps were undertaken to control for possible experimenter bias (Rosenthal, 1966). Following Rosenthal's suggestions, all hospitalized and nonhospitalized subjects were tested by persons other than the authors, and neither of the examiners had any knowledge of the hypotheses being tested in the study.

# 11

# Results and Discussion

Our review of the literature has suggested the importance of comparing hospitalized and nonhospitalized mothers in terms of the capacity for mature interpersonal relationships as well as in terms of attitudes toward a number of issues believed to be of central importance in the care of young children. Furthermore, we have seen that the mother's premorbid adjustment may be an important correlate both of her capacity for object relations and of her child care attitudes. In the present chapter we shall review our empirical data regarding these questions and shall also consider the relation between our measure of character, the Interpersonal Apperception Technique, and measures of both self-reported distress and child care attitudes in the patient and nonpatient groups.

## MATERNAL CHARACTER AND PSYCHOSOCIAL CONFLICT

Data regarding the differences between hospitalized and non-hospitalized women on the Interpersonal Apperception Technique are presented in table 12. Significant differences were obtained in conflict measures on three of the four dimensions for which predictions were made. In the case of two of these dimensions, sufficiency/dependency and trust/mistrust, these differences were significant at between the .05 and .01 significance levels, while in the case of mutuality/isolation this difference was significant at the .05 level. Additional data

TABLE 12. COMPARISON OF HOSPITALIZED AND NONHOSPITALIZED MOTHERS ON INTERPERSONAL APPERCEPTION TECHNIQUE

| Dimension | Hospitalized Mothers (N=33) | | Nonhospitalized Mothers (N=35) | | Welch | | |
|---|---|---|---|---|---|---|---|
| | Mean | Std. Dev. | Mean | Std. Dev. | t-test | df | p |
| Sufficiency vs. dependency | | | | | | | |
| 1. Salience | 3.46 | 1.77 | 3.40 | 1.54 | 0.14 | 63.5 | n.s. |
| 2. Ranks | 3.67 | 1.96 | 3.66 | 1.87 | 0.02 | 65.3 | n.s. |
| 3. Conflict | 50.65 | 8.75 | 45.78 | 2.04 | 2.04 | 64.5 | .025 |
| Trust vs. mistrust | | | | | | | |
| 1. Salience | 2.58 | 2.12 | 1.85 | 1.61 | 1.58 | 59.7 | .06 |
| 2. Ranks | 4.36 | 1.81 | 4.76 | 2.04 | 0.84 | 65.8 | n.s. |
| 3. Conflict | 45.73 | 17.32 | 34.23 | 21.51 | 2.43 | 64.5 | .01 |
| Anger vs. destructiveness | | | | | | | |
| 1. Salience | 2.09 | 1.91 | 2.20 | 1.62 | 0.25 | 63.0 | n.s. |
| 2. Ranks | 5.00 | 1.98 | 5.21 | 1.53 | 0.50 | 60.1 | n.s. |
| 3. Conflict | 43.65 | 20.65 | 42.54 | 15.49 | 0.24 | 57.4 | n.s. |
| Autonomy vs. control | | | | | | | |
| 1. Salience | 2.88 | 1.73 | 4.63 | 1.73 | 4.17 | 65.8 | .001[a] |
| 2. Ranks | 4.10 | 1.93 | 3.33 | 1.75 | 1.73 | 64.5 | .09[a] |
| 3. Conflict | 48.29 | 14.97 | 49.47 | 7.98 | 0.40 | 48.2 | n.s. |
| Self-esteem vs. inferiority | | | | | | | |
| 1. Salience | 2.55 | 2.14 | 2.86 | 1.93 | 0.63 | 64.3 | n.s. |
| 2. Ranks | 3.33 | 1.91 | 3.74 | 2.20 | 0.82 | 65.6 | n.s. |
| 3. Conflict | 46.71 | 16.79 | 42.83 | 15.44 | 0.99 | 64.7 | n.s. |
| Mutuality vs. isolation | | | | | | | |
| 1. Salience | 2.82 | 1.29 | 3.65 | 1.75 | 2.26 | 62.4 | .025 |
| 2. Ranks | 3.62 | 1.68 | 3.50 | 1.81 | 0.29 | 66.0 | n.s. |
| 3. Conflict | 51.55 | 9.41 | 48.17 | 6.90 | 1.68 | 58.5 | .05 |
| Nurturance vs. self-absorption | | | | | | | |
| 1. Salience | 3.06 | 1.32 | 3.54 | 1.17 | 1.69 | 64.0 | n.s. |
| 2. Ranks | 3.90 | 2.07 | 3.61 | 1.99 | 0.60 | 65.4 | n.s. |
| 3. Conflict | 50.67 | 9.78 | 49.56 | 7.28 | 0.48 | 59.0 | n.s. |
| Impairment in forming object relations | 0.358 | 0.882 | -0.337 | 1.013 | 3.02 | 65.6 | .004 |
| Dissatisfaction with mothering | -0.039 | 1.153 | 0.037 | 0.864 | 0.31 | 59.2 | n.s. |
| Feelings of inadequacy | -0.015 | 1.176 | 0.014 | 0.835 | 0.11 | 57.4 | n.s. |

[a]Two-tail test

regarding this specific prediction can be obtained from the examination of the summary factor scores. As might be expected, the first rotated Interpersonal Apperception Technique factor (that of impairment in forming object relations) differentiated between patients and nonpatients at greater than the .01 level. No differences were obtained on the other two factors. In the case of two phases, autonomy/control and mutuality/isolation, the differences between the hospitalized and non-hospitalized mothers were in the opposite direction. That is, nonhospitalized mothers indicated greater concern with these phases than was true for patients (number of salient stories), although they did not experience greater conflict.

## MATERNAL CHARACTER AND PSYCHOPATHOLOGY

We have seen that hospitalized mothers showed greater impairment in forming object relations than did nonhospitalized mothers. It was expected that the dimensions associated with the summary factor of impairment in forming object relations, as well as the summary factor itself, would be related to measures of social maladjustment and symptomatic distress. This expectation is confirmed when we consider the correlation between the IAT and measures of symptomatic distress derived from the MMPI. The thirteen scales derived by Wiggins (1966, 1969) from an analysis of the domains measured by the MMPI item pool served as the measure of psychopathology. In addition to these scales, the scales of ego-strength, anxiety or ego-resiliency, and social introversion from the traditionally scored scales were also used. To facilitate the present discussion, we have focused on the relation between these measures of psychopathology and the three summary IAT factors. Data regarding this relation are shown in table 13.

The first IAT factor, impairment in the capacity for object relations, shows the highest association with psychopathology as measured by the MMPI. Greater impairment in forming relations is related to greater social introversion or moving away from others, greater anxiety, psychotic symptoms such as dissociation, lowered mood, and interpersonal hostility. Women showing greater conflict on this first IAT factor can be described as behaving in unusual ways and feeling distant and aloof from others.

TABLE 13. CORRELATION OF IAT FACTORS AND MMPI SCALES

| MMPI Scale | IAT Factor | | |
| --- | --- | --- | --- |
| | Impairment of Object Relations | Dissatisfaction with Mothering | Feelings of Inadequacy |
| Si | .43** | .03 | .19 |
| Es | -.34** | .03 | -.20 |
| A | .41** | -.06 | .26* |
| SOC | .41** | .16 | .18 |
| DEP | .32** | .03 | .19 |
| FEM | -.12 | -.38** | .10 |
| MOR | .47** | .12 | .27* |
| REL | -.04 | .27* | .26* |
| AUT | .22 | .34** | .08 |
| PSY | .42** | -.12 | .21 |
| ORG | .22 | -.16 | .41** |
| FAM | .21 | .18 | .32** |
| HOS | .24* | .29* | .12 |
| PHO | .36** | .07 | .38** |
| HYP | .21 | .43** | .16 |
| HEA | .18 | .00 | .25* |

$*p < .05.$   $**p < .01.$

Dissatisfaction with mothering shows the fewest correlates with psychopathology. Women expressing greater dissatisfaction with mothering are less likely to identify with typical feminine interests, are more likely to express hostility toward others, and are more likely to be involved in authority conflicts and to flee from inner discomfort by compulsive activity. It could be that the demands of child care prevent these angry and active women from being able to deal with their discomfort through activity, so that child care makes them particularly uncomfortable.

Feelings of dissatisfaction as a woman are associated with a variety of MMPI scales said to reflect inner distress. While women feeling less self-regard are likely to experience greater anxiety, they are less likely to express this anxiety through psychotic symptoms, such as was the case with women shown to be more impaired in forming object relations and more likely to express this anxiety through conversion symptoms or psychosomatic illnesses. These women are more likely to deal with their own feelings of inadequacy by turning against the self than by turning against others, as is characteristic of women feeling greater dissatisfaction with the maternal role, or turning away from others, as is characteristic of women experiencing greater impairment in forming object relations (Horney, 1945). It would appear that the inadequacy factor is more closely related to psychopathology within the neurotic range, while greater conflict regarding the first factor is associated with more pervasive and profound psychopathology, including both social withdrawal and psychotic symptoms.

This pattern of relations between the picture-thematic and the self-report measures is consistent with the observations of psychoanalytic theorists—that impairment in the capacity for object relations, epigenetically among the earliest forms of conflict in psychosocial development, is associated with particularly serious and pervasive psychopathology, including greater vulnerability to psychosis. Problems in the development of feelings of self-esteem and autonomy are viewed as related more closely to the development of compromise formations or neurotic symptoms.

Finally, the different pattern of relations between the IAT factors and MMPI content scales shows that the IAT dimensions measure conflict regarding specific aspects of internal experience rather than some general trait of psychopathology. If the IAT were nothing more than a more complex form of scoring inner distress or anxiety, not only would the factor analysis have yielded a single factor rather than several factors but the relation between self-report and picture-thematic measures would have been nearly identical for each of the three factors.

The data reported in this chapter show, as predicted, that hospitalized mothers express greater conflict regarding epigenetically earlier issues in psychosocial development than do nonhospitalized mothers. The demand for greater differentiation and reciprocity such as is required by marriage appears to have been greater than these hospitalized mothers could accept. The fact that the nurturance/self-absorption phase did not show differences between the hospitalized and nonhospitalized mothers suggests that hospitalized mothers have experienced such intense conflict in resolving developmental tasks regarding mutuality/isolation that the later phase, involving resolution of conflict associated with nurturance/self-absorption, was not even salient for them.

Regarding two of these phases of psychosocial development, mutuality/isolation and autonomy/control, nonhospitalized mothers indicated greater concern (a larger number of scorable stories) than hospitalized mothers, although hospitalized mothers indicated greater conflict regarding mutuality/isolation. This finding suggests that nonhospitalized mothers are quite involved with these two developmental phases, even if such involvement has not led to increased difficulty in resolving the nuclear conflicts associated with the two phases. On the contrary, we see once more that recognition of the salience of a particular phase may lead to a greater ability to deal with it.

The advent of parenthood requires reorganization of the marital relationship and the extension of the love and care which husband and wife feel toward each other and toward their child. This is an aspect of what Fairbairn (1946) has termed "mature dependence." Such reorganization of the marital relationship evokes increased concern regarding the satisfactions which she seeks from her marriage (LeMasters, 1957; Dyer, 1963). Acknowledgment of this concern makes it possible to deal with it and may lead to a more satisfactory resolution of the nuclear conflict associated with the phase. This resolution, in turn, may lead to greater comfort in assuming the parental role.

The findings concerning autonomy versus control were consistent with our impression, while coding these materials, that there was greater concern with this developmental phase than would have been expected in advance. While the scores on this dimension were not coded according to the relationship figures, examination of the data suggests that many of the stories concerned a mother's relationship with her own mother. The majority of the subjects in both the patient and nonpatient samples had grown up in the New England area (73 percent and 79 percent, respectively).

Fischer and Fischer (1963), in their ethnographic account of a New England community, point out that most Orchard Town mothers lived near their own mothers if their husbands' jobs made it possible. The Fischers do not indicate whether such preference stemmed from the subjects' own expressed desires or merely indicated the extent of the ambivalence of the feelings of Orchard Town mothers in this regard.

Since the majority of women in the present study lived near their parents, proximity fostered more frequent contact with a woman's own mother, leading to renewed concern with the issue of standing on one's own feet and of expressing one's own will. A story told by a nonhospitalized mother, Mrs. L, to picture Si 3, which portrays a young woman, wearing a coat and carrying a handbag, who is about to go out the door, best describes the concern with the autonomy/control issue.

Mother leaving the daughter's house. Mother came for a visit to the daughter's place. Probably gave some advice to the daughter which was not taken very well as the girl's face appears rather unhappy and grim. Mother is trying to ease the daughter's life. Daughter is rebelling and thinking, "I'd rather do it myself." It is unfortunate that children will not make their lives on their parents' past experiences! I am sure that this tiff will blow over, especially if there has been a harmonious relationship between mother and daughter before.

This story was scored at the "2" level on autonomy versus control, and, in commenting on the story, one of the raters noted that "there was some evidence that the daughter felt forced to go along with her mother, but the story was resolved and an appropriate solution achieved."

We need to know a great deal more about the meaning for the subject of her relationship with her own mother, particularly regarding the autonomy/control dimension. It is possible that hospitalized women, since they showed greater conflict regarding sufficiency/dependency (Sampson et al., 1964), would term this a "crisis of separation," and are so preoccupied with the desire to be taken care of that the later battle of wills has not yet become salient for them. However, the problem needs to be studied in greater detail.

It should be noted that not all dimensions of the Interpersonal Apperception Technique differentiated between hospitalized and nonhospitalized mothers. This finding suggests once more that the IAT measures more than psychopathology or the tendency to admit to psychopathology. We have discussed this issue in commenting upon the Ginsparg (1956) study, using a similar technique to evaluate psychosocial development among hospitalized and nonhospitalized women.

While Ginsparg coded thematic materials across relationship figures rather than across developmental dimensions, the fact that the distribution of patient scores clustered around the lowest or "autistic" point on the scale suggests that Ginsparg was heavily influenced in her scoring by indices of psychopathology, such as bizarre content, rather than by the degree of resolution which was indicated regarding the several developmental phases. Subjective distress is not unrelated to conflict in psychosocial development, as we have indicated in the present instance; indeed, hospitalized mothers showed a greater deficit in their ability to form interpersonal relationships. However, this deficit is more subtle than the grossly apparent symptomatic distress which was evident upon first reading the thematic apperceptive data of the hospitalized mothers.

## MENTAL ILLNESS AND CHILD CARE ATTITUDES

It will be recalled that the original sample of hospitalized and nonhospitalized mothers consisted of thirty-five matched pairs, but that two of the hospitalized mothers left the study before the picture thematic data could be collected. Since complete attitude data was available for all subjects, it was possible to examine differences in the attitudes of hospitalized and nonhospitalized mothers by means of a t-test for paired observations (Edwards, 1967). One-tail tests of significance were employed since specific hypotheses had been formulated regarding differences between hospitalized and nonhospitalized mothers on this measure (Ferguson, 1959). The results of this matched group comparison are indicated in table 14.

Predicted differences were obtained for two of the five factors, encouragement of reciprocity and acceptance of emotional complexity. In the case of the third factor, appropriate closeness, the differences were in the predicted direction but not significant.

In the case of the fifth factor, comfort in meeting the baby's needs, the hypothesized results did not obtain, and, in fact, differences between the two groups were in the opposite direction. The predicted difference did obtain for the response set measure of independent versus conventional approach to the task. Hospitalized mothers indicated a significantly greater tendency than nonhospitalized mothers to answer items in the "typical" direction and to disagree with the items.

TABLE 14. COMPARISON OF HOSPITALIZED AND NONHOSPITALIZED MOTHERS ON MATERNAL ATTITUDES AND VARIABLES

| MAS Variable | Patients | | Control | | Mean of Difference | Std. Dev. Difference | t-test | p |
|---|---|---|---|---|---|---|---|---|
| | Mean | Std. Dev. | Mean | Std. Dev. | | | | |
| Summary factors: | | | | | | | | |
| 1. Appropriate control | 0.190 | 0.775 | 0.051 | 1.119 | 0.139 | 1.199 | 0.67 | n.s. |
| 2. Encouragement of reciprocity | -0.182 | 0.801 | 0.210 | 0.908 | 0.392 | 1.339 | 1.71 | .05[a] |
| 3. Appropriate closeness | -0.355 | 0.962 | -0.124 | 1.045 | -0.230 | 1.237 | 1.09 | n.s. |
| 4. Acceptance of complexity | -0.637 | 1.378 | -0.087 | 0.890 | -0.550 | 1.672 | 1.92 | .04[a] |
| 5. Comfort meeting baby's needs | 0.263 | 0.775 | -0.128 | 0.781 | 0.391 | 0.915 | 2.49 | .02[b] |
| Response sets and styles | | | | | | | | |
| 1. Agreement style | -1.961 | 4.456 | 0.140 | 3.100 | 2.102 | 0.931 | 2.25 | .05[b] |
| 2. Independence set | -1.408 | 2.864 | 0.161 | 1.479 | 1.570 | 0.553 | 2.84 | .01[a] |

[a]One-tail test, 34 df  [b]Two-tail test, 68 df

These results suggest an interesting paradox. On the one hand, contrasted with mothers in the nonhospitalized group, mothers in the hospitalized group approached the test with the intent of answering items in the manner which they believed characterized the typical mother. On the other hand, for three of the five factors, their attitudes were different from those of the mothers in the nonhospitalized group. Hospitalized mothers, to a greater extent than nonhospitalized mothers, denied that the typical mother has concerns regarding child rearing or that she is concerned with establishing a reciprocal mother-child relationship. Hospitalized mothers also tended to believe that mothers do not feel uncomfortable in learning to meet their infants' needs, while nonhospitalized mothers admitted to greater concern regarding this child care issue. These findings suggest that the hospitalized mothers do not have a realistic perception of the child care attitudes of the typical "normal" mother and that they express stereotyped and undifferentiated attitudes concerning these child care issues.

We have suggested that, as a result of the stress in our own culture upon the mother as the primary socialization agent, most women feel considerable doubt and concern about their competence to perform the maternal role. However, in order to respond appropriately to the conflicting role demands of wife and mother, and in order to resolve the variety of issues with which she is confronted in the first years of the child's life, a woman must be able to perceive and accept these doubts and concerns.

The fact that hospitalized mothers appeared to have such stereotyped and conventional attitudes toward child rearing indicated that these women were less able than nonhospitalized mothers to recognize and deal with these feelings, a factor which may have seriously impaired their ability to respond appropriately to these child care issues. Hartman (in part 2), in discussing her clinical findings concerning a program of therapeutic intervention designed to help hospitalized mothers care for their children, also noted the problems which these women had in admitting to their ambivalent feelings concerning child rearing and commented that one of the major goals of her work with these women was to help them acknowledge and accept this ambivalence.

These findings regarding the child care attitudes of hospitalized and nonhospitalized mothers also support the hypothesis that hospitalized mothers do not believe it is possible to establish a social relationship with a baby. It is not so much, as we had first believed, that these women perceived the child as a narcissistic extension of the self or felt unable to meet the baby's physical needs. Rather, hospitalized mothers viewed the child not as a separate being but as one who is passive and unable to communicate or achieve reciprocity with his mother. The implications of such attitudes for the child's emotional development have been discussed by Bettelheim (1967), who stresses the importance of the mother's being able to perceive and respond to the child's demand for reciprocity.

The importance of [permitting the child to feel the master of his fate] for the development of a self can hardly be overrated. With it, the ego expands from one that only acts into one that interacts, that responds to others and becomes slowly aware that it can modify their responses. . . . In order for this to happen, the mother must have wished all along to relate to the child in mutuality.... If the child has all along known the experience of mutuality ... it helps him to develop it in his personal relationships [1967, p. 26].

## HOSPITALIZATION AND "POSTPARTUM" ILLNESS

Conflict in psychosocial development has been shown to be associated both with hospitalization for mental illness and as a correlate of particular forms of self-reported psychopathology. However, even within the group of hospitalized mothers, there is considerable variation in factors associated with hospitalization itself, including the length of time between childbirth and hospitalization, as well as the adequacy of a woman's premorbid adjustment. Among factors related to premorbid adjustment, the one which has received the greatest attention in the literature concerns the time of the mother's hospitalization, considered in terms of the birth of her youngest or index child. While different authors have used a different definition of the postpartum period, work by Ginsparg (1956), LeMasters (1957), and Dyer (1963), has suggested that the first postpartum year may be a period of especially high risk for the subsequent development of emotional disturbance.

In the present instance, we have divided the sample of hospitalized mothers into those hospitalized within the first year of childbirth (early hospitalization) and those hospitalized at some later point (late hospitalization). It should be noted that this division into early and late hospitalization was independent of length of present hospitalization ($\chi^2 = 0.663$, 2 d.f.), premorbid social adjustment ($\chi^2 = 0.153$, 1, d.f.), or the total number of weeks ever hospitalized ($\chi^2 = 1.76$, 2 d.f.). There were, however, a number of personality differences between mothers hospitalized earlier and later after childbirth. These differences are indicated in table 15. Mothers hospitalized earlier after childbirth, when contrasted with mothers hospitalized later than one year after childbirth, showed less concern regarding sufficiency/dependency, less conflict concerning trust/mistrust, and greater concern (although not greater conflict) regarding nurturance/self-absorption. Mothers hospitalized earlier after childbirth indicated less impairment in the basic capacity to form relationships and also a tendency

TABLE 15. COMPARISON OF HOSPITALIZED MOTHERS ADMITTED EARLIER AND LATER AFTER CHILDBIRTH

| Variable | Early Admission ($N=20$) | | Late Admission ($N=13$) | | $t$-test[a] | $df$ | $p$ |
|---|---|---|---|---|---|---|---|
| | Mean | Std. Dev. | Mean | Std. Dev. | | | |
| Subject's age | 3.273 | 1.077 | 3.077 | 1.888 | 0.488 | 23.3 | n.s. |
| Number of children | 2.409 | 1.368 | 2.077 | 1.256 | 0.731 | 27.1 | n.s. |
| Number of boys in family | 1.273 | 0.827 | 0.692 | 0.630 | 2.337 | 30.7 | .03[b] |
| Sufficiency/ dependency, Salience | 3.050 | 1.877 | 4.077 | 1.441 | 1.772 | 30.7 | .08[b] |
| Trust/mistrust, Conflict | 40.915 | 19.646 | 53.124 | 9.549 | 2.380 | 29.2 | .01 |
| Nurturance/ self-absorption, salience | 3.482 | 1.387 | 2.530 | 1.121 | 2.169 | 29.4 | .04[b] |
| Impairment in forming object relations | 0.145 | 0.951 | 0.685 | 0.673 | 1.916 | 30.7 | .08 |
| Changes in psychological functioning in past six months | 2.364 | 1.364 | 3.016 | 1.687 | 1.633 | 28.2 | .06 |
| Total number of hospitalizations | 1.864 | 0.834 | 1.154 | 0.376 | 3.444 | 31.4 | .01[b] |
| Premorbid social adjustment | 2.364 | 1.049 | 2.538 | 1.127 | 0.455 | 23.9 | n.s. |
| Ego-strength (MMPI) | 46.909 | 12.000 | 39.769 | 10.963 | 1.797 | 27.2 | .09[b] |
| Anxiety (MMPI) | 59.211 | 11.758 | 64.793 | 9.366 | 1.540 | 29.9 | n.s. |
| Social Maladjustment (MMPI) | 11.818 | 5.491 | 16.385 | 6.305 | 2.176 | 22.6 | .02 |
| Psychoticism (MMPI) | 14.091 | 10.151 | 14.385 | 6.727 | 0.103 | 32.4 | n.s. |
| Depression (MMPI) | 14.955 | 8.203 | 20.308 | 6.156 | 2.192 | 30.9 | .03[b] |
| Poor morale (MMPI) | 12.136 | 6.034 | 16.308 | 3.816 | 2.501 | 32.8 | .01[b] |

[a]Welch correction used in computation of $t$-test
[b]Two-tail test

to greater change in psychological functioning in the six months prior to hospitalization; these mothers hospitalized earlier after childbirth also tended to have a greater number of prior hospitalizations. However, mothers hospitalized earlier indicated less social withdrawal, less depression, and better morale than mothers hospitalized later after childbirth.

It is interesting to note that while mothers hospitalized earlier after childbirth did not have more children and were not, as a group, older than mothers hospitalized later, there was a greater proportion of boys among their children than among the children of mothers hospitalized later following childbirth. Since there was little association between sex of the youngest child and the time of hospitalization ($\chi^2 = 0.005$, 1 d.f.), this finding reflects the total number of boys in the family, and not just the sex of the youngest child, as a factor associated with hospitalization among women hospitalized earlier after childbirth.

Consistent with the data reported by Ginsparg, LeMasters, and Dyer, the disturbance evident in the women who are hospitalized earlier after childbirth appears to be a reaction to the stress represented by pregnancy, delivery, and the postpartum period. While the disturbance is a recurrent one, these women are able to function adequately in the community until they once again become mothers, after which time they once more become disturbed and are hospitalized.

Mothers hospitalized later after childbirth showed no less psychotic symptomatology or social withdrawal, but they appeared lower in ego-strength and expressed a greater sense of futility about their lives. These women appeared to have experienced a long-term psychological deficit, even though they had avoided previous hospitalizations and seemed to be similar to Ginsparg's sample of hospitalized controls. These data are consistent with Hartman's findings, reported in this volume, and suggests that, for women hospitalized later after childbirth, issues involved in the assumption of the maternal role are less important in the development of a disturbance; the disturbance is much less a reaction to life events than to intrapsychic conflicts. Women who are hospitalized earlier after childbirth also appear to have a better prognosis, even though they may be hospitalized again following a subsequent delivery.

The finding that mothers hospitalized earlier after childbirth tended to have a greater number of sons than mothers hospitalized later is of particular interest. Psychoanalysts such as Zilboorg (1925) and Deutsch (1945), following a dreambook approach, have viewed the dynamics of emotional disturbance following childbirth primarily in terms of the penis-envy hypothesis, in which pregnancy represents a way of acquiring a phallus, which is then lost through childbirth. According to this dreambook approach, the birth of a boy is a particularly traumatic experience, since a woman is more directly confronted both with the opportunity and with the attendant loss. An ego-psychological approach, with its greater emphasis upon the interaction between person and environment, suggests a different interpretation of this finding. According to such an approach, the mother's disturbance would be viewed less in terms of such dynamics than in terms of a woman's feelings about assuming the nurturant role. According to several studies (Knof, 1946; Garn and Clark, 1953; Terman and Tyler, 1954; Moss, 1965; Garai and Scheinfeld, 1968), boys tend to cry more and are more fretful as infants, are awake for a larger part of the day, are more active, more prone to illness, and more variable in their overall development. These data suggest that caring for boys may be especially difficult for a woman who already feels ambivalent about becoming a mother. The advantage of an ego-psychological approach is that it considers not just character, but the interaction of character and the demands of the "average expectable environment" (Hartman, 1939).

## MATERNAL CHARACTER AND PREMORBID ADJUSTMENT

In addition to the time after childbirth at which the mother is hospitalized, work of Ginsparg (1956), Markham (1958, 1961), and Weiss et al. (1964) suggests that other aspects of premorbid adjustment are also associated with the amount, as well as with the particular area, of conflict in psychosocial development. These factors include the extent of changes in psychological functioning in the six months prior to admission, length of present and previous hospitalizations, and number of hospitalizations for mental illness. This conflict is expected to be particularly significant for the first two phases—sufficiency versus dependency and trust versus mistrust. As can be seen from table 16, this hypothesis received only partial support.

TABLE 16. CORRELATION BETWEEN PREMORBID ADJUSTMENT AND PSY-
CHOSOCIAL DEVELOPMENT

| IAT Dimensional Scores | Total Days of This Admission | Number of Changes in Past Six Months | Friends and Interests | Total Weeks Ever Spent in Hospital |
|---|---|---|---|---|
| Sufficiency/dependency:salience | .20 | .14 | .17 | .02 |
| Sufficiency/dependency:ranks | .15 | -.18 | .27 | -.01 |
| Sufficiency/dependency:conflict | .16 | .19 | -.05 | .12 |
| Trust/mistrust: salience | .07 | .15 | .03 | -.13 |
| Trust/mistrust: ranks | -.03 | -.02 | -.24 | -.19 |
| Trust/mistrust: conflict | .37* | .08 | .40** | .33* |
| Anger/destructiveness:salience | .13 | .19 | -.08 | -.11 |
| Anger/destructiveness:ranks | .03 | -.07 | -.20 | .29 |
| Anger/destructiveness: conflict | .37* | .03* | .33* | .28 |
| Autonomy/control: salience | -.13 | -.08 | -.08 | -.14 |
| Autonomy/control: ranks | -.67 | .04 | -.28 | -.02 |
| Autonomy/control: conflict | .37* | .03* | .33** | .28 |
| Self-esteem/inferiority: salience | .14 | .05 | -.09 | .03 |
| Self-esteem/inferiority: ranks | -.09 | -.16 | .01 | -.17 |
| Self-esteem/inferiority: conflict | .21 | .27 | .11 | .25 |
| Mutuality/isolation: salience | -.15 | .13 | .04 | -.01 |
| Mutuality/isolation: ranks | .26 | -.08 | .02 | -.01 |
| Mutuality/isolation: conflict | .23 | .23 | .21 | .26 |
| Nurturance/self-absorption:salience | -.23 | -.13 | .43* | -.27 |
| Nurturance/self-absorption: ranks | -.21 | .37 | .39* | .07 |
| Nurturance/self-absorption: conflict | .36* | -.15 | .11 | .07 |
| *IAT summary factors* | | | | |
| Impairment in forming object relations | -.21 | .08 | .18 | .26 |
| Dissatisfaction with mothering | .18 | -.04 | -.07 | -.17 |
| Feelings of Inadequacy | .34* | .31* | .20 | .31* |

$N=33$   *$p<.05$   **$p<.01$

A greater length of time spent in the hospital during the present admission was related to a greater conflict concerning the phase of trust/mistrust ($p<.025$), as well as to greater conflict concerning autonomy/control ($p<.05$), greater conflict concerning nurturance/self-absorption ($p<.05$), and greater feelings of devaluation of femininity ($p<.05$). Contrary to expectation, the report of a less significant shift in psychological functioning in the six months preceding hospitalization was related to greater conflict regarding autonomy/control ($p<.05$), and devaluation of femininity ($p<.05$). Greater social withdrawal prior to hospitalization was related to greater conflict concerning trust/mistrust ($p<.01$), but also *less* concern regarding nurturance/self-absorption ($p<.01$), while total weeks hospitalized was related only to greater conflict concerning trust/mistrust. In general, less adequate premorbid adjustment of measures related to less satisfactory premorbid adjustment and to a greater tendency to a chronic disturbance is related to some impairment in the capacity to form meaningful and satisfying interpersonal relationships. A less satisfactory premorbid adjustment was also related to greater conflict concerning one's adequacy as a woman, together with feelings of lessened capacity to stand on one's own feet.

Additional understanding of the association between character and premorbid adjustment is possible when we compare hospitalized women on the three configurations derived from the IAT summary factors. These configurations, which offer greater and more complex and multidimensional approaches than those provided by the use of single factors, were created on the basis of a woman's scores on the three summary IAT factors, relative to the mean of the score for all hospitalized women. Three separate patterns were possible: women whose scores were above the mean on any particular pair of factors, women whose scores were above the mean on one factor but below the mean on the other, and women whose scores were below the mean on both factors in the pair. Table 17 shows the mean

TABLE 17. LENGTH OF HOSPITALIZATION (IN DAYS) AMONG FOUR GROUPS OF MOTHERS DIFFERING ON IAT SUMMARY FACTORS

| Groups of Mothers | Mean | Standard Deviation |
|---|---|---|
| 1. Impaired object relations and feelings of inadequacy | 126.214 | 117.735 |
| 2. Capacity for object relations and positive self-regard | 93.333 | 60.411 |
| 3. Impaired object relations and positive self-regard | 42.714 | 35.094 |
| 4. Capacity for object relations and feelings of inadequacy | 68.667 | 62.53 |

$F$-ratio$=2.423$  $df=(3, 25.8)$  eta$=.53$  $p=.07$

Comparisons between groups

| Groups | t-ratio | df | p |
|---|---|---|---|
| 1 versus 2 | 0.822 | 17.1 | n.s. |
| 1 versus 3 | 2.445 | 16.9 | .026 |
| 1 versus 4 | 1.420 | 16.8 | n.s. |
| 2 versus 3 | 1.808 | 7.8 | n.s. |
| 2 versus 4 | 0.695 | 10.0 | n.s. |
| 3 versus 4 | 0.902 | 7.6 | n.s. |

number of days of hospitalization for women in the four groups formed by the pattern of impairment in forming object relations and feelings of inadequacy. The results suggest that women with greater impairment in forming object relations and greater feelings of inadequacy remained in the hospital for a longer period of time than did women with impaired object relations but with more positive self-regard. Mothers in the former group were likely to appear more acutely distressed, while mothers in the latter group were likely to show less concern with their disturbance, less affect, and less interest in obtaining help with their problems.

Mothers who showed a greater capacity for object relations and who showed more positive self-regard remained in the hospital almost as long as women showing more acute turmoil. However, in contrast to these more acutely troubled women, mothers showing both a greater capacity for forming object relations and a more positive self-regard are likely to be considered good treatment prospects and to have the potential for benefiting from psychotherapeutic intervention. Because they are such good treatment risks, they may be encouraged by their physicians to remain in the hospital longer in order to take advantage of the therapeutic resources which the hospital offers. This may also be true, although to a somewhat lesser extent, of those mothers with a greater capacity for forming object relations and greater feelings of inadequacy.

Additional support for this interpretation came from examination of premorbid social adjustment among mothers in these four groups, as shown in table 18. The poorest premorbid social functioning was demonstrated by the mothers with both greater impairment in the capacity for object relations and with greater feelings of inadequacy. A significant difference obtained between the mean ratings of the mothers in this first group and mothers who showed a greater capacity for forming object relations and more positive self-regard. Indeed, the mean premorbid adjustment score of the mothers in this second group was the lowest of the four groups, indicating that these women had the most favorable premorbid social adjustment. The mean premorbid adjustment ratings of the mothers in the other two groups were intermediate between the two extreme groups.

This interpretation of the findings regarding maternal character and length of stay in the hospital also received confirma-

TABLE 18. PREMORBID SOCIAL ADJUSTMENT AMONG FOUR GROUPS OF MOTHERS DIFFERING ON IAT SUMMARY FACTORS

| Groups of Mothers | Mean | Standard Deviation |
|---|---|---|
| 1. Impaired object relations and feelings of inadequacy | 3.000 | 0.877 |
| 2. Capacity for object relations and positive self-regard | 1.833 | 0.408 |
| 3. Impaired object relations and positive self-regard | 2.000 | 1.155 |
| 4. Capacity for object relations and feelings of inadequacy | 2.167 | 1.169 |

$F$-ratio $= 3.055$    $df = (3, 16.7)$    eta $= .60$    $p = .05$

Comparisons between groups

| Groups | t-ratio | df | p |
|---|---|---|---|
| 1 versus 2 | 4.056 | 17.7 | .001 |
| 1 versus 3 | 2.019 | 9.6 | .072 |
| 1 versus 4 | 1.567 | 7.5 | n.s. |
| 2 versus 3 | 0.357 | 7.7 | n.s. |
| 2 versus 4 | 0.659 | 6.2 | n.s. |
| 3 versus 4 | 0.258 | 10.7 | n.s. |

tion from the pattern formed by the IAT factors of impairment in forming object relations and maternal dissatisfaction. Table 19 shows that mothers with both greater impairment in the capacity for object relations and greater dissatisfaction with mothering stayed in the hospital longer than did women with impaired object relations but with greater satisfaction with mothering. Mothers with a greater capacity for object relations but less satisfaction in mothering had a mean length of hospitalization intermediate between these two groups.

The women who showed a greater impairment in forming object relations, as well as greater feelings of inadequacy, could be characterized as a group of quite disturbed and possibly destructive women who required the protective custody of the hospital. However, the women characterized by a greater impairment in forming object relations but greater satisfaction with mothering was a group for whom hospitalization may not have been profitable. Since these women had difficulty in forming object ties, it was more difficult to work with them in treatment; on the other hand, their feelings about mothering were not so destructive or their impulse control so poor as to require continued hospitalization.

The women marked by a greater capacity for object relations but dissatisfaction with mothering were more able to form a

TABLE 19. LENGTH OF HOSPITALIZATION (IN DAYS) AMONG THREE
GROUPS OF MOTHERS DIFFERING ON IAT SUMMARY FACTORS

| Groups of Mothers | Mean | Standard Deviation |
|---|---|---|
| 1. Impaired object relations and satisfaction with maternal role | 51.889 | 53.067 |
| 2. Impaired object relations and dissatisfaction with maternal role | 133.250 | 121.937 |
| 3. Capacity for object relations and dissatisfaction with maternal role | 78.444 | 54.402 |

$F$-ratio $= 2.819$    $df = (2, 20.4)$    eta $= .54$    $p = .083$

Comparison between groups

| Groups | t-ratio | df | p |
|---|---|---|---|
| 1 versus 2 | 2.067 | 15.9 | .056 |
| 1 versus 3 | 1.048 | 16.0 | n.s. |
| 2 versus 3 | 1.384 | 16.1 | n.s. |

therapeutic relationship and may have been a group of mothers whom the staff believed it could help. These results suggest that character is an important dimension to consider when studying the careers of mental hospital patients. It appears possible to differentiate women who respond more positively to the hospital and to psychotherapy from those requiring protective custody.

In general, the results concerning character and premorbid adjustment were consistent with our prior expectations. As expected, unresolved conflict concerning the trust/mistrust dimension was associated with greater social withdrawal prior to hospitalization and with a greater length of hospitalization. Length of hospitalization and degree of change in the six months prior to hospitalization was found unexpectedly to be correlated with conflict concerning the autonomy/control dimension and the summary factor of feelings of inadequacy. The data from this study suggest that women with a more limited sense of purpose or will, who feel less able to stand on their own feet, remain in the hospital for longer, while a greater sense of autonomy appears related to a shorter period of hospitalization. A longer period of hospitalization and less adequate premorbid social adjustment were found to be particularly characteristic of women who showed greater impairment in forming object relations and who felt more inadequate.

When impairment in forming object relations was accompanied by dissatisfaction with mothering, women were also likely to be hospitalized longer, possibly because of their destructive feelings regarding children and mothering. Women with a greater capacity for object relations and who also felt less inadequate remained in the hospital somewhat longer, perhaps because they could profit more from the resources which the hospital makes available. However, these findings should be replicated in subsequent studies which are focused more directly on the therapeutic careers of women while in the hospital.

The relation between premorbid adjustment and child care attitudes paralleled the findings regarding character and premorbid adjustment in several respects. Although there was no relation between premorbid social adjustment and three of the five attitude factors, a significant relation was found for two of these factors, encouragement of reciprocity $(r = -.33, p < .05)$ and appropriate closeness $(r = -.47, p < .01)$. That is, mothers who showed a less successful premorbid social adjustment were more likely to feel unable to achieve reciprocity with their baby, and were more likely to view the baby as a narcissistic extension of the self.

It is striking that maternal withdrawal from social relationships, over the years preceeding hospitalization, was associated not only with greater impairment in forming relations, but also with less adaptive attitudes regarding the establishment of reciprocity with the child. It would appear that conflict in being able to establish satisfying relationships which is observed among these women is reflected in feelings of being unable to establish a mutual relationship with the baby. At the same time, the withdrawn mother is more likely to view the baby as a narcissistic extension of herself and to use the baby as a way of gaining satisfaction of her own primitive needs.

# 12

# Summary and Conclusion

We have examined the relation between conflict in psychosocial development and resolution of conflict regarding the assumption of the maternal role among women who have been admitted to a mental hospital during the first years after the child's birth, as contrasted with a group of nonhospitalized mothers. In discussing the theoretical framework of this study, it was suggested that mothers experience more or less adaptive attitudes regarding a variety of "critical issues" in the child-rearing situation as a function of developmentally significant conflicts which have been reawakened within the mother herself.

This hypothesis, derived primarily from the work of Grete Bibring, Helene Deutsch, and Therese Benedek, is consistent with the genetic point of view in psychoanalytic theory, which conceptualizes the development of character (defined as the habitual mode of perceiving and structuring mental representations of significant relationships) in terms of the resolution of successive phases or stages of preadult and adult psychological development, leading to increasingly complex, differentiated, and appropriate perceptions of interpersonal relationships. Each of these phases is marked by a particular nuclear conflict determined by the prototypic mode of relating to others that is characteristic of the phase.

Fixation arises from the inability to resolve the nuclear

conflict associated with a given phase of psychosocial development. Regression to points of fixation at particular phases of
preadult psychosocial functioning arises when, at some later
point, the individual is unable to resolve the developmental
tasks posed by marriage and parenthood. This regression results
in an inappropriate mode of resolving the developmental tasks
associated with adulthood.

Psychopathology or particular forms of symptomatic distress
represent a visible manifestation of this regressive process, and
various forms of psychopathology develop. The attainment of
psychosocial maturity is indicated by the appropriate resolution
of the nuclear conflicts associated with the adult phases of
psychosocial development, and in a manner commensurate
with one's role as an adult.

The general hypothesis regarding maternal character as a
determinant both of adaptation to motherhood and of particular patterns of child-rearing attitudes, could best be tested
through the study of mothers who had suffered an emotional
disturbance and had been hospitalized at some point during the
first few years following childbirth. The mother's hospitalization
is regarded as an index of her inability to deal effectively with
the developmental tasks posed by marriage and parenthood.

This discussion pointed to a number of more specific
hypotheses which could be examined through empirical study.
Considering, first, the combined sample of hospitalized and
nonhospitalized mothers, predictions were made regarding
specific areas of conflict. When the two groups of mothers were
compared, it was predicted that, since the hospitalized mothers
had been relatively unable to resolve the developmental tasks of
maturity, these mothers would be characterized by greater
conflict regarding epigenetically *earlier* "critical issues" in the
mothering encounter.

When the group of hospitalized mothers was considered
alone, it was predicted that poor premorbid adjustment would
be associated with greater conflict regarding earlier phases in
psychosocial development and also with less adaptive attitudes
regarding earlier issues in the mothering encounter.

In order to study this problem in a more systematic way,
following a review of previous theoretical and empirical studies
of character development, a new method was constructed for

the assessment of character. This method, the Interpersonal Apperception Technique, consists of separate scales for rating the extent to which a woman has resolved nuclear conflicts associated with each of seven preadult and adult phases of character development.

Stories told in response to a number of pictures, including several constructed especially for the present study, were coded in such a manner as to provide an index both of the extent of the woman's concern with each phase and of the extent of unresolved conflict pertaining to that phase. A detailed manual was constructed with definitions of each scale and stories illustrative of each scale point. Subsequent correlational study of the conflict scores yielded three rotated factors, the interpretation of which was consistent with the theoretical formulation on which the study was based. The phases of psychosocial development and the summary factors are defined as follows:

### Phases of preadult character development

1. Sufficiency versus dependency: Feelings of satisfaction and an ability to receive help from others when appropriate, versus feelings of deprivation, helplessness, and longing.

2. Trust versus mistrust: Feelings of empathy and safety with others versus feelings of suspiciousness of others and their intent.

3. Anger versus destructiveness: Feeling that one can express anger in a moduiated manner versus feeling of lack of control in the expression of angry feelings.

4. Autonomy versus control: Feeling of exercise of will and of an ability to stand on one's own feet versus a feeling of domination in interpersonal relationships.

5. Self-esteem versus inferiority: Feeling of adequacy as a woman versus feeling of shattered self-regard.

### Phases of adult character development

6. Mutuality versus isolation: Feeling of investment in interpersonal relationships versus feelings of distance from others and a fear of involvement with them.

7. Nurturance versus self-absorption: Feelings of meaningful

participation versus feelings of self-sacrifice derived from caring for others.

*Summary factors*

A. Impairment in forming object relations: Feelings of deprivation, mistrust, and isolation from others.

B. Dissatisfaction with mothering: Feelings of resentment over the demands which the child makes.

C. Feelings of inadequacy and entrapment: Feelings of inadequacy as a woman and presentation of a poor self-image.

Attitudes toward child care were measured using the Maternal Attitude Scale, a paper-and-pencil inventory which assesses five issues believed to be of importance in the mother's relationship with her young child: appropriate versus inappropriate control of the child's aggression; discouragement versus encouragement of reciprocity; appropriate versus inappropriate closeness; acceptance versus denial of complexity in child rearing; comfort versus discomfort in meeting the baby's physical needs. Mothers in both groups were also administered the Minnesota Multiphasic Personality Inventory (MMPI), which was scored on a number of face-valid scales derived from an analysis of the substantive dimensions measured by this instrument. Hospitalized women were also scored on variables associated with premorbid adjustment, including the length of time between the onset of symptoms and hospitalization, as well as the severity of the disturbance at the time of hospitalization.

Two groups of mothers with children below the age of three served as subjects in the present study: the thirty-five mothers in the patient group represent nearly consecutive admissions to the wards of a research-oriented state mental hospital. Each hospitalized mother was individually matched with a non-hospitalized mother who had never sought psychiatric treatment, on the basis of education, religious preference, parity, husband's education, and age and sex of youngest child. All subjects were individually tested by an experienced examiner; all protocols were coded blind by the author and other experienced coders without knowledge of whether a subject was in the hospitalized or nonhospitalized group.

The results of this study can be examined in terms of three separate comparisons: (1) findings concerning the entire sample of hospitalized and nonhospitalized mothers; (2) findings concerning the subsamples; and (3) findings concerning chronicity and premorbid adjustment within the hospitalized subsample.

The dimensions comprising the Interpersonal Apperception Technique attained satisfactory inter-rater reliability. In general, these indices of character development were independent of such background factors as social class and intelligence. Hospitalized mothers indicated greater impairment in the capacity for close interpersonal relationships, while nonhospitalized mothers indicated greater concern, although not greater conflict, concerning the autonomy/control dimension.

Across the entire sample, greater impairment in forming object relations, and the phases related to this factor, were associated with self-reported psychopathology, particularly in areas of cognitive functioning and satisfaction derived from social relations. Devaluation of femininity, and the dimensions associated with this factor, were associated with less self-reported psychopathology.

Among hospitalized mothers, both greater impairment in interpersonal functioning and self-reported psychopathology were associated with impairment in forming object relations. Among nonhospitalized mothers, on the other hand, self-reported psychopathology was manifested in a more basic inability to establish meaningful interpersonal relationships, and was associated with feelings of self-doubt, concern about one's adequacy as a woman, and greater conflict with one's own parental family.

Consistent with this interpretation, the child care attitudes of the hospitalized mothers differed from those of nonhospitalized controls in the expected direction. Hospitalized women believed less than nonhospitalized controls that the infant could develop a reciprocal social relationship with its mother, and were more likely to deny concerns regarding child care. While believing that the baby was not a social being, however, these hospitalized mothers felt more certain than the nonhospitalized controls that they could meet and understand the baby's needs.

As to premorbid adjustment, mothers hospitalized sooner

after the baby's birth were more likely to express concern regarding the nurturance/self-absorption dimension, while mothers hospitalized later after childbirth were particularly conflict-ridden in regard to the trust/mistrust issue. This finding was consistent with other findings that suggested that women hospitalized sooner after childbirth were more involved in child care, even if the disturbance recurred following the birth of each new child, than were women who broke down at a later point after delivery. Women hospitalized later after childbirth tended to be particularly aloof and distant from others and unable to respond to the child's demand for a reciprocal relationship. These mothers were, in general, more depressed, more socially withdrawn, and more likely to have had prior hospitalizations. They showed lower ego-strength and felt more futile about their life. Also of interest was the finding that having a greater number of boys is associated with a greater risk of hospitalization. Boys appear to be particularly difficult to care for and present a cumulatively greater stress than caring for girls.

Women whose disturbance was observed for a longer period prior to hospitalization showed greater impairment in forming object relations than women who became ill more recently and whose illness was presumably more reactive. However, the number of days hospitalized did not show a linear relationship to conflict in psychosocial development, largely because women hospitalized for a long time may remain in the hospital either because they are able to profit from hospitalization or because they are so seriously disturbed that they cannot function outside the hospital. Comparison of length of hospitalization among women showing quite different patterns of conflict in psychosocial development showed that women with a greater sense of purpose were likely to be discharged from the hospital sooner, particularly when they also showed a greater capacity for object relations.

Our results suggest that the psychoanalytic theory of character development has utility not only in the study of the single case but also in the more systematic study of larger numbers of persons. They further suggest that an individual's perceptions of significant interpersonal relationships do seem to have some bearing on present psychosocial functioning. To the extent that a person perceives others in a manner which is developmentally inappropriate, there is likely to be a disturbance in present adjustment. The earlier this conflict occurs in the sequential phases of character development, the more serious are the implications for a person's subsequent psychosocial development, including the capacity to resolve developmental tasks associated with adulthood.

# References to Part 4

Abraham, K. (1916) 1960. The first pregenital stage of the libido. In K. Abraham, *Selected papers on psychoanalysis*. New York: Basic Books.

―――. (1921) 1960. Contributions to the theory of the anal character. in ibid., pp. 248-79.

―――. (1924a). The influence of oral eroticism on character formation. In ibid., pp. 393-406.

―――. (1924b). A short study of the development of the libido, viewed in the light of mental disorders. In ibid., pp. 418-502.

―――. (1925). Character formation on the genital level of the libido. In ibid., pp. 407-17.

Anderson, E. W. 1933. A study of the sexual life in psychoses associated with childbirth. *Journal of Mental Science* 79: 137-49.

Anthony, E. and Benedek, T., eds. 1970. *Parenthood: Its psychology and psychopathology*. Boston: Little, Brown.

Armor, D. and Couch, A. 1972. *Data-text primer*. New York: Free Press and Macmillan.

Atkinson, J. W. 1950. Studies in projective measurement of achievement motivation. Unpublished doctoral dissertation, University of Michigan.

Balint, M. (1932) 1965. Character analysis and the new beginning. In M. Balint, *Primary love and psychoanalytic technique*. New York: Liveright.

―――. (1947) 1965. On genital love. In ibid., pp. 109-20.

―――. (1951) 1965. On love and hate. In ibid., pp. 121-35.

Benedek, T. 1959. Parenthood as a developmental phase. *Journal of the American Psychoanalytic Association* 7: 389-417.

―――. 1970. The family as a psychologic field. In E. Anthony and T. Benedek, eds., *Parenthood: Its psychology and psychopathology*, pp. 109-36. Boston: Little, Brown.

Bettelheim, B. 1967. *The empty fortress*. New York: Free Press.

Bibring, E. 1953. The mechanism of depression. In P. Greenacre, ed., *Affective disorders*, pp. 13–48. New York: International Universities Press.

Bibring, G. 1959. Some considerations of the psychological processes in pregnancy. *Psychoanalytic Study of the Child* 14: 113–21.

Bibring, G. et al. 1961. A study of the psychological processes of pregnancy and of the earliest mother-child relationship. *Psychoanalytic Study of the Child* 16: 9–22.

Blum, G. 1949. A study of the psychoanalytic theory of psychosexual development. *Genetic Psychology Monographs* 39: 3–99.

———. 1962. A guide for the research use of the Blacky pictures. *Journal of Projective Techniques* 26: 3–29.

Bonaparte, M. 1953. *Female sexuality*. New York: International Universities Press.

Caldwell, B. 1964. The effects of infant care. In M. Hoffman and L. Hoffman, eds., *Review of child development research*, pp. 9–88. New York: The Russell Sage Foundation.

Caplan, G. and Grunebaum, H. 1967. Perspectives on primary prevention: A review. *Archives of General Psychiatry* 17: 331–46.

Cohler, B.; Woolsey, S.; Weiss, J.; and Grunebaum, H. 1968. Childrearing attitudes and adjustment among mothers volunteering and revolunteering to participate in a psychological study. *Psychological Reports* 23: 603–12.

Cohler, B.; Weiss, J.; and Grunebaum, H. 1970. Childcare attitudes and emotional disturbance among mothers of young children. *Genetic Psychology Monographs* 82: 3–47.

Cohler, B. 1973. Manual for the interpersonal apperception technique. Unpublished manuscript, Committee on Human Development, University of Chicago.

Cronbach, L. 1951. Coefficient alpha and the internal structure of tests. *Psychometrika* 16: 297–334.

Dahlstrom, E. and Welsh, G. S. 1960. *An MMPI handbook*. Minneapolis: University of Minnesota Press.

Deutsch, H. 1945. *The psychology of women*. Vol. 2: *Motherhood*. New York: Grune and Stratton.

———. 1948. An introduction to the discussion of the psychological problems of pregnancy. In M. Senn, ed., *Problems of early infancy*. New York: Macy Foundation.

———. (1925) 1948. The psychology of women in relation to the functions of reproduction. In R. Fliess, *The psychoanalytic reader*, pp. 165–80. New York: International Universities Press.

Dreeben, R. 1962. Organization and environment: The relationship between mental hospitals and district courts. Unpublished doctoral dissertation, Harvard University.

Dyer, E. D. 1963. Parenthood as crisis: A re-study. *Marriage and Family Living* 25: 190–201.

Edgcumbe, R. and Burgner, M. 1973. Some problems in the conceptualization of early object relationships: I. The concepts of need satisfaction and need-satisfying relationships. *Psychoanalytic Study of the Child* 27: 283–314.

Edwards, A. 1967. *Statistical methods*. New York: Holt, Rinehart and Winston.

Erikson, E. 1959. Identity and the life cycle. *Psychological Issues* 1: 1.
———. 1963. *Childhood and society*, rev. ed. New York: Norton.
———. 1964. *Insight and responsibility*. New York: Norton.
Fairbairn, W. (1946) 1952. Object relations and dynamic structure. In W. Fairbairn, *Psychoanalytic studies of the personality*, pp. 137–51. London: Tavistock Press.
———. (1949) 1952. Steps in the development of an object relations theory of personality. In ibid., pp. 152–61.
———. 1952. *Psychoanalytic studies of the personality*. London: Tavistock Press.
Fenichel, O. 1945. *The psychoanalytic theory of the neuroses*. New York: Norton.
Ferguson, G. 1959. *Statistical analysis in psychology and education*. New York: McGraw-Hill.
Fischer, J. and Fischer, A. 1963. The New Englanders of Orchard Town, U.S.A. In B. Whiting, ed., *Six cultures: Studies of childrearing*, pp. 869–1010. New York: John Wiley.
Freud, S. (1905). *Three contributions to the theory of sex*. Standard Edition of the Complete Psychological Works of Sigmund Freud, vol. 7, p. 125.
———. (1908) 1956. Character and anal eroticism. In S. Freud, *Collected papers*, vol. 2, pp. 45–50. London: Hogarth Press.
———. (1911) 1956. Psychoanalytic notes upon an autobiographical account of paranoia, dementia paranoides. In ibid., vol. 3, pp. 390–472.
———. (1913a) 1956. The excretory functions in psychoanalysis and folklore. In ibid., vol. 5, pp. 88–91.
———. (1913b) 1956. The predisposition to obsessional neurosis. In ibid., vol. 2, pp. 122–31.
———. (1916) 1956. On the transformation of instincts, with special reference to anal eroticism. In ibid., vol. 2, pp. 164–71.
———. (1917a) 1956. Mourning and melancholia. In ibid., vol. 4, pp. 152–72.
———. (1917b). *Introductory lectures on psychoanalysis*. Standard Edition, vol. 15, p. 3.
———. (1923). *The ego and the id*. Standard Edition, vol. 19, p. 3.
———. (1925) 1956. Some psychological consequences of the anatomical distinction between the sexes. In *Collected papers*, vol. 5, pp. 186–97.
Garai, J. and Scheinfeld, A. 1968. Sex differences in mental and behavioral traits. *Genetic Psychology Monographs* 77: 169–299.
Garn, S. and Clark, L. 1953. The sex difference in the basic metabolic rate. *Child Development* 24: 215–24.
Ginsparg, S. 1956. Post-partum psychoses. Unpublished doctoral dissertation, Washington University.
Glover, E. (1924). Notes on oral character formation. In E. Glover, *On the early development of the mind, collected papers*, vol. 1.
Gloye, E. and Zimmerman, I. 1967. MMPI item changes by college students under ideal-self response set. *Journal of Projective Techniques* 31: 63–69
Goodrich, W. 1968. Toward a taxonomy of marriage. In J. Marmor, ed., *Modern psychoanalysis*. New York: Basic Books.
Gottheil, E.; Paredes, A.; and Exline, R. 1968. Parental schemata in emotionally disturbed women. *Journal of Abnormal Psychology* 73: 416–19.

Gruen, W. 1964. Adult personality: An empirical study of Erikson's theory of ego-development. In B. Neugarten, ed., Personality in middle and late life, pp. 1–14. New York: Atherton Press.

Grummon, D. and Jones, E. 1954. Changes over client-centered therapy evaluated in psychoanalytically based thematic apperception test scales. In C. Rogers and R. Dymond, eds., Psychotherapy and personality change. Chicago: University of Chicago Press.

Gruntrip, H. 1961. Personality structure and human interaction. New York: International Universities Press.

Hamilton, J. A. 1962. Postpartum psychiatric problems. St. Louis: C. Mosby.

Hartmann, H. (1939) 1958. Ego psychology and the problem of adaptation. New York: International Universities Press.

———. (1953) 1964. Contribution to the metapsychology of schizophrenia. In H. Hartmann, Essays on ego psychology, pp. 186–206. New York: International Universities Press.

Henry. W. E. 1956. The analysis of fantasy. New York: Wiley.

Hilgard, R. 1953. Anniversary reactions in parents, precipitated by children. Psychiatry. 16: 13–80.

Hilgard, S. and Newman, M. 1959. Anniversaries in mental illness. Psychiatry 22: 113–21.

Hilgard, J. and Fisk, F. 1960. Disruption of adult ego identity as related to childhood loss of a mother through hospitalization for psychosis. Journal of Nervous and Mental Disease 131: 47–57.

Horney, K. 1945. Our inner conflicts. New York: Norton.

Hurvich, M. and Bellak, L. 1968. Ego function patterns in schizophrenics. Psychological Reports 22: 299–308.

Isaacs, S. 1952. The nature and function of fantasy. In M. Klein, P. Heimann, S. Isaacs, and J. Riviere, eds., Developments in psychoanalysis, pp. 67–121. London: Hogarth Press.

Jacobson, E. 1964. The self and the object world. New York: International Universities Press.

———. 1967. Psychotic conflict and reality. New York: International Universities Press.

John, E. J. 1953. Mental health and the principle of least effort. Unpublished doctoral dissertation, University of Chicago.

Jones, E. (1918) 1961. Anal-erotic character traits. In E. Jones, Papers on psychoanalysis, 5th ed., pp. 413–37. Boston: Beacon Press.

Kagan, J. 1959. The stability of TAT fantasy and stimulus ambiguity. Journal of Consulting Psychology 23: 266–71.

Kenny, D. T. 1964. Stimulus functions in projective techniques. In B. Maher, ed., Progress in experimental personality research, pp. 285–354. New York: Academic Press.

Klein, M. (1932) 1960. The psychoanalysis of children. New York: Grove Press.

Knof, C. A. 1946. The dynamics of newly born babies. Journal of Pediatrics 29: 721–28

Lanyon, R. 1968. A handbook of MMPI group profiles. Minneapolis: University of Minnesota Press.

LeMasters, E. E. 1957. Parenthood as crisis. Marriage and Family Living 19: 352–55.

Lesser, G. 1961. Custom-making projective tests for research. *Journal of Projective Techniques* 25: 21–31.

Linn, L. and Polatin, P. 1950. Psychiatric problems of the puerperium from the standpoint of prophylaxis. *Psychiatric Quarterly* 24: 376–84.

Markham, S. 1958. Dynamics of post-partum pathological reactions as revealed in psychological tests. *Journal of the Hillside Hospital* 7: 178–89.

———. 1961. A comparative evaluation of psychotic and nonpsychotic reactions to childbirth. *American Journal of Orthopsychiatry* 31: 565–78.

McClelland, D. 1958. Methods of measuring human motivation. In J. Atkinson, ed. *Motives in fantasy action and society*, pp. 7–42. Princeton, N.J.: Van Nostrand.

Melges, F. T. 1965. Postpartum psychiatric syndromes. Paper presented at Annual Meeting, American Orthopsychiatric Association, New York.

Milrod, D. 1954. Some prognostic factors in schizophrenia related to childbirth. *Journal of the Hillside Hospital* 3: 107–25.

Modell, A. H. 1968. *Object love and reality*. New York: International Universities Press.

Monroe, K. L. 1966. The estimation of the full-scale WAIS I.A. *Journal of Clinical Psychology* 22: 79–81.

Moss, H. A. 1965. Methodological issues in studying mother-infant interaction. *American Journal of Orthopsychiatry* 35: 382–486.

Murray, H. et al. (1938) 1962. *Explorations in personality*. New York: Science Editions.

Murray, H. 1943. *The thematic apperception test*. Cambridge: Harvard University Press.

Murstein, B. 1961. The role of the stimulus in the manifestation of fantasy. In J. Kagan and G. Lesser, *Contemporary approaches to thematic apperception methods*, pp. 229–73. Springfield, Ill.: Charles Thomas.

———. 1963. *Theory and research in projective techniques, emphasizing the TAT*. New York: John Wiley and Sons.

Nagera, H. 1964. Arrest in development, fixation, and regression. *Psychoanalytic Study of the Child* 19: 222–39.

Nunberg, H. (1932) 1955. *Principles of psychoanalysis*. New York: International Universities Press.

Parsons, T.; Bales, R. F.; et al. 1955. *Family socialization and interaction*. New York: Free Press.

Pavenstedt, E. 1961. A study of immature mothers and their children. In G. Caplan, *Prevention of mental disorders in children*, pp. 192–217. New York: Basic Books.

Phillips, L. 1953. Case history data and prognosis in schizophrenia. *Journal of Nervous and Mental Disease* 117: 515–25.

Piker, P. 1938. Psychoses complicating childrearing. *American Journal of Obstetrics and Gynecology* 35: 901–9.

Prelinger, E. and Zimet, C. 1964. *An ego-psychological approach to character assessment*. New York: Free Press.

Rangell, L. 1965. Some comments on psychoanalytic nosology. In M. Schur, ed., *Drive, affects, behavior*, vol. 2, pp. 128–60. New York: International Universities Press.

Rapoport, R. 1963. Normal crises, family structure, and mental health. *Family Process* 2: 68–80.

———. 1967. The study of marriage as a critical transition for family and personality development. In P. Lomas, *The predicament of the family*, pp. 169–206. New York: International Universities Press.

Rapoport, R. and Rapoport, R. 1965. Work and family in contemporary society. *American sociological Review* 30: 381–94.

Reich, W. (1933) 1949. *Character analysis.* New York: Noonday Press.

Rheingold, H. L. 1964. *Maternal destructiveness: The fear of being a woman.* New York: Grune and Stratton.

Ribble, M. 1943. *The rights of infants.* New York: Columbia University Press.

Ritvo, S. et al. 1962. Object relations. *Journal of the American Psychoanalytic Association* 10: 102–17.

Robinson, S. A. and Hendrix, V. 1966. The Blacky test and psychoanalytic theory: Another factor-analytic approach to validity. *Journal of Projective Techniques and Personality Assessment* 30: 597–603.

Robinson, W. S. 1957. The statistical measurement of agreement. *American Sociological Review* 22: 17–25.

Rosberg, J. and Karon, B. 1959. A direct analytic contribution to the understanding of postpartum psychoses. *Psychiatric Quarterly* 33: 296–304.

Rosenthal, R. 1966. *Experimenter effects in behavioral research.* New York: Appleton-Century-Crofts.

Ryle, A. 1961. The psychological disturbances associated with 345 pregnancies in 137 women. *Journal of Mental Sciences* 107: 279–86.

Sampson, H.; Messinger, S.; and Towne, R. 1964. *Schizophrenic women: Studies in marital crisis.* New York: Atherton Press and Prentice-Hall.

Sander, L. 1962. Issues in early mother-child interaction. *Journal of the American Academy of Child Psychiatry* 2: 141–66.

———. 1964. Adaptive relationships in early mother-child interaction. *Journal of the American Academy of Child Psychiatry* 3: 221–63.

———. 1969. The longitudinal course of early mother-child interaction: Cross-case comparison in a sample of mother-child pairs. In B. Foss, ed., *Determinants of infant behavior*, vol. 4, pp. 189–228. London: Methuen and Company.

Saunders, E. 1929. Association of psychoses with the puerperium. *American Journal of Psychiatry* 86: 715–19.

Shapiro, D. 1965. *Neurotic styles.* New York: Basic Books.

Smith, M. B.; Bruner, J.; and White, R. W. 1956. *Opinions and personality.* New York: John Wiley and Sons.

Spitz, R. 1959. *A genetic field theory of ego formation: Its implications for pathology.* New York: International Universities Press.

Sullivan, H. S. 1953. *The interpersonal theory of psychiatry.* New York: Norton.

Taft, R. (1959) 1962. Multiple methods of personality assessment. In I. Sarason, ed., *Contemporary research in personality*, pp. 84–98.

Terman, L. and Tyler, L. 1954. Psychological sex differences. In L. Carmichael, ed., *Manual of child psychology*, 2d. ed., pp. 1064–1114. New York: John Wiley and Sons.

Vaillant, G. 1962. Prediction of recovery in schizophrenia. *Journal of Nervous*

*Disorders* 135: 534–43.

———. 1964. Prediction of schizophrenia remission. *Archives of General Psychiatry* 11: 509–18.

Waxler, N. 1959. Defense mechanisms in interpersonal behavior. Unpublished doctoral dissertation, Harvard University.

Weiss, J. L.; Grunebaum, H. U.; and Schell, R. E. 1964. Psychotic mothers and their young children. II: Psychological studies of mothers caring for their infants in a psychiatric hospital. *Archives of General Psychiatry* 11: 90–98.

Western Psychological Services. 1963. *Shipley Institute of Living Scale, manual of directions and scoring key.* Beverly Hills, Cal.: Western Psychological Services.

Wiggins, J. 1969. Content dimensions in the MMPI. In J. Butcher, *MMPI: Research developments and clinical applications,* pp. 127–80. New York: McGraw-Hill.

Zigler, E., and Phillips, L. 1962. The process-reactive distinction in psychopathology. *Journal of Abnormal and Social Psychology* 65: 215–22.

Zilboorg, G. 1928. Post-partum schizophrenias. *Journal of Nervous and Mental Disease* 68: 370–83.

Zubin, J.; Eron, L.; and Schumer, F. 1965. *An experimental approach to projective techniques.* New York: John Wiley and Sons.

# part 5

## conclusion

*Henry Grunebaum,*
*Justin L. Weiss,*
*Bertram J. Cohler,*
*Carol R. Hartman, and*
*David H. Gallant*

# Conclusion

Hospitalization for an emotional disturbance during the first months after childbirth is a stressful event not only for the patient herself but for her child, her husband, and other members of the family. Hospitalization typically means that a mother has to separate from her child, who is then exposed to surrogate care which is often both transient and confusing. As disruptive as hospitalization may be at other points in the life cycle, it is especially difficult for the new mother. Feeling ambivalent over the burdens imposed by having had to care for the baby during her decompensation, and guilty over her apparent abandonment of the maternal role, she finds it difficult to take advantage of the treatment resources which the hospital has to offer, yet she finds it impossible to manage outside the hospital.

Joint admission was designed to resolve this conflict. Bringing the child into the hospital at some point during the mother's stay makes it possible for the mother to have the protection and support which the hospital provides while she resumes the maternal care which is so important both to her child and to herself. In addition, the mother and her therapist are able to utilize in treatment important observations of her feelings and actions which would be unavailable if the baby were not in the hospital. If this aspect of the mother's treatment is neglected, when she returns home and resumes her maternal respon-

sibilities, she must face, often without help, intense feelings of
rage, guilt, jealousy, and ambivalence which may be over-
powering.

## JOINT ADMISSION AS A TREATMENT PROCESS

This book began with a description of a young mother who was
admitted to a mental hospital in a psychotic state, whose
progress toward recovery was slow, who was enabled to care for
her child on the ward where she was an inpatient, and who then
made rapid strides forward, returning home to resume her life. It
is appropriate to remind ourselves of Mrs. P at this point
because it was the issues she brought to our attention which led
to the studies reported here: How does the staff determine
which psychotic mothers can be assisted by joint admission?
How can psychotic mothers be helped to resume the care of
their young children? Does uniting a mother and baby during
the time of her hospitalization adversely affect the child? How
can the treatment program facilitate a more healthy mother-
child relationship? How does one encourage a family evolution
which permits the patient's positive change? What special
difficulties in mothering attitudes, motivations, and practices
characterize mentally ill women? We have sought answers to
these questions and discussed them at length in the preceding
chapters.

   In the course of preparing the conclusion to this book, it
occurred to us to write to Mrs. P and ask how life had fared for
her and Bobby. She replied to our letter at length and with
warmth, reporting that she and her husband now had four
"marvelous children," that their marriage had weathered some
stormy times but was now "really smooth sailing," and that the
conflicts between the demands of home with which her
husband is little help and the desire to be active in a career or in
school are still alive and sometimes stressful. She commented
retrospectively about her experience in our hospital that "its
saving grace was having Bobby with me, for I could be
productive during that long period." On the other hand, she has
had two brief hospitalizations (less than one month each) since
the birth of her fourth child and felt at these times that a respite
from the burdens of the home was welcome.

From the outset, we have seen the mother and her child as located in a psychosocial world, dealing with critical life issues in ways which are determined both by the immediate situation and by more enduring aspects of personality. Central to the whole idea of joint admission is the concept of the patient as an active and responsible person living in a world inhabited by other people important to her. There would be no point in asking her to care for her child on a psychiatric ward if we did not believe that problems in living with others are best approached, whenever possible, by working on their resolution in a setting in which one is engaged with rather than disengaged from significant others. The salience of this viewpoint for our work is to be seen in the nursing approach to the mother, which is focused on her relationships with the treatment staff as well as with the primary people in her life. Our investigations of mothers and their babies have suggested several important directions for the continuation of these efforts.

Intervention with populations at risk cannot be done without collaborative efforts to evaluate the situation and its potential for deviant development. The mothers and fathers were remarkably open to our concerns and became close allies in developing methods for replicating our observations in a more systematic way. The same holds true for evaluating the impact of our clinical efforts with the mothers, even in those situations which we deemed unsuccessful. Initially this approach may appear to be inconsistent with the rigor and "purity" of research design, but the realities implied by our treatment approach demand openness and the cooperation of those participating in the study. A patient caring for her baby on the ward brings forcefully to our attention her mothering behavior and feelings and the nature of her interaction with her child. We learn about—and we must deal with—emotionally powerful realities which are simply not seen by examining diagnoses, dynamics, or verbal reports. This is the only way in which deficits in her mothering can be understood and treated. Directing our efforts toward ongoing forces in a mother's life requires concomitant evaluation and research with the most complete possible participation in order to prevent premature or invalid judgments as to cause and effect.

Conceptualizing the intervention process and putting it into action, assessing maternal character and maternal attitudes in terms of naturally evolving sequences or states of development, and relating these sequences to success or failure in joint admission, have led to certain implications for practice. Three models of joint admission have been described. Our own "intermediate" model unites the mother and baby rather early in the mother's hospital experience, though not immediately. In this model the mother has primary responsibility for her baby, with therapeutic efforts directed toward enhancing her ability to sustain that responsibility and to develop a more favorable attitude toward the care of her child. The two other models are each in part a function of staffing patterns. The "early" model keeps the mother and baby together by providing twenty-four-hour nursery facilities for the child from the time of the mother's hospitalization until she takes full responsibility (England, Cassell Hospital). The other, or "late," model, unites mother and baby just in the last days before the mother leaves the hospital to return home (U.S.A., Medfield State Hospital).

In general, we found that our "intermediate" model was not harmful to the babies and was reasonably helpful to the majority of the mothers who participated in the project. When we directed our attention to the correlates of success in joint admission, we saw that certain dynamic characteristics of family life and certain dimensions of individual personality and pathology provided better predictors than did the traditional diagnostic categories. Family histories for both mother and father which indicated instability and strife across several generations were linked to a more chronic patterning of deviant behavior within the marriage and in individual styles of relating. However, when some of the mothers, together with their husbands, accepted the continuation of treatment in the home, important gains were possible.

The outline of maternal issues involved in the therapeutic care of joint admission mothers provides an initial interpersonal orientation for assessing the ongoing interaction of the mother and other important people as they work together. This framework allows us to anticipate and plan for the needs and concerns of *all* joint admission patients in terms of palpable, immediate interpersonal problems which must be faced, and to consider how the responses of *each* patient may be related to more enduring patterns of individual behavior. Complementing the intervention process is research which demonstrates the enduring quality of certain character patterns of mothers, manifest in more and less adaptive child-rearing attitudes. Study of the children indicates that cognitive development can be favorably influenced by intervention, despite uneven development and attentional deficits. Nevertheless, intervention has been less successful in fostering a greater capacity for relatedness in the child.

## INTERPERSONAL RELATEDNESS AND THE TREATMENT PROCESS

Of central importance throughout this book—in our theoretical framework, in our clinical and empirical assessments of mothers, their babies, and their marriages, and in our therapeutic approach—has been the concept of interpersonal relatedness. We have been concerned with individual differences in the *capacity* for relatedness; with various *styles* of relating; with the *development* of critical aspects of interpersonal relationships as these are expressed in personality, attitudes, and behavior; and with the *facilitation* or reactivation of adaptive modes of relating.

This emphasis is consistent with the epigenetic nature of our thinking about human growth and human crisis, as formulated by Erikson (1963). We have constructed research instruments within an interpersonal orientation, such as the maternal attitude scale which drew much of its content from the sequential tasks of mother-child interaction as described by Sander (1962).

Mahler (1968) has emphasized the developmental sequence of *attachment, separation,* and *individuation* in her conceptualizations of serious emotional disturbances in childhood. We regard these three processes as the cornerstones of human development and believe that the satisfactory accomplishment of later interpersonal and intrapsychic integrative tasks depends to a significant degree upon how well the foundation has been built in the child's earliest relationships. Failure in the continued activation of these processes within a person and within a family can come from many sources. Stability of development depends upon growth in one's capacity for attachment to others, for appropriate separation from others, and for differentiation which allows one to combine closeness and separation. Evaluation of such processes can be approached through the integrated use of systematic research instruments and clinical observations, which, in turn, should facilitate the development of more effective means for both psychiatric and nursing intervention.

In our own work, analysis of the nursing observations indicates that mothers who have developed more adaptive ways of attaching, separating, and differentiating themselves in relation to others are more likely to make successful use of joint admission. Hostile, disaffiliating patterns of relating to others are associated with the failure to resolve critical issues in treatment.

Analysis of the character and maternal attitudes of hospitalized mothers affirms the correlation between length of treatment and a mother's capacity to relate more or less positively to others. The marriages of the patients in our study reflected differences in the strength of the capacity for attaching, separating, and differentiating; such differences greatly influence patterns of parenting. Problems within the nuclear family and the extended family can be traced to qualitative differences in these adaptive processes. Examples of the styles of mothering and therapeutic encounters around critical nursing issues, both in the hospital and in the home, deal with the activating of these three processes so that the mother can move toward a clearer definition of herself and her abilities.

Pervasive egocentricity at earlier stages of psychosocial development has been found to be associated with more conflicted maternal attitudes. The relation between maternal psychopathology and impairment of the child's capacity for relating to others also lends support to the view that long-standing deviations in a parent's patterns of relating are associated with similar deviations in the child, though a causal connection is not yet definitively established.

## MOTHERHOOD AS A DEVELOPMENTAL ROLE CRISIS

A second major concept which unites much of the material of

this volume is that of the developmental role crisis involved in motherhood. The women we have studied found it necessary to confront the conflicting and complex requirements of multiple roles—those of patient, wife, mother, daughter, neighbor, and so forth—and our experience has given us a new appreciation of the difficulties which face the new or recent mother (Rossi, 1968).

As Lopata (1971) has pointed out, motherhood is a stage in the life cycle which, even for women without predisposition to mental illness, permits little preparation and arrives with shocking suddenness. Perhaps only widowhood or other losses by death evoke a greater crisis for the American housewife. The psychoanalyst Grete Bibring (1959) has observed that crisis refers to a developmental "point-of-no-return" in an individual's life. Caplan (1961) defines a psychological crisis in the following way: "A crisis is a state provoked when a person faces an obstacle to important life goals that is, for a time, insurmountable through the utilization of customary methods of problem-solving. A period of disorganization ensues, a period of upset, during which many different abortive attempts at solution are made. Eventually some kind of adaptation is achieved which may or may not be in the best interest of that person and his fellows" (p. 18). Consistent with this view of crises as the testing ground of psychological health, Caplan and Grunebaum (1967) observe that: "the individual may emerge from the crisis with increased adaptive capacities. . . . On the other hand, he may emerge with lower adaptive capacities and a greater vulnerability to mental disorder. . . . crises represent mental health turning points" (p. 337).

Motherhood is an almost classic example of such a crisis. During pregnancy, a woman, her husband, and their extended families can prepare for the new role, but no preparation can anticipate the full reality of the event itself. With the baby's birth, the mother must have the welfare of another uppermost in her thoughts: at least in our culture, concern for self is explicitly secondary to concern for another for the first time in a woman's life. Time, energy, and emotional resources must be shared, and even sleep is sacrificed for the baby's welfare. Caplan (1960) and Kaplan and Mason (1960) have documented the phases of this crisis and its resolution among mothers of prematures.

Less detailed study of women with babies of at least average birth weight suggests that mothers of prematures are not alone in experiencing motherhood as a crisis. Dyer (1963) replicated an earlier and less carefully executed study of LeMasters (1957), and found that nearly all mothers felt exhausted and inadequate in the months following delivery. After almost one year, half of these women continued to feel uncertain and inadequate as mothers. Similar findings have been reported by Hobbs (1965) and by Meyerowitz and Feldman (1960). Pugh and his associates (1963) studied all first admissions to Massachusetts mental hospitals in one calendar year and found temporal associations between risk of emotional breakdown and certain critical time periods. The risk of mental illness is actually lower during pregnancy than would be expected by chance alone, but is significantly greater than chance for the first three postpartum months, lower than would be expected by chance during the fourth through sixth postpartum months, and significantly greater than would be expected by chance at the end of the first postpartum year. Similar findings have been reported by Paffenbarger and McCabe (1966). These studies demonstrate a clear association between the assumption of the maternal role and the development of mental illness during the postpartum period.

Even among nonhospitalized women, some psychiatric symptoms are quite common in the months following childbirth. Jacobson, Kaij, and Nilsson (1965) report that depression, fatigue, and irritability were present in well over one-third of the postpartum women in their sample. Yalom and his associates (1968) report that more than half the women in their normal postpartum sample showed signs of depression, including crying, during the first weeks after delivery. Yalom and his colleagues noted other evidence of postpartum emotional distress, including undue concern about the baby, fatigue, irritability, and insomnia. Melges (1968) notes a common syndrome in postpartum women, consisting of feelings of shame, helplessness, and confusion. Melges also notes that laboratory studies ruled out the possibility of endocrine factors as a determinant of this postpartum emotional distress. Especially interesting in the context of the present discussion, the same syndrome was noted among women adopting a baby as was noted among women delivering a baby. While this may represent modeling in conformity to culturally expected patterns of reacting to childbirth, it is clear that, even among women referred to by Robertson (1958) as "ordinary devoted mothers," transition to motherhood is a unique developmental crisis in the life cycle.

A recent study by a group of Scandinavian investigators (Malmquist and Kaij, 1971) has used an ingenious twin design in examining this hypothesis. A sample was gathered consisting of monozygous twins, of whom one had married and had one child, and the other had not yet had a child. Twins with children showed a significantly greater number of psychiatric symptoms than those who had not yet had a child, and these symptoms were especially noticeable among younger women who, it was believed, felt especially burdened by the conflicting demands of marriage and parenthood. Even when both twins were married, the twin with children showed a greater number of psychiatric symptoms. Mothers with two children showed a greater number of symptoms than those with one child, suggesting the cumulative stress which occurs with increasing numbers of children.

Becoming a mother can be viewed from several perspectives, and although our focus is largely on the psychological issues involved, it is useful to consider this developmental stage from the perspective of a role transition. Cottrell (1942) has suggested that several factors influence the ease of adjustment to a new role. In particular, role transition is likely to be facilitated by anticipatory socialization, which may be defined as the process of learning the norms or expectations of a role before one is actually called upon to act in that role. It seems likely that there is little opportunity in our society with its smaller families for young women to participate by observing and sharing in child care. The years for baby-sitting are over, and this activity tends to involve entertaining and putting children to bed who are often toddlers before they are entrusted to a teen-aged girl.

Cottrell further contends that role transitions are facilitated when the role can be clearly defined and there is little conflict with other roles. Neither of these conditions is usually met when one becomes a mother; the norms are poorly defined, success is difficult to assess, the end point for deciding one has done a good job recedes into the future as each stage is negotiated, and clearly there are real conflicts between the role of mother and that of wife. The young woman does not know how well she is doing or, in fact, what is to be considered "doing well"— self-assessments which are more easily made in school and at work. And her husband is likely to be of little help in this assessment, since to some degree her working at mothering interferes with the time she can devote to him and his needs. But the transition to motherhood involves in addition profound psychological adjustments so that it is often considered a key example of a "life crisis."

Among factors contributing to making the transition to motherhood such a crisis is the set of expectations of the maternal role held by mothers, their husbands, and their own and their husbands' families. As we have noted earlier, in discussing the Fischers' (1963) study of Orchard Town, New England, American women are expected to be the primary agents in the child's socialization. To the extent that the child develops a good "moral character," his achievements are believed to be directly related to the manner in which his mother raised him. While the philosophy of "open marriage," together with "women's liberation," is designed to alter the distribution of responsibility within the family, for the majority of American women the values described by the Fischers continue to guide maternal conduct.

American mothers have also been described as isolated from their own extended families in obtaining assistance during the first difficult months after delivery. This factor is cited by the Gordons (1958, 1959, 1960) as an especially important source of emotional distress in the first postpartum year. However, data provided by Litwak (1960a, 1960b) support Sussman's (1959, 1965) concept of the modified extended family in America in which, typically, a couple's parents provide both help and financial support during the earlier years of marriage in exchange for similar support later on in life during their own old age. While it may be that some mothers are particularly vulnerable to feelings of isolation from their own kinship group in transient suburban homes, the majority of mothers live within a day's drive of their own parents. For example, more than three-quarters of the mothers studied by our research group were born within ten miles of their present residence.

The problem is not primarily that women are isolated from their own kinship group. More important is the fact that women frequently experience such conflict with their own families that, while they receive help and are provided with baby-sitting and advice, this help is received with mixed feelings. In Melges's (1968) study of normal parturient women, fully half the mothers interviewed spoke of their fear of becoming more like their own mothers as a result of having a child of their own; a substantial number of women in our culture have highly ambivalent feelings about their own mothers.

Such data suggest that it is too easy to attribute the difficulties of motherhood solely to the isolation of the nuclear family. Just as significant is a woman's relationship with her own family. As we have seen in discussing the relationships of the women in the present study with their extended families, even where a woman does not have such relatives, she tends to find some older women to stand *in loco parentis*.

Particularly among mothers in the joint admission project who were better able to make use of their hospitalization, these "crises of identification" were of the greatest importance in their treatment. As they cared for their babies on the ward, the women recalled similarities between the ways in which they were raising their children and the ways in which their mothers had raised them. Frequently, they were frightened by the realization that, even though they intended to do things differently from their mothers, they found themselves reacting in the same ways. Such feelings could then be brought to their therapists while still fresh and intense. Feeling frightened of becoming like her mother, and uncertain about even the possibility of becoming fully a woman and a mother, a woman cannot sustain an appropriate relationship with her child, and is even less able to maintain an appropriate relationship with her husband.

Our data suggest that, while the husband-wife relationship is critical to the way in which the patient is able to adapt to her home environment after hospitalization, such problems between husband and wife can only be adequately resolved after a woman has been able to work through problems between herself and her own parents. Indeed, the stability of the nuclear family itself, among these postpartum women, is dependent on the support which women receive from their own extended families.

In the first place, most families arrange for the maternal

grandmother to provide surrogate care when hospitalization of the mother is necessary and before the joint admission plan is formulated. In the second place, women who have maintained little relationship with their own families tend to feel greater inner emptiness and are less able to sustain interpersonal relationships with any significant figures in their lives. It is significant in this regard that, while hospitalized mothers have to struggle to form close and satisfying relationships, a more important problem for nonhospitalized women is that of attaining a more stable balance between seeking their own mothers' help and being able to take an independent stance. Before this issue of autonomy can be resolved, a woman must first be able to become close to important persons in her life without feeling afraid of such closeness. In the third place, as a woman becomes more aware of her feelings and attitudes toward significant figures in her life, her parents provide a more secure starting point for reevaluating these relationships than her husband, for she spends less time with her parents, and so less depends upon her success in resolving these relationships.

If a woman is to be able to relate to her husband in a more mature manner, she must be able to resolve interpersonal conflicts which first arose with her parents. This view is supported by the fact that, in our own data, the dimensions of sufficiency/dependency and trust/mistrust, symbolic of pre-adult psychosocial relationships, are associated with the resolution of mutuality/isolation, a dimension of primary importance in the husband-wife relationship.

Becoming a mother frequently disturbs relationships with both a woman's husband and her friends. To the extent that a mother is able to resolve the developmental crisis of motherhood, she must be able to talk with her husband and to achieve mutual recognition of the problems between them created by this new role. As LeMasters (1970) has observed in his review of the problems associated with the assumption of the maternal role, the difficulty in achieving a transition from a two-person system to a three-person system is enormous. A woman's husband now has to compete with his baby for his wife's time and must subordinate his own needs to those of the baby. Sexual relations between husband and wife become complex as the couple no longer has the privacy and freedom of earlier days. With pre-school and school-aged children, the choice of a time for such intimacies is less often governed by mutual desires.

Furthermore, with the wife feeling exhausted and depressed, husband and wife may be uninterested in or unwilling to listen to each other's problems. Husbands in American culture typically feel that their wives withdraw into themselves after the baby is born. As his wife becomes increasingly self-absorbed, the husband becomes increasingly interested in hobbies and civic activities outside the home during his free hours in the evening and on weekends.

In our own work with hospitalized mothers and their husbands, the relationship between the patient and her husband proved to be a critical determinant of the degree to which a patient was able to profit from hospitalization and to use the joint admission program constructively. As we have already noted, most women requiring hospitalization showed serious conflicts with their own husbands. For many of these women, pregnancy and parenthood had come too soon after marriage, and husband and wife had not been able to create a stable two-person system before they had to accommodate a new member of the family. The couple's parents still played an influential role in many of these new marriages, making it necessary for the wife to resolve the frequent conflicts between her own parents, her husband's parents, and her husband and herself, all at the same time. Such conflicts are difficult enough for a woman to cope with even without having to learn how to care for a baby at the same time.

The need to make a decision about joint admission helped these young people to work together at a common task while enjoying the support of the psychiatrist, the social worker, and the nurse, who offered help with regard to the specific task of joint admission as well as with the larger problems in their marriage. In a similar manner, for couples with more long-standing but unstable and conflicted marriages, having to work together on the problems involved in planning and carrying out a joint admission provided both husband and wife with one of the first opportunities in their marriage to learn to work together at a common task and to receive help with the conflicts which kept them apart. Husband and wife learned how to support and understand each other, often for the first time. Husbands in these unstable or imbalanced marriages were able to discuss how they felt about the way their wives cared for the children, and both husband and wife had an opportunity to learn to work together as a couple and as parents. Husbands began to appreciate the importance of being more available to their wives, and tried, often for the first time, to share in the task of being a parent. Under conditions which supported growth, husband and wife were able to work together toward greater mutuality.

Relations with friends and neighbors also became strained by the experience of becoming a mother, while at the same time the new mother urgently needs peer support and advice in her role. Couples who have no children tend to arrange their day according to a different schedule, staying up later at night and sleeping later during the day over weekends and holidays. Women who have to be up during the night and early in the morning with their babies often become fatigued by staying out late at night and, as the family's social clock becomes increasingly discrepant from that of friends without children, they see these friends less and less often. The problem of having to arrange for baby-sitting means that it is less possible to make spontaneous plans. The cost of the baby-sitter also adds appreciably to the expenses for an evening's outing. More and more of a woman's life is restricted to that with close neighbors with children who lead similar lives and whose children offer playmates, helping to occupy some part of the day for both mother and child. Because of the difficulties sometimes involved in arranging for baby-sitting, it is even hard to spend time alone with other couples who have children. Special events planned well in advance are often called off at the last minute because a child of one couple or the other is sick.

The mentally ill women in the present study were largely deficient in the ability to form friendships or to rely on neighbors for help during periods of crisis. Being able to talk with friends and neighbors about child care provides important information about how to care for children, and also reduces feelings of frustration, isolation, and alienation. Among the women who made better use of hospitalization and the joint admission project, those who did not have close family ties were able to turn to friends and neighbors who often took the place of family members.

The goal of the nursing and psychiatric intervention during the post-discharge period was to support the development of social ties. Therapeutic efforts during hospitalization had been directed toward helping women to develop more satisfying relationships with others. Special support was often required during the period immediately following hospitalization in order to help women to realize the gains they had made during hospitalization in being able to become closer to others and actually to establish new relationships.

As we have noted, it is especially important to encourage women to experiment with new modes of social relationships after discharge. Our data and the work of other investigators indicate that women who feel isolated from friends and neighbors are especially vulnerable to subsequent illness and rehospitalization and have greater difficulty in being able to use therapeutic resources after discharge.

Increased demands on a woman's time and energies, the necessity of considering the baby's needs ahead of her own, the problem of coming to terms with her feelings about her own mother and her similarity to her mother, decreased intimacy with her husband, and loss of friends who were important in the days before becoming a mother—all these factors contribute to the crisis of assuming the maternal role. Many of the problems are accentuated in the woman who develops a serious emotional disturbance in the first months after childbirth.

Data published by the Gordons (1958, 1959, 1960, 1965) suggest that women more vulnerable to postpartum disturbances have fewer friends than other new mothers, are more preoccupied with providing a neat and well-run home, are less able to care for the baby while continuing some activities outside the home, are less able to arrange for help in caring for the baby, and are less able to resolve conflicts with their husbands, who, in turn, are less willing to compromise their own outside interests in order to help their wives. Particularly predictive of later breakdown among pregnant women are a previous history of emotional instability among both husband and wife, considerable difference in age between husband and wife, and physical complications during pregnancy and childbirth.

The Gordons also found (1958) that approximately 30 percent of suburban primiparae show symptoms during the first months following childbirth of such severity as to require psychiatric treatment. Confirming the Gordons' earlier work in this area, later papers suggest that stress is cumulative, and that the more difficulties a woman experiences, both intrapsychically and interpersonally, the greater is the probability that she will show psychiatric impairment in the first months following delivery. Reviewing their work, the Gordons comment:

As a rule, emotionally ill new mothers (1) have usually suffered greater numbers of generally stressful experiences—events such as serious personal or familial illness or parental or personal divorce; (2) have had poorer preparation in the personal, economic, and social skills needed for coping with their responsibilities and more difficulties adjusting to their specific life roles; and (3) were likely to recover or improve from their emotional disorders when their social environment could be improved, either by their own spontaneous efforts or with the help of psychiatrists and others [1965, p. 168].

In our own work, we have found two specific factors, birth complications and the sex of the offspring, to be significant sources of stress. For most women, childbirth is a frightening experience. Being in the hospital, experiencing pain, submitting to surgical procedures, and postoperative exhaustion all lead to feelings of stress. However, unlike other surgical procedures this experience culminates in a new life. Not only are most mothers concerned about their adequacy as women and ambivalent about having a child, giving rise to unacceptable feelings of hostility and exaggerated worries about the baby's health (Levy, 1943), but most women are quite worried about whether they will be able to deliver a "normal" baby, and about the short- and long-term effects of birth complications on the baby's development. For this reason, birth complications provide a particularly significant source of stress for both mother and baby. Breech presentation, the need for high forceps, anoxia, and other problems during delivery leave the mother feeling especially guilty, worried, and inadequate. In addition, the impact of these birth complications on the child's subsequent neurological development may lead him to be an especially difficult child to care for, and to increase the child's vulnerability to subsequent mental illness. Our clinical data also suggest that such birth complications are associated with less successful outcome of joint admission and posthospital treatment.

The other factor which differentiates mentally ill women from non-psychiatric controls in the studies reported in this volume is the number of boys a woman has in her family; cumulative stress appears to develop as a result of having had to raise a greater number of boys, and clinical and research findings both point in this direction. This difference between the proportion of boys in the families of hospitalized and nonhospitalized women is significant at the .01 level. Mothers with a greater number of boys are also less able to profit from the joint admission program, and infant boys are more difficult to care for on the wards of a mental hospital.

Boys provide a greater stress for their mothers than girls because they are so much more difficult to care for during the first years of life. Moss (1967) has shown that infant boys fret more easily, are more irritable, are more difficult to console when upset, and sleep less than infant girls. Other data suggest that boys are less neurologically competent at birth and that myelinization of the male nervous system proceeds more slowly. We may infer that it is more difficult for a woman to derive a sense of maternal competence from raising boys; the more boys a woman has, the more she may feel at her "wit's end" when confronted with yet one more boy to raise.

Clearly, the stress associated with the maternal role is particularly great among women who have just had their first child, and much of our discussion has concerned the relation between mental illness and childbearing among women who have become parents for the first time. However, as Flohil (1967) reminds us, many women are able to manage the care of their first child, and only become mentally ill in some manner that requires psychiatric intervention after the second or third child. Each pregnancy adds to the total amount of stress which a woman feels, and, for that reason, adds to the greater risk of mental illness with each birth.

Flohil observes that, among the women in his sample, some already showed psychiatric impairment after the birth of the first child. These women were emotionally immature, married early, and felt overwhelmed by the demands of child care. Another group of women, approximately ten years older than these new mothers, only began to show psychiatric symptoms after the second or third child was born. These women were exhausted from housework, child care, economic instability, and marital conflicts, and showed problems similar to those of women described by Gavron (1966) in her work on "the captive wife," and Cooper and McNeill (1968) in their study of "house-proud" housewives whose days were filled with housekeeping tasks.

While Flohil's description of a bimodal distribution is in accord with our own clinical observations, other large-scale studies are less convincing. According to Gozali and Demorest's (1970) review, most studies find a higher rate of mental illness among mothers having their first child. Obviously there is a statistical artifact in studies reported by Vislie (1956), and by Gordon and Gordon (1959), for, as Gozali and Demorest note, following White et al. (1957), there are more firstborns than later-borns, so that the population at risk is much greater. In the studies we have reported of women with young children admitted to the Massachusetts Mental Health Center over a one-year period, about one-third of the mothers were primi-parae, a figure which agrees quite closely with that which would be expected if the risk of psychiatric illness were equal for each pregnancy.

We may summarize this discussion of the difficulties involved in assuming the maternal role by stating generally that becoming a mother presents a very real crisis for women in our society, and that even ordinary mothers experience a variety of observable psychiatric symptoms in the first year following childbirth. As a result of conflicts with their own families and those of their husbands, intense marital conflict, and feelings of isolation, alienation, and resentment, some emotionally immature women become psychiatrically impaired after the birth of the first baby. Other women are able to manage with one child but, as a result of the increased stress of having two or more children to care for (a problem which is particularly significant if the children are all boys), either show increasing impairment with each new child or suddenly become overwhelmed by their burdens and require psychiatric hospitalization. Studies of woman throughout the years when they are caring for young children are needed in order to understand why some women become mentally ill after the birth of the first child while others become disturbed only after the birth of a second or third child.

## CRITICAL PERIODS IN DEVELOPMENT AND TREATMENT

A third concept which has been basic to the studies presented in this volume is that of "sensitive" or "critical" periods of development; this concept applies equally to the mother's personality development, her child's intellectual and socio-emotional development, and the course of hospitalization and home treatment. This term first gained currency during the thirties, as Konrad Lorenz (1935) began to describe the development of attachment patterns among infant animals and their mothers.

Lorenz had become interested in the question of how it was possible for a member of a species to identify himself as such and, in addition, to follow one species member identified as a caretaker. Lorenz had previously observed that, even among birds, infants develop a pattern of attachment or affiliation to the mother, and follow and recognize her. This following behavior was explained by the mechanism of "imprinting"— the unique pattern of learning by which an animal develops the capacity for recognition of and attachment to a particular other in order to follow the other and obtain certain need satisfaction. What is particularly important about imprinting as a mechanism is that the process can take place only during a very limited period of time within the first hours after birth; beyond this time of maximum sensitivity, such an attachment response cannot develop.

Not only has this process been observed to take place during a very brief and critical time, but it is irreversible and affects subsequent patterns of behavior which have not yet developed (Bowlby, 1969). The concept of the critical period derives its power from the fact that there is a certain point in development during which a process must occur, and if this process does not occur during the specific interval, it is difficult or impossible for it to take place at any later point. Data of Hess (1959), Gray (1958), Harlow and Zimmerman (1959), Thorpe (1963), Bowlby (1969), Ainsworth (1967, 1969, 1973), Ainsworth, Bell, and

Stayton (1971), and Stayton, Hogan, and Ainsworth (1971), all point to the importance of events occurring in earliest infancy as determinants of the later capacity for social relationships, among both humans and other animals.

Imprinting is but one of the many phenomena which demonstrate the concept of critical periods in human development. The discrimination between human and nonhuman stimuli in the first hours following birth, the development of the smiling response in infants, and stranger or eight-month anxiety, are all phenomena which occur at a time of maximum sensitivity. In discussing this concept of the critical period, and its importance in understanding personality development, Sutherland observes that

This kind of behavior [psychoneurotic conflicts in adulthood] appears to imply processes which the clinician considers must give a perspective to the study of what goes on in early development. First, certain frustration experiences with his objects seem to set up sub-systems in the person which, though their aims may be unrecognized, remain as active systems constantly seeking expression despite the pressure of other, more central systems which try to inhibit them. Second, these sub-systems are relatively little influenced by subsequent training. (They constitute in fact the so-called "fixations.") There is, however, a curious feature of their activity in that, although the relationships they seek are so inappropriate to the adult, they can influence in a profound way all the processes of the central part of the person, his perception of, his thinking and feeling about, and his action towards the world around him [1963, p. 236].

Behavior systems that have their origins in events taking place within these critical periods are likely to develop rapidly and to be relatively irreversible at some point later. For example, among the hospitalized women we have studied, deficits in the capacity for forming close relationships, as measured by our Interpersonal Apperception Technique scales, probably appeared early in the women's lives. As a result of frustrations suffered by them in their early relationships with others, discussed at length with the project nurse, these women perceived others as unsatisfying or as destructive and attacking

(Klein, 1932; Riviere, 1952; Guntrip, 1961). At later points in the life cycle, we find these women are unable to feel close to their husbands or to achieve mature heterosexual relationships. The same factors are at work throughout their marriage which first caused them to select as husbands men with similar conflicts about achieving closeness. Thus, a highly stressful situation which fosters the development of psychiatric symptoms arises from the cumulative impact of marital conflicts, continuing difficulties with their own families, and feelings of being unable to achieve reciprocity with their babies.

What is particularly important about this conflict in relating to others is that it does not arise *de novo* during adulthood, but appears to be determined by the manner in which these women were cared for during those very early critical or sensitive periods in the first months of life in which the later capacity for mutuality is established.

Critical learning experiences early in life may thus be viewed as establishing the preconditions and the upper and lower limits of the success with which much later challenges will be resolved. It is possible that the same deficits in interpersonal relationships which occur among these women will prevent them from being able to resolve important psychological issues during critical periods in the development of their children. Given that many of the children of mentally ill mothers are likely to have genetic predispositions which make them particularly vulnerable to the subsequent development of psychopathology, the positive and negative features of their psychosocial environment take on greater significance. For this reason we have been especially concerned about the socioemotional and cognitive development of the children. For this same reason we were concerned that the process of joint admission should not adversely affect the child's early development or contribute to difficulties later in life.

Interesting but troubling findings emerged from our data comparing joint admission children with those who had surrogate home care instead, and with those whose mothers had no psychiatric history. Both groups of children of psychotic mothers showed deficits in the capacity for close interpersonal relationships, and both groups of children preferred things to people and preferred instrumental rather than intrinsic or expressive relationships. The children of nonhospitalized women showed much less deficit in these areas. It is possible that the sphere of interpersonal relationships is particularly sensitive to stress and that the mother's illness and hospitalization had taken their toll on the child's capacity for relatedness. It is also possible that the critical period for determining this capacity for closeness had already come and gone, and that we were actually observing precursors of significant psychopathology in later childhood and adulthood.

Our data suggest that being with their mothers in the hospital had a facilitating or enriching effect on the cognitive develop- ment of the joint admission children. They showed a higher level of active and passive language development, perceptual- motor behavior, and object manipulation than did either the chil- dren of non-joint admission psychotic mothers or the children of "normal" controls. Only long-term follow-up studies of these children will reveal the extent to which the impairment in social development which we have observed in early childhood is actually predictive of subsequent psychopathology in later childhood and adulthood.

As is true for personality development, there are critical periods in the treatment process itself. The outcome of both the joint admission and post-discharge phases of treatment depends upon the manner in which earlier issues in the mother's hospitalization are resolved. For example, if the mother and the therapist are unable to establish a good working alliance at the time of hospitalization, a poor outcome from treatment can be expected. In a similar manner, if a mother cannot differentiate herself from her child to the extent of considering the effects of a mental hospital on him (seen particularly in mothers who can not part from the baby at the time of hospitalization), joint admission will later tend to be unsuccessful. Furthermore, these issues must be considered at the time of admission to the hospital, and must be resolved at that time, in order for the mother to be able to deal with later and more complex problems. For hospitalization and psychotherapy, as for per- sonality development as a whole, it might be said that "in the beginning is the end."

We should like to end this book with one final thought. Our interests in children involve the conviction that the decision to bring a child into the world should be entered into by genuine mutual consent of the parties who will share responsibility for that child with acknowledgment that the help of others may be needed at times. In the real world it does not always happen that way, but the ideal is worth striving for because of its dividends in human dignity, and because commitment is usually stronger to that which we undertake voluntarily than to that which is thrust upon us, because a sense of mastery leads to greater self-esteem than a feeling of helplessness or victimization, and because the feeling of "wantedness" enhances the feeling of "belongingness."

There are clear parallels to be drawn in the case of the hospitalized psychotic mother of a young child. We have repeatedly emphasized the importance of arriving at a genuine, mutual agreement about a joint admission by the patient, her husband, relevant family members, and the treatment staff. In the world of the mental hospital, where the clinical staff is in a position to see that agreements are genuine and mutual, it *must* happen that way if the treatment plan is to succeed. Properly prepared for and timed, this specialized therapeutic arrangement has the potential for making the hospital experience one of increased dignity, commitment, mastery, self-esteem, and belongingness.

# References to Conclusion

Ainsworth, M. 1967. *Infancy in Uganda: Infant care and the growth of love.* Baltimore: Johns Hopkins Press.

———. 1969. Object relations, dependency, and attachment: A theoretical review of the mother-infant relationship. *Child Development* 40: 969–1025.

———. 1973. The development of infant-mother attachment. In B. Caldwell and H. Ricciuti, eds., *Review of child development research,* pp. 1–94. Chicago: University of Chicago Press.

Ainsworth, M.; Bell, S.; Stayton, D. 1971. Individual differences in strange-situation behavior of one-year olds. In H. Schaffer, ed., *The origins of human social relations,* pp. 17–52. London: Academic Press.

Bibring, G. 1959. Some considerations of the psychological processes in pregnancy. *Psychoanalytic Study of the Child* 14: 113–21.

Bowlby, J. 1969. Attachment. Vol. 1: *Attachment and loss.* New York: Basic Books.

Caplan, G. 1960. Patterns of parental response to the crisis of premature birth. *Psychiatry* 23: 365–74.

———. 1961. *An approach to community mental health.* New York: Grune and Stratton.

Caplan, G., and Grunebaum, H. 1967. Perspectives on primary prevention: A review. *Archives of General Psychiatry* 17: 331–46.

Cooper, J., and McNeill, J. 1968. A study of houseproud housewives and their interaction with their children. *Journal of Child Psychology and Psychiatry* 9: 173–88.

Cottrell, L. S. Jr. 1942. The adjustment of the individual to his age and sex roles. *American Sociological Review* 7: 617–20.

Dyer, E. D. 1963. Parenthood as crisis: A re-study. *Journal of Marriage and Family Living* 25: 196–201.

Erikson, E. 1963. *Childhood and Society* (rev. ed.). New York: Norton.

Fischer, J., and Fischer, A. 1963. The New Englanders of Orchard Town, U.S.A. In B. Whiting, ed., *Six cultures: Studies of child-rearing*, pp. 869–1010. New York: John Wiley.

Flohil, J. M. 1967. A preliminary study of the interrelationships of certain clinical data in post-partum psychoses. *Psychiatrica, Neurologia, Neurochirurgia* 70: 191–96.

Gavron, H. 1966. *The captive wife: Conflicts of housebound mothers*. London: Routledge and Kegan Paul.

Gordon, R., and Gordon, K. 1958. Psychiatric problems of a rapidly growing suburb. *Archives of Neurology and Psychiatry* 79: 543–48.

———. 1959. Social factors in the prediction and treatment of emotional disorders of pregnancy. *American Journal of Obstetrics and Gynecology* 77: 1074–83.

———. 1960. Social factors in prevention of post-partum emotional problems. *Obstetrics and Gynecology* 15: 433–38.

Gordon, R.; Eli, E.; and Gordon, K. 1965. Factors in post-partum emotional adjustment. *Obstetrics and Gynecology* 25: 158–66.

Gozali, J., and Demorest, A. 1970. *A review of the literature on postpartal mental disorders*. Milwaukee: Jewish Vocational Service.

Gray, P. H. 1958. Theory and evidence of imprinting in human infants. *Journal of Psychology* 46: 155–66.

Guntrip, H. 1961. *Personality structure and human interaction*. New York: International Universities Press.

Hamilton, J. A. 1962. *Post-partum psychiatric problems*. St. Louis: C.V. Mosby Co.

Harlow, H., and Zimmerman, R. 1959. Affectional responses in the infant monkey. *Science* 130: 676–84.

Hess, E. H. 1959. Imprinting. *Science* 130: 133–41.

Hobbs, D. 1965. Parenthood as crisis: A third study. *Marriage and Family Living* 27: 367–72.

Jacobson, L.; Kaij, L.; and Nilsson, A. 1965. Post-partum mental disorders in an unselected sample: Frequency of symptoms and predisposing factors. *British Medical Journal* 1: 1640–43.

Kaplan, D. and Mason, E. 1960. Maternal reactions to premature birth viewed as an acute emotional disorder. *American Journal of Orthopsychiatry* 30: 539–52.

Klein, M. (1932) 1948. *The Psychoanalysis of Children*. London: Hogarth Press.

LeMasters, E. E. 1957. Parenthood as crisis. *Marriage and Family Living* 19: 352–55.

———. 1970. *Parents in Modern America*. Homewood, Ill.: Dorsey Press.

Levy, D. 1943. *Maternal overprotection*. New York: Columbia University Press.

Litwak, E. 1960a. Occupational mobility and extended family cohesion. *American Sociological Review* 25: 9–21.

———. 1960b. Geographic mobility and extended family cohesion. *American Sociological Review* 26: 258–71.

Lopata, H. 1966. The life cycle of the social role of the housewife. *Sociology and Social Research* 51: 2–22.

———. 1971. *Occupation: housewife*. New York: Oxford University Press.

Lorenz, K. 1935. Companionship in bird life. in C. H. Schiller, ed., *Instinctive Behavior*, pp. 83–128. London: Methuen.

Mahler, M. 1968. *On human symbiosis and the vicissitudes of individuation.* New York: International Universities Press.

Malmquist, A., and Kaij, L. 1971. Motherhood and childlessness in monozygous twins. Part II: The influence of motherhood on health. *British Journal of Psychiatry.* 118: 11–28.

Melges, F. 1968. Post-partum psychiatric syndromes. *Psychosomatic Medicine* 30: 95–108.

Moss, H. 1967. Sex, age and state as determinants of mother-infant interaction. *Merrill-Palmer Quarterly* 13: 1935.

Meyerowitz, J., and Feldman, H. 1966. Transition to parenthood. *Psychiatric Research Reports* 20: 78–84.

Paffenbarger, R., Jr., and McCabe, L. 1966. The effect of obstetric and perinatal events on risk of mental illness in women of childbearing age. *American Journal of Public Health* 56: 400–407.

Pugh, T.; Jerath, B.; Schmidt, W.; and Reed, R. 1963. Rates of mental illness related to childbearing. *New England Journal of Medicine* 268: 1224–28.

Riviere, J. 1952. On the genesis of psychical conflict in earliest infancy. In M Klein, P. Heimann, S. Isaacs, and J. Riviere, *Developments in psychoanalysis.* London: Hogarth Press.

Robertson, J. 1962. Mothering as an influence on early development. *Psychoanalytic Study of the Child* 17: 245–64.

Rossi, A. 1968. Transition to parenthood. *Journal of Marriage and the Family* 30: 26–39.

Sander, L. 1962. Issues in early mother-child interaction. *Journal of the American Academy of Child Psychiatry* 2: 141–66.

Stayton, D.; Hogan, R.; and Ainsworth, M. 1971. Infant obedience and maternal behavior: The origins of socialization reconsidered. *Child Development* 42: 1057–69.

Sussman, M. 1959. The isolated nuclear family: Fact or fiction? *Social Problems* 6: 333–40.

———. 1965. Relationships of adult children with their parents in the United States. In E. Shanas and G. Streib, eds., *Social structure and the family: Intergenerational relationships*, pp. 62–92. Englewood Cliffs, N.J.: Prentice-Hall.

Sutherland, J. D. 1963. The concepts of imprinting and critical period from a psychoanalytic viewpoint. In B. M. Foss, *Determinants of infant behavior*, pp. 235–37. London: Methuen.

Thorpe, W. H. 1963. *Learning and instinct in animals.* 2d ed. London: Methuen.

Vislie, H. 1956. Puerperal mental disorders. *Acta Psychiatrica et Neurologica Scandinavica* 31, suppl. 111.

White, M.; Prout, C.; Fixsen, C.; and Founderur, M. 1957. Obstetricians' role in post-partum mental illness. *Journal of the American Medical Association* 165: 138–43.

Yalom, I.: Lunde, D.; Moos, R.; and Hamburg, D. 1968. Post-partum "blues" syndrome: A description and related variables. *Archives of General Psychiatry* 18: 16–27.

# Index